Batten's SOUTH SOMERSET — VILLAGES —

VIZ.,

BARWICK,
CHILTON CANTELO,
SUTTON BINGHAM,
EAST COKER,

BRYMPTON,
HOUNDSTONE,
PRESTON PLUCKNETT,
LIMINGTON,

WITH NOTICES OF

WEST COKER AND HARDINGTON MANDEVILLE.

BY

JOHN BATTEN, F. S. A.

Somerset Books

© Somerset Books

Originally published as
*Historical and Topographical Collections relating
to the Early History of Parts of South Somerset,*
by Whitby and Son, Yeovil, and
Simpkin, Marshall & Co., Paternoster Row,
London, 1894

Facsimile edition by
Somerset Books, 1994

ISBN 0 86183 270 1

British Library Cataloguing-in-Publication Data
CIP data for this book is available from the British Library

SOMERSET BOOKS
Halsgrove House
Lower Moor Way
Tiverton EX16 6SS

Tel: 01884 243242
Fax: 01884 243325

Printed and bound in Great Britain by
Bookcraft (Bath) Ltd., Midsomer Norton.

FOREWORD

For half a century there were two schools of thought among Somerset's local historians. All enthusiastically supported the newly-formed county Archaeological and Natural History Society which from its inception in 1849 had set about forming a museum and library. Its general aim was to collect materials for a county history, but here the difference of opinion became apparent. Some, and perhaps the most numerous and influential, wanted to begin afresh, setting aside what they considered to be the inadequate work John Collinson had published in 1791. Others, and John Batten was among them, continued to believe that Collinson provided a good base from which to proceed.

So, in his remarks 'To The Reader' at the beginning of this volume, Batten insists that his work is simply 'a collection of materials ... additional to Collinson's History of the County ... which ... may be a useful contribution towards the much needed new edition of that valuable work'.

No new edition ever materialised, though the Archaeological Society later published a comprehensive index and a supplement. Instead the Victoria History of Somerset was born, part of a national enterprise which still continues. The then General Editor of the History wrote on 30 November 1900 to Somerset's leading figures. Despite his opinions about Collinson, Batten would surely have been among the first to be asked for his support. He had, however, died three weeks earlier.

In its topographical progress through the county since 1967 the V.C.H. has not yet come to the hundred of Houndsborough, Barwick and Coker for one particular reason, namely that the parishes at the heart of that area already have a history, pioneer in its time and still recognised as of outstanding quality. The republication of this volume is most welcome.

Robert Dunning,
Editor, Victoria History of Somerset

INTRODUCTION

John Batten, J.P., D.L., F.S.A., was born in Yeovil on 17 February 1815, the eldest son of John Batten (1775-1854), a prominent local solicitor and banker, and member of a family already established for two generations in the town, probably at Church House in Church Lane (now Church Street), still the home of Batten & Co.[1] John Batten the elder was at the forefront of the local campaign for municipal reform for over two decades and died a few days before the Yeovil Improvement Act received the Royal Assent.

The working life of his son John was also devoted to the legal profession and in addition he held numerous public appointments including registrar of the county court, clerk to the county justices and clerk to the commissioners of taxes. He was also a deputy lieutenant for Somerset and a justice of the peace in both Somerset and Dorset. Following the creation of the municipal borough he served as Yeovil's first town clerk from 1854 to 1876.

Batten's interests were also in historical research, and as early as 1833 he 'made a rough drawing of three heraldic tiles' in Tintinhull church.[2] In 1866 he was elected a Fellow of the Society of Antiquaries of London on the grounds that he 'has a taste for and takes great interest in local antiquities and archaeology generally'. He was already a member of the Somerset Archaeological Society and a member of the (Royal) Archaeological Institute. Among his sponsors for his Fellowship were the antiquarian Francis Henry Dickinson of Kingweston, the historian Thomas Hugo, man-of-letters Henry Reeve, James, Baron Talbot de Malahide, another antiquarian, of Evercreech and Charles Old Goodford, provost of Eton, from Chilton Cantelo.[3]

Most of Batten's historical writing was carried out in his active retirement after 1876. His contributions to the *Proceedings* of the Archaeological Society spanned practically half a century and were almost exclusively devoted to south Somerset subjects. He was one of the society's earliest members, acted as local secretary for Yeovil from 1865, ably served as president in 1886 and thereafter was one of its vice-presidents until his death.

His presidential address delivered in Yeovil Town Hall in 1886 perhaps best reveals something of the personality of the man: regretful that he was 'quite incompetent to speak' about Natural History in order 'to excite greater attention to this most interesting science'; hopeful that the 'many young friends amongst us today ... will be induced to join our ranks and lend a helping hand to our agreeable labours'; optimistic that the 'abundant and varied store' of material 'must be worked with energy and perseverance, before we can pronounce the topography and history of Somersetshire to be complete'; and restrained on the subject of genealogy, ' a study that must be pursued with great caution, or it will soon degenerate into pedigree making'.[4]

This present volume, encapsulating much of Batten's life-time of research, and published when the author was nearly eighty years old, is his *magnum opus*. Amidst the comprehensive text covering manors, manor houses, churches, chapels, mills and lists of incumbents are occasional and unexpected flashes of humour, such as the comment on railways and railway travel (p.33), the merits of repair versus restoration (p.35), the problems of farming versus archaeology and tourism (p.107), and the pitfalls of local topography and local tradition (pp.173-4).

The book was originally published in an edition of 200 copies and could be purchased from messrs. E. Whitby & Son of 8 Princes Street, Yeovil. It sold for the princely sum of 6s. 6d. (£0.33p). One contemporary reviewer commented that it was 'pleasantly written, with no trace of dryness, and will be read with profit and interest by all who are acquainted with the locality ...'.[5] The photographer is unknown, though it was possibly Henry Stiby, whose glass negatives are deposited with the Museum of South Somerset, Yeovil.

John Batten remained active to the very end of his long life, continuing to contribute articles to the Archaeological Society's *Proceedings* up to the year before his death. He also found time to submit items to *Somerset and Dorset Notes and Queries*, an historical miscellany which he had instigated in 1888 and which endures as his lasting memorial.[6]

He died in Weymouth on 8 November 1900 at the age of eighty five and was buried at Barwick. His five children by his wife Grace Eleanor White all survived him. The obituary in the Archaeological Society's *Proceedings* paid fulsome tribute:

> Mr Batten's last appearance at our Annual Meetings was at Sherborne in 1896, when those who heard his paper read in the open air in the churchyard of Poyntington, upon the Descent of that Manor, will not readily forget his vigorous and 'smart' appearance, and manner, and his clear enunciation, which would have done credit to a man 20 years his junior ... His death will leave a blank in the public life of the district, which cannot fail to make itself felt.[7]

The *Western Gazette* summed him up as follows:

> ... he was widely known as a clever lawyer, and a man of keen perception. He possessed a retentive memory, and he maintained all his faculties unimpaired in the least degree up to the last. As an ardent antiquarian nothing gave him more delight than to delve into the past, to trace the history of one of the old county families, or of some old estate... He was the owner of ... Aldon House and grounds, a beautifully situated domain, better known ... in the locality as 'Nine Springs'. In summer months he threw his grounds open to the public, and the opportunity of a stroll through this picturesquely wooded and watered spot was taken advantage of by many. His long connection with Yeovil won for him the respect of all. He was a gentleman of the old school, and he will be missed in many quarters.[8]

Robin Ansell,
Reference Librarian, Yeovil

References:
1. J.B. Burke, *Landed Gentry* iii (1972), pp. 48-9.
2. *P(roceedings of the) S(omerset) A(rchaeological and) N(atural) H(istory) S(ociety)* xxxii (1886), pt.i. 70-1.
3. Society of Antiquaries of London, certificate of candidate for election, 41 (7 June 1866).
4. *PSANHS* xxxii (1886), pt.i. 11-28.
5. *S(omerset and) D(orset) N(otes and) Q(ueries)* iv (1895), p.48.
6. *SDNQ* xxxii (1991), pp.641-3.
7. *PSANHS* xlvi (1900), pt.ii. 202.
8. *Western Gazette*, 9 November 1900, p.6; see also *SDNQ* vii (1901), p.171.

JOHN BATTEN'S PRINCIPAL WRITINGS

'Somersetshire Sequestrations during the Civil War', *P(roceedings of the) S(omerset) A(rchaeological and) N(atural) H(istory) S(ociety)* iv (1853),pt.ii. 60-77

'Somersetshire Sequestrations', ibid. xvi (1870), pt.ii. 13-34

'Trent', ibid. xx (1874), pt.ii. 113-39

'Inaugural Address', ibid. xxxii (1886), pt.i. 11-28

Notes on Barwick and its Church (Western Chronicle Historical Series no. 1), Yeovil, Western Chronicle, 1887

'The Early Owners of Limington', *PSANHS* xxxiii (1887), pt.ii. 137-45

Descriptive and Historical Notes on Sutton Bingham, Brympton, and the Ancient Yeovil Chapelries (Western Chronicle Historical Series nos. 2, 3 and 4), Yeovil, Western Chronicle, 1890

'The Barony of Beauchamp of Somerset', *PSANHS* xxxvi (1890), pt.ii. 20-59

'Additional Notes on Barrington and the Strodes', ibid. xxxvii (1891) pt.ii. 40-3

'Fishing in the Tone and Parrett', *S(omerset and) D(orset) N(otes and) Q(ueries)* iii (1893), p.181-2

'Malet of Enmore, Somerset', ibid. pp.255-8

'The Pedigree of King of West Hall, Folke ...', ibid. p.260

Historical and Topographical Collections relating to the Early History of Parts of South Somerset, viz. Barwick, Chilton Cantelo, Sutton Bingham, East Coker, Brympton, Houndston, Preston, Limington, with Notices of West Coker and Hardington Mandeville, Yeovil, Whitby, 1894

'Stoke under Hamdon in connection with Sir Matthew de Gournay, Kt., and the Duchy of Cornwall', *PSANHS* xi (1894), pt.ii. 236-71

'Notes on North Perrot', ibid. xli (1895), pt.ii. 73-91

'Arms of de Mandeville of Coker: Sir William Pole's MSS.' *SDNQ* iv (1895), pp. 170-3

'The Lady of Poyntington', *PSANHS* xlii (1896), pt.ii. 1-5

'The Horsey Family' ibid. xliii (1897), pt.ii. 84-93

'Rental of Lydlinch Manor', *SDNQ* v (1897), pp.17-8

'Stocklinch Ottersey near Ilminster, Somerset', ibid. pp. 42-3

'Deer Parks in Dorset and Somerset', ibid. pp.83-7

'Who wrote Coker's Survey of Dorsetshire?', ibid. pp.97-102

'Burial in Sherborne Abbey Church', ibid. p.225

'Fifehead Magdalen cum Cokerford', ibid. pp.289-91

'An Early Chapter of the History of Yeovil', *PSANHS* xliv (1898), pt.ii. 203-23

'Mudford and its Church', ibid. xlv (1899), pt.ii. 179-92

'Craucombe Carew', *SDNQ* vi (1899), pp.49-56

'Hinton House Portraits', ibid. pp.306-14

'Manor of Preston Bowyer, in Milverton Parish, Somerset', ibid. pp.327-36

'The Royal Peculiar of Ilminster', ibid. vii (1901), pp.13-7

'Treating at Elections', ibid. pp.30-1

'Alhampton, Churchill and Pokerleston (Puxton)', ibid. pp.69-72

'Hundreds of Stone and Catash, Somerset', ibid. pp.120-6

'Alfoxton, Wordeston, Burton and Tokeswell: Copies of Old Deeds ...', ibid. pp.149-50

APPENDIX 1: SIMPLIFIED FAMILY TREE (BASED ON BURKE'S LANDED GENTRY 1972)

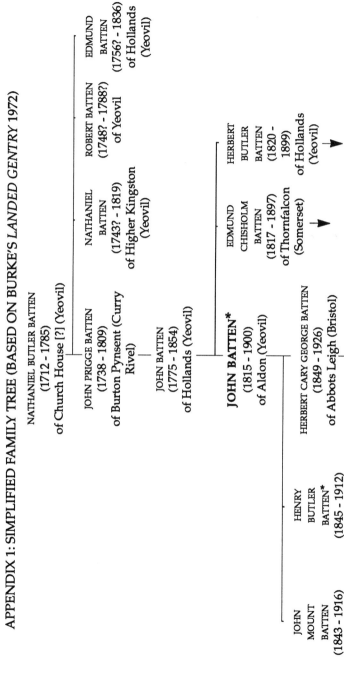

NATHANIEL BUTLER BATTEN
(1712 - 1785)
of Church House [?] (Yeovil)

JOHN PRIGGE BATTEN
(1738 - 1809)
of Burton Pynsent (Curry Rivel)

NATHANIEL BATTEN
(1743? - 1819)
of Higher Kingston (Yeovil)

ROBERT BATTEN
(1748? - 1788?)
of Yeovil

EDMUND BATTEN
(1756? - 1836)
of Hollands (Yeovil)

JOHN BATTEN
(1775 - 1854)
of Hollands (Yeovil)

EDMUND CHISHOLM BATTEN
(1817 - 1897)
of Thornfalcon (Somerset)

HERBERT BUTLER BATTEN
(1820 - 1899)
of Hollands (Yeovil)

JOHN BATTEN*
(1815 - 1900)
of Aldon (Yeovil)

HERBERT CARY GEORGE BATTEN
(1849 - 1926)
of Abbots Leigh (Bristol)

HERBERT COPELAND CARY BATTEN*
(1884 - 1963)
of Aldon (Yeovil)

HENRY BUTLER BATTEN*
(1845 - 1912)
of Aldon (Yeovil)

JOHN MOUNT BATTEN
(1843 - 1916)
of Up Cerne (Dorset)

WILLIAM HENRY BATTEN
(1926 -)
of Aldon (Yeovil) and
Ryme Intrinseca (Dorset)

(* = served as Yeovil Town Clerk)

TO THE READER.

I T is only necessary for the author—or rather compiler—of this little work to say, by way of preface, that he does not profess it to be a complete history of the places described, but only a collection of materials relating to them, hitherto unpublished, which inclination and opportunity have enabled him to gather together as additions to Collinson's History of the County, and which, he hopes, may be a useful contribution towards the much needed new edition of that valuable work.

It is not improbable that some of his friends, after glancing at the table of contents, may express their surprise that he should have devoted his time and energies in the pursuit of objects of little general interest, or practical utility. To such critics he would venture to excuse himself in the words of Dr. Johnson,—who in one of his papers in "The Rambler" (no. 161) observes :—"It is not easy to discover how it concerns him that gathers the produce, or receives the rent, of an estate to know through what families the land has passed—who is registered in the Conqueror's Survey as its possessor—how often it has been forfeited by treason—or how often sold by prodigality. The power or wealth of the present inhabitants of a country cannot be much increased by an enquiry after the names of those barbarians who destroyed one another twenty centuries ago, in contest for the shelter of woods or convenience of pasturage.

"Yet we see that no man can be at rest in the enjoyment of a new purchase, till he has learned the history of his grounds from the ancient inhabitants of the parish ; and that no nation omits to record the actions of their ancestors, however bloody, savage, and rapacious."

TABLE OF CONTENTS.

in East Coker Church—Chapel of "Our Lady of Burton"—Description
of Church—Effigies—Heraldic Glass—James, Earl of Wilts, and Avice
his wife—Description of Coker Court—Notice of Archdeacon Helyar—
Letter of Sir Walter Raleigh in his favour—Court Rolls—Manor Survey in
1321—Services of Tenants—several Manors held under Coker—Borough of
Murifield—part of North Coker held by Richard de Argentine—disputes
between him and Geoffry de Mandeville settled temp. Ric. I—Pavyots Mill
held of Manor by De Montacute—"St. Clere's land"—Hymerford House in
North Coker—Families of Hymerford and Hambridge—Chelworth Farm—
La Hurne—Nash—Description of the old Mansion there—Title and Devolu-
tion of the Estate—Bubspool—Family of Penny..................p. 105 to p. 181.

CHAPTER VIII.
LIMINGTON.

Roger de Curcell, Domesday Tenant of Manor—descended to Malet and
Beauchamp—Division into three parts—one-third held by Fitz-Bernard—
—descended to De Givernay—Family of De Givernay—Chantry Chapel in
Church—Effigies of De Givernay—another Third held by De Tudenham—
sold to D'Aumarle and descended to Bonville—remaining one-third in
possession of Geoffry St. Martin, who gave it to Priory of Bradenstock.

LIST OF ILLUSTRATIONS.

CHAPTER I.

BARWICK.

ARWICK or Berewick is not mentioned in the Præ Domesday "Inquisitio Gheldi" or in the Domesday Survey itself. In all probability it was included in Yeovil, as part of the Hundred of "Givelea" in the former survey, and of the Manor of "Iula" in the latter. Indeed this is tolerably certain, as it did form part of The Hundred of Stone, which nearly corresponded with that of "Givelea," as late as the reign of Henry III., when William de Cantilupe, the Lord, had withdrawn it from the jurisdiction of that hundred.[1] It may be presumed that this obliged Cantilupe to obtain Royal licence to hold his manor of Barwick and Chilton Cantelo as a separate liberty or hundred, and these two parishes still constitute the Hundred of Barwick.

Collinson in his history of Somerset says "The Manor of Barwick soon after the conquest came into the possession of the family of Courtenay, of whom was William de Courtenay the founder of the Priory of Woodspring (near Weston-super-Mare), A.D. 1210. In the 26th Henry III. the lands of Robert [William] de Courtenay, Lord of this Manor, were divided between Vitalis Engain and William de Cantilupe, *and in that partition Barwick was allotted to the latter,* who died seized thereof 35 Henry III., leaving William de Cantilupe his son and heir."[2]

---

[1] Rot. Hund. II., 125.   [2] Coll. Som. II., 337.

The learned Mr. Eyton also in his "Somerset Domesday," following Collinson, says," Barwick was sometimes held by the Courtenay Lords of the Honour of Montgomery, from whom it descended to Cantilupe as Courtenay's heir." No documentary evidence is adduced to justify these statements. The Fine Roll of 26 Henry III., to which Collinson refers, only shows that William de Cantilupe and Vitalis Engain, claiming as heirs of William de Courtenay, paid a fine on having seisin of a manor in Suffolk, part of the Honour of Montgomery; and although Dugdale in his Baronage certainly says, on the authority of a private MS., that partition was made 26 Henry III., between William de Cantilupe and Vitalis Engain—he is speaking generally "of the Lands and Fees which have descended to them from William de Courtenay," not specifying Barwick or any other manors. Indeed, there is no evidence that Barwick ever was part of the Honour of Montgomery, or held by a Courtenay.*

The history of this early period is so enveloped in darkness that it is little more than a series of probabilities, but if Barwick was originally part of the great Manor of Yeovil, it would have escheated to the Crown on the attainder either of William de Eu or William Earl of Mortain (between whom the manor was divided), and afterwards may have been granted to Cantilupe. This idea is strengthened by the Pipe Roll of 6 Richard I., which, under

---

* This William de Courtenay (whose immediate connection with the family of Courtenay, Earl of Devon, is rather uncertain) was the only son of Robert de Courtenay by his wife Matilda, only child of Reginald Fitzurse, of Williton, in this county, one of the assassins of Thomas á Becket. Reginald's father was Richard Fitzurse, whose wife was another Matilda, daughter and eventual heiress of Baldwin de Bullers, by his wife Sybil de Falaise, a natural daughter of Henry I., who enriched her with the Honour of Montgomery on her marriage. Failing the male line of de Bullers, the honour descended to William de Courtenay, whose right may have been founded not only on his heirship to Matilda his mother (Oblata, John a.m. 12) but possibly also *jure uxoris*, she being Wentleana de Bullers, supposed to be a daughter of Robert de Bullers.[3] On the death of William de Courtenay without issue in 1214, the Honour was claimed by Vitalis Engain and others[4] but King John apparently treated it as an escheat, and in 1216 granted the greater portion to his steward, William de Cantilupe.[5] The relationship, if any, between Cantilupe and Courtenay is not known, but it is probable there was some, as it will be seen that the Fitzurse family held their estate at Williton under William de Cantilupe as Over-Lord. Another action was pending relating to the Courtenay inheritance between Vitalis Engain and William de Cantilupe and Mazilia his wife.[6] Possibly she may have been a sister of William de Courtenay.

[3] Bracton's Note Book, case 96.
[4] Plac apud Westm. 9 and 10 Henry III., m. 3 dors.
[5] See Eyton's Hist. Shropshire, xi., 128; Notes and Queries, 4th ser., vii. 268.
[6] Bracton's Note Book.

the head of "Wards and Escheats," says : "William de St. Mary Church [the Crown Receiver, Archdeacon of London] accounts for £4 for the *Farm at Berewic* of *Walter de Cantelu* for half a year and for 16s. 3d. for certain land of *Kocre* for half a year, and for 33s. 9d. for the Farm of *Hardinton* for one-quarter of a year." Walter not only held Berewic, but Chilton Cantelo also, and his relationship to William de Cantilupe is proved from the Close Roll 6 John, which records a writ to the sheriff of Norfolk to deliver to Walter certain lands in that county which the King had previously committed to the custody of *William his son*. There is little doubt, therefore, that William de Cantilupe did not acquire Barwick as co-heir of Courtenay, but as the heir of his own father.

William de Cantilupe was a person of great influence, holding several high offices under King John, until he broke out in rebellion in 1223-4. He soon, however, obtained his pardon, and died at an advanced age in 1239, having previously, by license from the Crown, transferred his estate to his son William de Cantilupe, junior, the second of that name.

He was also a faithful friend of the King, and steward of the Royal Household, and, dying in 1251, left his son William, the third of that name, his successor ;—" a rich, handsome young man," who was cut off, " to the grief of many," in 1254. He married Eva, one of the four daughters and co-heiresses of William de Braose, jun., and became, *jure uxoris*, owner of one-third of the manor of Trent, which he and his wife bestowed on the Priory of Studley, in Warwickshire, and of the manor of Little Marston, in the parish of West Camel, which, with Barwick, descended to their son George, who at his father's death was only three years old. He also died at an early age in 1272, and being unmarried, his heirs were his sister and his nephew, son of another sister who had predeceased him.

The inquisition taken after his death gives such a minute description of his property, and such an insight into the value of land and labour in those early times, that a summary of its contents will be interesting.

It is an inquisition and survey of the manor of Berewyk, in the county of Somerset, late of George de Cantilupe, made at Berewyk, Wednesday next after the Epiphany, 2nd Edward I., before Roger de Crofte, clerk, Master Richard de Clifford, and Robert Radinton, subescheator of the said county, by Roger de Merston and 11 other jurors, who on their oaths say that the said George held the said Manor of Berewyk of Lord John de Burg in chief, by the service of half a knight's fee, and there is there a certain well-built messuage, for the repair of which, nevertheless, 30 marks will not suffice, and it is worth, with the gardens, dovehouse, and service of courts, 20s. And there are there in demesne 151 acres of arable, which pay 75s. 6d. a year, 6d. for each acre, and 17 acres of demesne meadow, which pay 34s. a year; 2s. for each acre. And there is there a certain several pasture for the Lord's oxen, containing four acres, which pay 2s. a year, 6d. for each acre ; and the value of the pasture of the said meadow after the hay is carried, if the Lord's oxen do not have it, is 2s. a year. And there is there a certain park, containing 40 acres and the herbage thereof which pays 10s. a year ; and the pannage of the said park pays 12d. a year. And the feed of 34 acres of the said park if sold once £10 4s., 6s. for each acre ; and the soil of the said park pays if the underwood is cut 10s. a year, for each acre 3d. ; and there are rents of assise of free tenants 47s. 6d., namely, of Henry de Woolavington for the 4th part of one knight's fee 31s., of Henry le Franc, for half a virgate of land 3s., of Walter Warin for the like 12d., of John Baret for the like 10s., of Geoffry de la More for the like 14s., of Richard Baudewyne for the like 18d., of Henry the Clerk for one fourth part of a virgate of 12d., of Walter de Halsinge for the like 12d., of the Tythingman of Chilton 5s.

And there are there eight customary tenants, each of whom holds half a virgate of land, and pays 8s. rent of assise, and one customary tenant holding half a virgate paying 7s. 8d., and two customary tenants holding half a virgate and the fourth part of the virgate and paying 12s., 6s. for each, and the said 11 customary tenants are bound to weed the lord's corn, and that service is worth for each of them 1½d.—and to mow the lord's meadow, and that service is worth for each 2d.—and to carry and rick the lord's hay, and that service is worth for each 1¾d., and they are bound also to do divers works in the autumn which are worth for each 2s. 2¼d.

And there are there four cottagers, each holding one cottage, the rent of each being 2s. a year, and one holding one cottage at 2s. 6d. a year, and two holding two at 20d. a year, and two holding two at 8d. each a year, and four at 10d. each a year—and one cottager holding one decayed cottage at 6d. a year, and one other at 18d.— and each of the said cottagers is bound to weed the lord's corn for one day, which service is worth ¼d. ; and they are also bound to carry and rick the lord's hay, which service is worth for each 1¼d. ; and each of them is bound to mow the lord's corn in the autumn for one day, which service is worth for each 1d., and there are two water mills which pay 66s. 8d. a year, and pleas and perquisites of courts, reliefs and other casuals are worth by the year 6s. 8d.

And the jurors say :

That Richard de Cantilupe holds the ville of Chilton of the said Manor of Berewyk by the service of one knight's fee, and owes suit of Court from three weeks to three weeks.

That William de Mohun holds the fourth part of one knight's fee in the ville of Overateberg [Adbere in parish of Mudford or Queen Camel] and owes suit of Court as aforesaid.

That William de Cantilupe holds the fourth part of one knight's fee in the ville of Cammel Regis and owes suit of Court as aforesaid.

That William Lord Reyny holds the manor of Duniford [in the parish of St. Decumans] by the service of one knight's fee, and owes suit of Court twice a year, and oftener if need be, and

That John Fitzurse holds half a knight's fee in Williton, and owes suit in the lord's court at Berewyk twice a year, and oftener if need be.

And that the Advowson of the Chapel at Berwyk belongs to the Lord of that place, and that the said chapel is worth 66s. 8d. a year. The total annual value of the manor is £26 6s. 6½d.

Little Merston.—And the jurors say that the said George held the Manor of Merston of our lord the king in chief by the service of one-fourth part of a knight's fee, and there is a certain manor house (curia), newly built, containing, with the garden, three acres, which, together with a dilapidated dovecot, are valued at 4s., and there are in demesne 129½ acres of arable, worth £4 6s. 4d. a year; and 17 acres of meadow, worth £6 0s. 4d. a year; and three acres of inclosed pasture, worth 3s. a year; and rents of assize from free tenements 13s. 7d. a year, viz., Henry of Little Merston for half a virgate of land 1d.; Peter the Merchant, for a house and curtilage, 1d.; Henry Dolling, for six acres of land, 1d.; and Henry of Little Merston for half a virgate of land 13¼d.; all of whom owe suit at the Lord's Court, and there is one customary tenant who holds the fourth part of one virgate of land, paying yearly a rent of assize of 5s.; and there are two cottagers who hold two cottages at rent of 2s. each a year; and two others at 18d. each a year; and the said customary tenant and cottagers are bound to mow and rick the Lord's hay, and reap his corn, which works are valued at 4½d. for each. The total annual value of Little Merston is £7 14s. 9½d.

Then the document proceeds : "The survey and inquisition of the borough of Stoford, in the county aforesaid, which belonged to the said George de Cantilupe, made at Berewyk the day and year aforesaid, by the said jurors and by 12 burgesses of the said borough, namely, Robert the Clerk, Nicholas de Ponte, Robert Smith (Faber), Philip Abbote, David le Hopere, Richard Baudewyne, Roger Merchant, William Halewell, Geoffrey de la More, Hugh Cook, John

Le Chaloner, William Baudewyne, and Robert le Tregetur [carrier?],
jurors, who, on their oaths, say that the Borough of Stoford is free
in itself as the Borough of Yvelcestre; nevertheless, it is part
(membrum) of the said Manor of Berewyke, and there are there 74
burgages and a-half which pay 72s. 1d. a year, namely, 10d. for each
burgage. And there are within the said borough not less than five
houses built in the market place [in mercato], one of which pays 2s.
a year, the second 16d., the third 8d., the fourth 8d. and half a pound
of cinnamon (price ½d.), and the fifth 6d.; and there are two plots
(placie) which pay 2d. a year.

" And there is a fair there on the feast of St. Mary Magdalen,
worth in tolls and other issues 13s. 4d. a year, and the pleas and
perquisites of the said borough are worth 13s. 4d. a year.

" And all the jurors say that Milisand (Millicent), wife of Eudo
la Zuche (of full age) and sister of the said George, and John de
Hastings, son and heir of Henry and Joan de Hastings (another
sister of the said George), are his next heirs, and the said John is
under age and in ward to the King."[7]

The right or franchise of the fair had been granted 12 Henry III.
to the father or grandfather of George, there being an entry on the
Close Rolls of that year (m. 7) that the King, by charter dated at
Windsor 12th June, granted to William de Cantilupe license to hold
a fair every year at the Manor of Berewic for three days, namely,
the vigil, the feast, and the morrow of the Feast of St. Mary
Magdalene[8], and three years after, he obtained, by a fresh charter,
license for holding a market every Tuesday.[9] This charter was
probably a confirmation of an existing market, as, if it had been an
entirely new franchise, it would naturally have been included in the
first charter, and circumstances point to a much earlier date for its
foundation.

The discovery in 1826 (noticed in the Somerset Archæological
Society's proceedings for 1884) of a British interment on the eminence
a little to the north of Stoford, and other indications on the ground,
suggest that it may have been the site of primæval dwellings, which
after passing through successive stages of civilisation, would at
length be developed into a Saxon village, and the inhabitants into a
village community. Situated on the ancient packway, or road towards London, close to the *Stone Ford* through the small river
dividing the shires (whence the softened name of *Stoford* is derived),
the village naturally become a halting place and rendezvous for

---

[7] Esch. 1 Edward I., No. 16.   [8] Close Rolls, 12 Henry III. m. 7.

[9] Charter Rolls, 15 Henry III., m. 8.

carriers of merchandise and travellers generally, and the interchange of traffic which would be the ordinary result of these meetings would lead to the establishment of some kind of market tending to increase the importance of the place and the number of the inhabitants. But other consequences would follow from such a state of things; and amongst them the growth of the village into, what is termed in the Inquisition,

The Free Borough of Stoford.—The term borough is sometimes applied to towns or villes not properly corporate; and when so used means a place where the owners of tenements within it held them of their lord, by a tenure which, prevailing in towns of the same class, was generally known as *burgage tenure*, the owners being called *burgesses*, and the place itself a *borough*. Under this tenure both the lord, as the grantee of the Crown, and his tenants, possessed certain reciprocal rights, by which the manor was exempted from the jurisdiction of the ordinary officers of the Crown, and placed under the milder sway of its own lord. For this reason it was called sometimes, as at Stoford, a *free borough*, and sometimes, as at Yeovil, a *liberty*, and at both we find all the attributes of a separate jurisdiction—a Court Leet instead of the Sheriff's Hundred Court; a Court for the recovery of debts, instead of the Sheriff's County Court; and a Court for the trial of actions relating to real property within its jurisdiction, without resorting to the superior Courts of the Crown.†

A necessary and important element in the self-government of such a community was the provision of executive officers, for securing its due administration, and as we find here a portreeve and bailiffs discharging their functions, from the reign of Henry III. down to the middle of the last century, it is fair to presume that their offices were coeval with the borough, and that their duties were derived from those of their Saxon predecessors.‡ For although the picture we have drawn may seem to point more properly to the feudal economy after the Norman conquest, the indicia of self-government may, we think, be found in many places at an earlier period of our national history. Under the Norman system this mode of administration

---

† The jurisdiction of the Manorial Court of Barwick certainly extended to lands within the Manor, for in the reign of Edward I. an assize was held to try whether Hugh Fitz Richard de Modiford and others had disseized Robert Onneife and his wife of lands in Stoford which had been recovered by writ of right in the Court of George de Cantilupe.[10]

‡ It appears from deeds still extant that 11 Ric. II., John Cade was Portreeve (prepositus) " of the ville," 15 Ric. II. William Ford, 3 Henry VI. William Pounset was Portreeve and John Bluwe and John Spyndelere were the bailiffs, and 9 Henry V. Thomas Tanner was Portreeve.

10 Assize Rolls, Div. Co. 2 and 3 Edw. I.

was not destroyed, but modified. The Lords to whom the Conqueror had granted any of these favoured manors found it politic to interfere as little as possible with the internal arrangements prevailing in them, and communities and tenants gladly acquiesced in a material acknowledgment of feudal seigniority of their Lord in return for his guarantee of their fundamental privileges, and their security from attacks on their lives and property which unaided they were not powerful enough to resist.

The borough of Stoford must have been of considerable size and importance at the commencement of the reign of Edward I., as it appears by the Cantilupe inquisition that there were not less than 74 burgages in it, besides customary tenements and cottages; and it should be observed that so tenacious were the burgesses of their rights that they would not allow the inquisition to be taken before a jury of the county alone, but required an additional jury of their own inhabitants to be associated with it; and the main feature of the verdict was that, although part of the manor of Berwyk, Stoford was free in itself, as Yvelcestre was free. The popular name of this quasi corporate body was "the Commonalty," as in a conveyance, 5 Henry V., a burgage in Stoford is said to be bounded on one side by a messuage of the Commonalty of the same ville.

The Borough had its Guildhall, or "Zuldhous." This appears from a deed, dated Monday after the Epiphany, 26 Edward III., whereby John Galyot, of Stovorde, and Alice his wife, grant to William Payn and 16 other persons therein named, one house with the curtilage adjoining, called the *Zuldhous*, situate in Stovorde before two great elms (aute duos magnos ulnos) on the west side between the tenement of John Galyot and the tenement of John Hywes, rendering a rent of 2s. to the Lord of the fee. This document is very important, as it proves that the Burgesses had not acquired the true element of a corporation, by which the Guildhall would have passed by law to the members for the time being; but that it was necessary to convey it to certain persons as feoffees or trustees. John Galyot was, probably, the survivor of a previous set of feoffees.

It is worth noticing that, down to a recent period, the hollow stump of an aged elm tree remained near the mediæval house with the pointed arched doorway at the eastern end of the village green, and possibly it was one of the ulni mentioned in the deed ; if so, the house, which bears its age well, was no doubt the Guildhall.

A Borough would be nothing without a common seal, and Stoford, rightly or wrongly, had one. It was circular, the design being

GUILDHALL, STAFFORD

To face p. 8

merely lines forming two squares, one lying angle fashion on the other, with a device of a daisy or star in the centre, and a legend round,

" s. COMVNE BURGENTES STOFORD,"

which, notwithstanding the error in the word Burgentes, evidently means, " the common seal of the Burgesses of Stoford." There are several instances of the use of a common seal in mediæval times in " villes," not strictly corporate, but it is difficult to account for them consistently with well-known principles of law. One possible solution may be found in the statute concerning bakers passed about the year 1285. That Act directs that standard measures shall be kept in all towns by the Mayor and bailiffs ; which, when examined and found correct, shall be marked with *the seal of the Commonalty of the town.* This may have been construed into a permission, if not a direction, to the authorities to provide a seal, and then it would naturally be used for other purposes. The document to which this seal was attached is a conveyance, dated 13 July, 1 Ric. III., of a burgage in the free borough *(in libero burgo)* of Stoford on the south side of South Street, between the King's Highway called Grene Street on the west, and the land of the Lord of the Manor on the east, together with a close of land adjoining, from Thomas Colyns to three Trustees, for the use and benefit of the poor people in the almshouse of Yevele, and, because his seal was unknown, he (Colyns) caused the official seal of the Portreeve of the ville of Stoford to be affixed thereto.*

The descent of the Manor is fully set out by Collinson, and it will suffice to state that in the partition of the estates of George de Cantilupe between his heirs, Barwick fell to the lot of his nephew, John de Hastings, afterwards first Lord Hastings, whose grandson Lawrence was raised to the title of Earl of Pembroke. It continued in the possession of this family for several generations, but John, Earl of Pembroke, who was killed accidentally at a tournament, 13 Richard II. (1390), dying without issue, his great estates descended, after much litigation, to Reginald, Lord Grey de Ruthin, who established his claim as heir of the whole blood, and consequently became the owner of Barwick. He did not, however, retain it long, for 7 Henry IV., by indentures of Fine between John Roger, of Bridport, and others, Plaintiffs, and the above Reginald Lord Grey, Defendant, the Manor of Barwick was, in consideration of 100 marks of silver, conveyed to John Roger and his heirs. The family of Roger, or Rogers, whose chief seat

---

* The foregoing deeds are taken from a transcript made many years ago by the writer from the originals then in the possession of the feoffees of Woborne's Almshouse, Yeovil, but since unfortunately lost.

was at Bryanston, Dorset,‡ held Barwick for six generations, extending to the latter part of the reign of Queen Elizabeth, when Sir Richard Rogers, knight, sold the manor and advowson to William Symes, of Chard, merchant.

This gentleman married Elizabeth, daughter of Robert Hill, of Poundisford, near Taunton, a representative of a very old Somerset-shire family, and he was succeeded at his death by his son and heir, John Symes, who at the close of his life left Poundisford for the residence of his son, at Winterbourne, in the parish of Frampton Cotterell, Gloucestershire, where he died and was buried. His remarkable career is minutely detailed in the monumental inscription in Frampton Church, engraved on a brass plate surmounted with the arms of Symes—*Azure three escallops in pale Or*, impaling those of Horner—*Sab three Talbots passant argent two and one.*

" Here lyeth the body of John Symes of Poundisford, in the parish of Pitminster in the county of Somerset, Esquire ; he was born on the 4th day of March, 1572 (in the 12th year of Queen Elizabeth). He lived soberly, righteously and godly, and died on the 21st day of October, 1661.

" Reader, thou treadest on the sacred ashes of John Symes, Esq., who, in the late unhappy times of rebellion, was forced (for his signal loyalty to his Prince) to leave his former habitation at Poundisford, in the parish of Pitminster, in the county of Somerset, and to seek a repose for his old age in this parish. He was a man greatly renowned for wisdom, justice, integrity, and sobriety, which talents he did not hide in a napkin, but religiously exercised in the whole conduct of his life, especially in the government of that county, wherein he bore all the honourable offices incident to a country gentleman as Knight of the shire, (elected *nem. con.*), for the Parliament held at Westminster in the 21st year of King James, High Sheriff, Deputy Lieutenant for many years, and Justice of the Peace for 40 years and upwards, and as he was careful and solicitous to discharge his duties to God, his soveraigne, and his country, so God was pleased to bestow on him several badges (also) of his special favour, as length of days, accompanied with a most healthy constitution of body for above 80 years, and of his mind to the last, as also a numerous posterity even of children and children's children, to the number of 100 and upwards, descended from his loynes (by his only wife Amy, the daughter of Thomas Horner, of Cloford, in the county of Somerset, Esquire).

" And when he was full of days and honour, having lived 88 years 7 months and 17 days, and seen the safe return of his Prince to his

‡ Hutch. Dors. 1. 250.

crown and kingdom, after a long and horrible exile, and thereby the flourishing condition both of Church and State. Having finished his work on earth, he cheerfully resigned his soul to God that gave it, the 21st day of October, anno domini 1661, in full assurance of a joyful resurrection."

The grandson of this extraordinary old gentleman was Thomas Symes, who resided at Barwick, and obtained, 23 Chas. II., a Charter for a second fair, to be held on the 17th of September. He renewed the alliance with the Horner family by his marriage with Merilla, younger daughter of Sir John Horner, of Mells, and died in 1681, leaving his wife and only son, John Symes, surviving, and was buried in Barwick Church. Against the west end of the north aisle of the church was a mural monument to his memory, surmounted with the arms of Symes and Horner, and the following inscription :[11]

" Heic subter sepultus jacet Thomas Symes armiger annos natus 46 a febri ereptus 22 die Novembris anno Verbi Incarnati 1681; mæstissimam reliquit viduam Merillam, filiam natu minorem Johannis Horner de Mells in Agro Somersetensi equitis aurati per quam filium unicum Johannem et unicam filiam habuit quorum hœc infans 6 die Septembris 1671, occubuit, heic etiam sepulta, ille, una cum matre superstite monumentum hoc posuit ; pientissima conjux, memoriam mariti sui pie colens hunc etiam sui locum sepulchri statuens cum Deo. opt. Max. visum fuerit."

The remains of the mourning widow were, in accordance with her wish so pathetically expressed, deposited by the side of her husband in the vault immediately beneath this monument, but we regret to say that during the recent restoration of the church the monument itself has been unceremoniously taken down and shifted to the opposite side of the church, where—the opening words of the inscription being no longer applicable—like another more celebrated one, it " lifts its head and lies." The only extenuation for the offenders probably is that they did not understand Latin.

It cannot be too strongly insisted that this removal was a clear violation of the law. Whatever may be done by the Bishop, in the exercise of a wise discretion with regard to a monument recently erected without his license, the law will presume an ancient one to have been lawfully set up, and (subject to rare exceptions) no authority, civil or ecclesiastical, can justify its removal or disturbance without the consent of the family of the deceased (in this case by no means extinct), to whom it absolutely belongs.

John Symes, only son of the above Thomas, survived his father but a few years. He was intended for the Bar, but was carried off by small-pox, in 1687, when only 20 years of age, and his fond mother

---

[11] Coll. Som. ii., 838.

recorded his many virtues and talents on a monument erected by her to his memory in Exeter College Chapel. A copy of the Latin inscription will be found in "Le Neve's, Mon. Angl." * As this young man died unmarried, Barwick, under a family settlement, devolved, first, on his cousin, John Symes, of Mount Serrat, in the West Indies, and then on his nephew, Samuel Parry, who assumed the name of Symes. His co-heiresses sold it in 1750 to John Newman, father of the worthy gentleman of that name, who enjoyed it for his long life, respected by all who had the good fortune to know him.

There were some small estates in Barwick not belonging to the manor, and amongst them one belonging to a gild at Shepton Mallet, which was granted to John Horner, of Cloford.[12] Amongst other owners of land in the parish were the Kelways, a branch of a most ancient and knightly family, who, springing originally from Devonshire, had large possessions in the western counties. Thomas Kelway, a landowner in Barwick, was living at Stoford in 1591. He was son of William Kelway, of Stalbridge, and Eleanor his wife, daughter of John Coker, and grandson of Thomas Kelway, of Sherborne, who married a daughter of the ancient house of Lewston, of Lewston. His uncle, Robert Kelway, was Surveyor of the Court of Wards and Liveries. By his wife, Elizabeth, daughter of Davy Jones, Thomas Kelway left a son, Richard Kelway, of Westminster, gentleman, who, with his mother, in 1613 conveyed their lands in Barwick to Henry Woolmington, then of Hardington, and afterwards of Barwick, gentleman. Descendants of both the families are, or lately were, resident in Barwick. The arms of Kelway were *Arg., two glazier's clipping irons in saltire sab between four Kelway Pears ppr quartering Ramsey and Byset.*

The military annals of Barwick are scanty. From a return to a commission 11 Elizabeth (1569) for certifying the number of able men with their arms in Somerset it appears that in the tything of Barwick there were nine, viz., three archers, three billmen, and three pikemen; and in the borough of Stoford nine also, viz., four archers, three billmen, and two pikemen. Armour—three corslets with pikes and seven almain revetts. In this return the names of the resident gentry are given, but as none are mentioned in Barwick we conclude the owner was non-resident. In a certificate from the Deputy Lieutenants of Somerset in 1584, 16 able men, bearing arms of different kinds, are returned for the hundred of Barwick. In a muster roll for Somerset, October, 1586, of "The Bande of Sir John

---

* Vol. III., p. 91.　　　　　　　　[12] Pat. Roll 2, Ed. VI., 3 pt. m. 42.

To face p. 13

BARWICK CHURCH.

Clifton, Kt.," in the hundred of Barwick, John Tayler, John Lockier, and John Wiseman are entered as pikemen, and Walter Miller (the tythingman), Thomas Scott, Walter Burford, and George Clarke as "shott." Lastly, in 1636, the hundred of Barwick was assessed to a rate for raising £8,000 for providing a ship of 800 tons at the sum of £44, to which Barwick was rated at £15 3s. 4d., Stoford £5 5s., and "Mr. Barrett, Vicar," £1 6s. 8d.

The church was erected at different periods of the Perpendicular style of architecture. As the building stood before the late restoration, the oldest portions were the south aisle and part of the nave. The chancel had evidently been from time to time much pulled about, and is now entirely rebuilt. In the east wall was a three-light window with Perpendicular tracery, but it had been blocked up by a plaster screen, after the fashion of the last century. That window has now been re-introduced and filled with painted glass, and the two square-headed two-light windows in the side walls, hitherto also blocked up, are again restored; but the height of the chancel has been so much increased that these windows are now quite out of proportion and character, and, with the stained high pitched roof, the stone reredos, the painted east window, and the bare stone walls, render the chancel far too dark. It is also questionable whether the floor level should have been so much raised. The chancel was, probably, the site of the original chapel, which was founded in the thirteenth century; and an early Decorated piscina, found encased in the angle of the east and south walls, probably belonged to it. The north aisle is much later than the south aisle, the piers and arches being plain chamfered ashlar, quite rude in execution; whereas those of the north aisle are much superior in design, and ornamented with trefoiled panels. The exterior of this north aisle is the most attractive feature of the whole building. Seldom does a small rural church exhibit so rich an example of the Perpendicular style. Viewed from the road below, it is very striking. The character of the work is not unlike that of the mother church of Yeovil, and it may be surmised that the rectors of that church (the abbess and convent of Syon) contributed to the enlargement of the chapel. Indeed at a later period (4 Henry VII.), their bailiff credits himself, in his accounts, with 40s. given out of charity *(ex elimōs)* of the Lady Abbess " to the Parishioners of the Chapel (capelle) of Berewyk, in part relief of the costs and expences of the said Parishioners in building the said chapel *(in edific̃ d̃ce capelle)* on the humble petition of the said Parishioners." This cannot refer to the whole structure, but it may mean the north aisle, and although Henry the 7th's reign would be very late for Perpendicular work, the architect may have introduced it by particular instructions. There is an arched doorway into the tower from the chancel, the jambs and head of which are made up of an old sepulchral slab, on which parts of an incised floriated cross are still visible. This doorway probably existed as an entrance before the tower was built, but there were indications of another entrance in the old south wall of the chancel, which would be the usual position for it. Afterwards the north doorway was closed, no doubt for comfort, and access to the tower made from the outside. It is now re-opened, and the base of the tower converted into a vestry. In the interior of the church the great puzzle is to account for the present level of the floor. It would seem to have been at one time several feet lower. The sills of the windows are within a foot of the ground. A walled-up doorway, opening into the porch on the south side, is not above five feet in height, if so much ; and a trefoil arched piscina, at the east end of the south aisle, of a later period than that in the chancel, is now only one foot above the floor. If the ground outside has always been of the same general level, there must have been a descent of several steps into the church, and to prevent this inconvenience and to make the church dryer it is probable that when fixed seats were introduced, after the Reformation, the floor was raised. The position of this second piscina indicates a side altar there. To whom it was dedicated cannot now be discovered, but close to it on the south wall is a fragment of a mural fresco painting which represents a stately draped figure, standing on a chequered black and white floor, and bending over a female whose head only is visible, and on which his hand appears to be laid ; but there is not sufficent of the subject left to afford any clue to the legend intended to exhibit. It probably related to the saint whose altar adjoined. There is no documentary trace of the foundation of a chantry in this church, but there were frequently two side altars in churches besides the high altar. A chantry is certainly mentioned in the records, but that seems to have been used as another term for the chapel itself, which, at its original foundation, was little more than a chantry chapel.

The church at one time had a very elegant carved Perpendicular oak screen dividing the nave from the chancel ; but only the base of it, to the height of the pews, remained, on which traces of colour in red, blue, and white were apparent. Other parts were found, cut up by village vandals, for supports and sill pieces to the seats. On the north side of the entrance to the chancel, in the angle of the tower wall, are the steps to the rood loft ; and on the south side a plain rude squint or hagioscope opening into the south aisle. There was found also, embedded in the walls of the chancel, a very small but delicately-carved head, which was, no doubt, a corbel end of a window label. The features are sharply cut and well defined ; the hair flowing, encircled with a fillet of lozenges, and the neck dress, or collar, is fastened by two straps.

The carvings on the massive bench ends are unusually rich examples of church furniture introduced soon after the Reformation. Other examples are to be found in this county, but nowhere so varied and perfect as here. The exact date of their erection is known, as W.H., 1533, is carved on the door of the reading-desk, originally a bench end. W.H. means William Hoper, the patron who, in 1521, presented John Gryme to the living. On another door is a shield with these arms carved on it, viz., *1 and 6, a mullet and in chief a fleur de lys (Rogers) ; 2 and 4 (———) ; 3 and 5, fretty (de Echyngham) impaling quarterly ; 1 and 4, six roundles ; 2 and 3, three camels.* On the door of a pew, that was the clerk's pew, are *Rogers and de Echyngham again quarterly, impaling Courtenay,* being the arms of Sir John Rogers, Knight, who died about 1547, and Elizabeth, his first wife, daughter of Sir William Courtenay, Knight. The oak pulpit is ornamented with carving, and in one panel are the initials E.M., 1619, for Eustace Moore, who was the incumbent.

There are no ancient monuments in the church. On the floor are some large sepulchral slabs with incised crosses, one with initials. In the nave was a flat stone in memory of Thomas Bicknell, who died February 25th, 1629 ; and on another, in the north aisle, inscribed I.G., 1517. Outside, leaning against the wall, close to the north door, is (or rather was, for it has been removed) a large slab to the memory of Richard Slade, who died 15th June, 1636 ; and another, close by, to Jane, wife of Samuel Gyles, daughter of Richard and Margaret Slade, " who lived with him in the estate of matri- mony, June 15th, 38 years, 1673."

In mediæval times, when a church was consecrated, the bishop went thrice round it in procession, and with a branch of hyssop sprinkled holy water on the walls at certain points, which were indicated to him by marks made beforehand. Afterwards crosses—called consecration crosses,—generally of the form termed in heraldry crosses pattee—were cut in the stone, and remained as a memorial of the event. At Barwick they are still well preserved. Round the exterior are at least seven such crosses, and one on the south inside jamb of the west door. There are two crosses on the chancel buttresses and two on the south aisle, and it is very probable that although the primary object of the ceremony was the conse- cration of the new north aisle, the whole fabric was reconciled (as it was termed), as the church may have been profaned during the progress of the works.

There are two bells in the tower. On the treble bell is the legend :—" Vox Augustine sonat in aure Dei," and an elegant cross fleurettèe, encircled with this inscription :—"Jhu merci Ladi help." The two other shields on it are trade marks. The second bell has similar marks with the legend :—" Sancta Katerina ora pro nobis." These marks are not those of a local bell founder, which are well known, but of a London manufacturer, and are to be found in nearly every county. If the bells were the gift of the ladies of Syon they would probably employ a London founder, and the invocation to St. Augustine would be an appropriate allusion to their society, which was of the order of that saint.

The earliest parish register commences in 1560, 13 years after Edward VI. ordered registers to be kept. The following entries occur in one of them :—" Memorandum a pulpit cloak, a cushion, and carpet, given by Merral Symes, lady of the manor, in the year 1708, and a Communion table, bought in the year 1708, likewise. Item : A large silver flagon, given to ye Church of Barwick by Mrs. Merril Symes, lady of the manor, ye 25th of December in ye year 1709, having her cress engraved thereon. Memorandum : A gallery set up in the year 1709, at the charge of the singers, with consent of Merral Symes, lady of the manor of Barwick, and Mr. Sydenham Burch, Mr. William Pearse, rector, and George William, churchwarden, and on consideration of its being an ornament to the Church they do agree and own it to be there own as land for them for ever, and their heirs after them without obstruction."

Several entries relate to the family of Horner, whose chief seat was at Mells, in this county, and who, as already mentioned, became connected with Barwick by the marriage of Merilla Horner with Thomas Symes. John Horner, a nephew of Merilla, married Ann, one of the two daughters and co-heiresses of Edward Phelips, of Preston Plucknett, and took up his residence at Barwick, and several of the following extracts relate to his children.

1729.—Edith, daughter of John Horner, Esq., was baptized Sept. 19.

1731.—W. Horner's daughter, of Barwick, was buried Nov. 3rd.

1735.—Merriall, the daughter of John Horner, was baptized April 26.

1737.—Thomas, the son of John Horner, Esq., of Barwick, was baptized Sept. 24th.

1738.—Johannah, daughter of Richard Picher, Esquire, of Cayford [Keyford], was baptized Oct. 12th.

1739.—George, the son of John Horner, Esq.,was baptized Sept. 8th.

1740.—Richard, the son of Richard Picher, of Cayford, was baptized Aug. 7th.

1741.—Anne, daughter of John Horner, Esq., was buried July 14.

1741.—Elizabeth, daughter of John Horner, Esq., of Barwick, was baptized July 19.

1742.—George, the son of John Horner, Esq., was buried April 13th.

1748.————— 8th then married Mr. Robert Marks and Mrs. Alice Bullock Mr. Marks of the parish of Thorn. Mrs. Alice Bullock of ye parish of East Coker.

1773.—John, son of John Newman, Esq., and Grace, his wife, brought to church (having been before privately baptized), Aug 30.

Barwick being, originally, only a hamlet, in the parish of Yeovil, the rector of that parish was charged with the sole cure of souls therein, and the inhabitants resorted to his church for Divine offices, and for such ceremonies of public worship as were then enjoined or sanctioned by the authority of the Church. This was a manifest inconvenience to the inhabitants of Barwick and Stoford, which increased with the growth of population, and in the reign of Henry III. a chapel had been erected by the Lord of the Manor for the accommodation of his tenants and dependents. Preston in Yeovil was also made a chapelry, but with this difference, that, while the rector retained the patronage of Preston, which was never separately endowed, he relinquished that of Barwick to the lord of the manor in consideration of his foundation and endowment of the chapel; and, moreover, gave up certain tithes to the chaplain in return for being relieved of the charge of providing a chaplain himself. By the general law no oratory or chapel could be legally founded in any parish without the consent of the bishop, the patron, and the incumbent of the mother church, and this rule was in force as far back as A.D. 1182, when a chapel founded in a parish in the county of Oxford was dissolved by the Pope, having been illegally built without the consent of the parties interested.[18] But, with this consent, they were frequently established in hamlets of parishes lying at a distance from their mother church, and endowed by the Lord of the Manor and others. Sometimes the privilege of administering the Sacrament and of burial was conferred on them, and then they became parochial chapels, the chaplain taking an oath of obedience or affiliation to the rector of the mother church. That seems to have been the case at Barwick.

In the year 1406, John Gamull, Canon of Wells, rector of the church of Yeovil, having occasion to investigate his relative position to the Incumbent of Barwick, procured certain official authenticated copies from the Bishop's registers, which copies are now preserved in the Public Record Office. They must have been handed over as part of the title deeds when the rectory of Yeovil was appropriated, about the year 1413, to the Abbey of Syon; and on the dissolution of monasteries, in the reign of Henry VIII., they were swept into the Augmentation Office, and have ever since remained there. The

---

[18] Kennett, Par. Ant., ii., 267.

earliest document is an agreement, not dated, between the Rector of Yeovil and the Lord of Barwick. The Rector was Walerand le Tyes (or Teutonicus, the German), who held the living in 1219, and Sir William de Cantilupe was the first of that name, who died in 1239, so that the approximate date may be fixed in the early part of the reign of Henry III. William de Cantilupe is called patron of the chapel by reason of foundation and endowment assigned thereto. ("Patronus Capelle de Berwyke racione fundacionis et dotis eidem assignate.")

The following is a translation of the agreement from the Latin text:

" To all sons of Holy Mother Church, to whom the present writing shall come, the Prior of Saint Augustine and Dean of Bristol greeting in the Lord. Whereas between Sir Wallrand, the German, rector of the Church of Gyvele of the one part, and William de Cantulupe, knight, patron of the chapel of Berwyke, by reason of foundation and endowment assigned thereto, and Thomas, chaplain [capellanus] of the said chapel, of the other part, a question arose in our presence by authority of letters of the Lord the Pope, concerning tithes of hay and of the mill of the manor of the same, and tithe of one virgate of land assigned to the said chapel for endowment and oblations at the feast of St. Mary Magdalen [to whom the chapel was dedicated] and the eve of the same. At length the dispute was amicably quieted in this wise, that is to say, that the said W. Knight, for himself and his men, hath acknowledged the tithes as well of the mill as of hay [to belong] to the said rector, as the right of his church. Also the said W. Knight and his successors shall, as patrons of the said chapel, freely present to the Bishop, without gainsaying whatsoever, a chaplain for the said chapel, when the same shall chance to be void. And because as well the said Rector as his successors are bound to find in the same chapel a chaplain, who shall dilligently celebrate therein divine service for the parishioners, the said W. Rector for himself and his successors hath granted that the Chaplain who for the time being shall be admitted by the Bishop on the presentation of the said W. Knight and his successors shall have and receive the oblations of which mention was above made and all other the oblations coming to the said chapel, also the tithe of the aforesaid virgate of land and all small tithes of the whole manor, also the tithe of the mill and a moiety of the tithe of demenes hay of the said knight and patron. But the said chaplain for the time being shall swear fealty and canonical obedience to the said Rector and his successors, and if he shall contravene his oath he shall be bound to pay one besant under the name of a penalty to the aforesaid church; and in the name of the said Rector and Patron he shall honourably serve or cause to be served in the said chapel, so that it shall not behove the said Rector to find in the said chapel another who shall serve therein, or to assign for their service to the chaplains more than is above said."

Not many years after, another dispute arose between the Rector of Yeovil and the Incumbent of Barwick. In the year 1286, Philip de Stanton, Rector of the Church of Ievele, instituted proceedings in the Bishop's Court at Wells, complaining that John de Bergeveny had been presented and instituted to the vicarage of the chapel of Berwyke, and the second time to the chantry of the said chapel, and behaved himself as Rector thereof, whereas the same appertained in full right to the mother church of Ievele. Wherefore the said Philip prayed, in his own name and in the name of his said church, that the admission of the said John to the Chapel of Berwyke should be pronounced null and void, and that the said John be by definite sentence removed from the said Chapel. The said John de Bergeveny, by his answer, admitted that he had been presented by Lord John de Hastinge first to the vicarage of the Chapel of Berwyke, and the second time to the chantry of the same and never to the chapel of Berwyke, and also that he had been admitted to the said chapel and instituted rector of the same. After hearing the case and the evidence adduced, the Bishop's Commissary pronounced judgment to this effect: " In the name of God, Amen. We, Alexander de la Knolle, Canon of Wells, Commissary of the venerable father, Lord R., by the grace of God Bishop of Bath and Wells, in this behalf the merits being known and fully understood of the cause which is depending between Master Philip de Stanton, Precentor of Wells, rector of the Church of Ievele, plaintiff of one part, and John de Bergeveny, defendant of the other part, concerning the unjust or surreptitious admission of the said John to the Chapel of Berwyke, the libel of the said Philip, and the answer of the said John to the same being read, the authentic instruments before noted being seen also before us judicially, pronounce the admission of the said John to the chapel of Berwyke, his institution and induction into corporal possession of the same chapel, to have been obtained not without the sin of falsehood by stealth, and we revoke, quash, or make void the same admission, institution, and induction as false or surreptitious, and by definite sentence remove the said John from the aforesaid chapel of Berwyke, which he *de facto* unjustly and surreptitiously detains by occupation, and we impose perpetual silence upon the said John concerning the said chapel of Berwike, since he has no right in the same, and by definite sentence we declare that the said chapel of Berwike ought to belong, and also by full right to appertain to the aforesaid mother church of Ievele, and the Rector of the same. And

[14] Cart. Ant. Aug. off. F. 7.

we declare that the said John de Bergeveny ought to be content with the portions [in this] wise under written, appertaining to the chantry of the chapel of Berwyke, which portions consist (to wit) in one virgate of land with . . . tithes of Berwyke and of Staford, and in a moiety of the hay from the demense of the lord of Berwyke, according to what is contained in the Inquisition made at the first presentation of him, the said John."

The record is endorsed in a later hand : " Contains the sentence given in the year of the Lord 1286 upon the right of the Chapel of Berwyke, appertaining to the Church of Yevelle, heard before the Commissary of the Bishop of Bath and Wells, and that it is not a rectory in itself, but is appurtenant to the said church of Yevelle." [15]

Besides the foregoing documents, the Rector, John Gamull, produced from the Bishop's registry the two following presentations.

On the ninth before the Kalends of July, 1373, the Bishop admitted Sir William Vinegyre, priest, to the chapel of Berewyke of his diocese, void by the death of John Bonewylle, last chaplain, to which he was presented by Walter Amyas Ralph de Walsham and John Malyns, attorneys of the Earl of Pembroke, the true patrons of the said chapel, this turn, and instituted him perpetual chaplain according to the form of the ordinance of the said chapel. And immediately after such institution, the said William, the Holy Gospels being touched by him, then and there swore to do to Sir Robert Samborne, rector of the church of Ievele, those things to which he is bounden according to the form and effect of the ordinance and composition of the said chapel ; Sir Thomas Aumenet and John Carsse being present.

Also on the 27th of February, 1374, the Bishop admitted Sir Robert Poleyn to the chantry of the chapel of Berwyke, through the resignation of Sir William Vynegre, last chaplain of the same, by reason of exchange with the church of Loketone (Lufton), which the said Robert first obtained, to which he was presented by Sirs Walter Amyas and Ralph de Walsham, the attorneys of the Earl of Pembroke, and instituted him perpetual chaplain. And the said Robert, after the institution aforesaid, the Holy Gospels being touched by him, swore a corporal oath to the Rector of the Church of Ievele, according to the form of the ordinance and composition of the chantry of the chapel aforesaid, John Brimpton and Sir Thomas Horne being present.[16]

In Pope Nicholas' Taxation, A.D. 1341, 14 Edward III.,[17] Barwick

---

[15] Cart. Antiq. Aug. off. M. 89.   Deeds various.   G. Box 9, Tray 27.

[16] Cart. Ant. Aug. off. No. 1.   [17] Exch. Lay Subsidies 169-14, m. 7.

is not described as a separate benefice, but is included under the head of " Ievele," and the jury, consisting of John Vage and others, parishioners of Ievele, say that the court [*i.e.*, house or manse], curtilage, and garden of the Vicar of Berewyk, within the parish aforesaid, together with mortuaries, oblations, and other small tithes there, are worth by the year £4.

John de Hastings, Earl of Pembroke, who died in 1376, had enfeoffed three Feoffees of the manor of Berewyk and Stoford, and the said Earl held the advowson of the chantry of Berewyk, which is worth nothing beyond the service of the chaplain serving there daily.[18]

At the commencement of the reign of Henry V. the Rectory of Yeovil was sold by the Arundel family to the Crown, and granted to the newly-founded monastery of Syon, and it continued in the possession of that society until the dissolution of monasteries by Henry VIII. One of the first acts of the Ladies of Syon was to procure the Rectory to be legally appropriated to their house, and this was effected by a bull of Pope Martin V., A.D. 1418. Upon every appropriation provision was made for the permanent endowment of the Vicar, on whom the performance of the services of the church devolved; and this was effected by agreement between the parties, which, when sanctioned by the Bishop, was called the ordination of the vicarage. In Yeovil there had always been a vicar or curate, maintained by the Rector, who was not necessarily in holy orders himself. Walerand le Tyes was in fact a layman, and probably held the Rectory for the King, in whose service he was. The ordination of the vicarage of Yeovil was made by an agreement confirmed 12th February, 1438, by John (Stafford), then Bishop of Bath and Wells, between the Abbess and Convent of the Monastery of Syon, " Rectors and Proprietors of the Parish Church of Yevel," of the one part, and Richard Stone, perpetual Vicar of Yevel, of the other part; and amongst other things it was agreed that the Vicar should be entitled to all the small tithes of the parish, " except the small tithes arising from the villages and hamlets of Berwyk and Stoford, which the perpetual chaplain (capellanus perpetuus) of Berwyk is accustomed to receive as in right of his chapelry."

From this it will be seen that at this time Barwick was still part of the ecclesiastical parish of Yeovil, and the incumbent was styled Perpetual Curate.

Notwithstanding he appears to have been popularly called Rector, as in the Yeovil Churchwardens' accounts for 36 Henry VI., 1457-8, the parish is credited with a fee paid by the " Vicar of Yeovil for the cross, cope, and thurible which he took with him to the funeral

---

[18] Esch. 49 Edw. III. No. 70.

of the late Rector of Berwyke." This was Nicholas Baker, who
died 1457 ; he was instituted to the " Parish Church or Chantry of
Berwyke."

Nearly 100 years after the incumbent is still called Rector. In
the Valor Ecclesiasticus 26 Henry VIII. (1535), the entry is as
follows :—" Berwyke, John Gryme rector there. The Rectory is
worth in demesne lands 43s. 4d. In predial tithes, 32s. ; in tithe of
wool and land, 20s. 4d. ; in personal tithes, with other casuals, 61s.
4d. ; total, £7 17s. Whereof are paid to the Archdeacon of Wells,
for procurations and synodals, 2s. 5½d., leaving clear, £7 14s. 6½d."
In the Wells Registry, Barwick is still called a rectory, and the incumbents are instituted as rectors.§

The Impropriate Rectory of Yeovil, after the dissolution, remained
a long time in the hands of the Crown and its lessees, but in 1560 it
was granted by James I. to Sir Thomas Freke and Henry
Sterr, who sold it to Sir Edward Phelips and his son, Sir Robert
Phelips. In 1637, Sir Robert sold off the tithes in portions, Thomas
Compton, of Sutton Bingham, being the purchaser of those
arising in Barwick and Stoford, and they descended from him to the
late Mr. George Harbin, of Newton. Mr. Harbin, a few years ago,
sold these tithes, except those of his farm, called Court Farm, and
covenanted with the purchaser for the repair of the chancel, the
liability to which had always fallen upon him and his predecessors,
as the freeholder ; but it may be very questionable whether the
freehold of this Church and of the church of Preston also has not
descended to the heirs of Sir Robert Phelips, inasmuch as he only
sold certain portions of the great tithes, but not the impropriate
Rectory of Yeovil.

The following list of the Incumbents was compiled before the
publication of Mr. Weaver's valuable work, " Somersetshire Incumbents," but the two accounts substantially agree.

1219 to 1239.—Thomas . . . . the chaplain of the Chapel. Patron, Sir
Wm. de Cantilupe.

1310.—Adam Trap was presented, and the custody of the Church granted to
him. Patron, not stated.

Henry de Havresham. Patron, not stated.

1311.—Henry de Strowe, to the Chapel of Borwyk, vice Henry de Havresham,
resigned. Patron, John Lord Hastings.

---

§ In a return, made by the commissioners for carrying out the Act 1 Edw. VI.
for the dissolution of Chantries &c., of lead, bells, &c., belonging to chantries in
the County of Somerset, there is an entry :—" Barwick—Two little bells belonging to the Chapel of Stowford, containing xi. lbs." No trace of the existence of
any such chantry can be discovered, and the explanation probably is that the
Commissioners treated Barwick as a Chantry Chapel coming within the meaning
of the Act, instead of a Parish Church as stated in the Valor Eccl.

1322.—Roger Bradesnesch, to the Chapel. John Bonewylle, Chaplain. Patron Philip de Columbers.

1373.—William Vynegre instituted Chaplain, vice Bonewylle, deceased. Patron, the Earl of Pembroke.

1374.—Robert Poleyn, to Chantry of the Chapel, vice Vynegre resigned. Patron, the Earl of Pembroke. John Wymyngham.

1436.—John Capron, vice Wymyngham, resigned. Patron, John Rogers, Lord of Barwick.

1444.—Nicholas Baker, Chaplain, vice Capron, resigned. Admitted to the Parish Church or Chantry of Berwyke, Ralph De Audley, Sir John Beauchamp, Edward Hulle, and Wm. Walberton, Patrons for this turn.

1457.—Thomas Poole, vice Baker, deceased. Patron, John Audley, in right of his wife, widow of John Roger, Esq.

1461.—Thomas Kymer, vice Pole, resigned. Patrons, John Audley and Annie, his wife.

1501.—John . . . . vice Kymer, deceased. Patron, Henry Rogers. Walter Perrott.

1521.—John Gryme, admitted to the Church of Berwkye, vice Perrott, deceased. Wm. Hoper, patron for this turn by grant of John Rogers, Esq.

1551.—Henry Lurbecke, instituted to Rectory. Patron, not stated.

1574.—John Rawlyns, vice Lurbecke, deceased. Patron, Richard Rogers, of Brianston, Esq.

1605.—Eustice Moore, vice Rawlyns, deceased. Patron, Humphrey Colles, of Chard.

1630.—Tobias Barrett, instituted to Rectory, vice Moore, deceased. Patron, not stated.

1643.—John Harvie or Harford, A.M., presented to the Rectory. Patron, John Symes, Esq.

"Richard Heymore, A.M., took this Church in the time of the Civil Commotions 'adeptus' in 1662, but retained in his possession, being constituted in both orders by the Bishop in 1660." Extract from Register Hugo MSS., British Museum.

1703.—W. Preston, vice Highmore, deceased. Patron, Merilla Symes, deceased.

1708.—Wm. Pearce, vice Preston, resigned. Patron, Merilla Symes, widow.

1721.—Henry Michell, vice Pearce, resigned. Patron, Nathaniel Carpenter.

1730.—Thomas Elmes, vice Michell, deceased. Patron, Thomas Thornbury.

INSCRIPTIONS UPON THE GRAVE-STONES IN BARWICK CHURCHYARD.

In pavement at west end:—

(1.) " Here lieth also the body of Mary Coad, the wife of Joshua Coad, who died the 12th day of December, 1740." (Verse at bottom imperfect.)*

(2.) " Here lyeth ye body of Jane, daughter of William Highmore, who died the 15th of October, 1758."

" Here lyeth the body of William Highmore, who departed this life the 17th day of ——, 1783, aged 58." (Verse imperfect.)

(3.) " Here lyeth the body of Hannah, the wife of Bryan Griffin (?), who died the —— of November, 1733, aged 96 years.

> " Behold the place where I do lye ;
> As thou art now, so once was I ;
> As I am now, so shalt thou be ;
> Prepare to ———, and follow me."

(4.) " Here lieth ye body of Mary, ye wife of John Abbot, who departed this life October ye 2nd, 1773, aged 36 years. Sacred to the memory of Roberu Guppy, who departed this life Feb. 15, 1826, aged 82 years. Also Ann Guppy, his wife, who departed this life October 5, 1825, aged 85 years."

(Much mutilated.)

(5.) " Here lieth the Body of James ——, son, who died November 27, aged 33.

"And also here lieth ye Body of Sarah Fathers, daughter of John Woollmington.

" Here lieth the body of Isaac, son of John Woollmington, who died December (?) the 10th."

(Other names and verses all very imperfect.)

(6.) " Here lieth the Body of Mary, wife of Edward Porter, who departed this life Nov. 1st, 1784, aged 73 years.

> " Weep not, my husband dear, I pray ;
> At God's appointed time we must obey."
>   William Kimber, fecit, Yeovil."

* Probably they were the father and mother of John Coad, a pious carpenter, who was born at Stoford, and joining as a zealous Protestant in the Monmouth Rising was convicted and left for execution by Judge Jefferies, but escaping the gallows by " woman's wit," he was exiled to Jamaica, and released after the Revolution in 1688. He left an account of the march and defeat of Monmouth and of his own sufferings, describing it as—" Memorandum of the wonderful Providences of God to a poor unworthy creature during the time of the Duke of Monmouth's Rebellion, by John Coad."   It was published a few years ago by Longman & Co.

(7.) " Here lieth the body of Mary, the wife of John Highmore, who departed this life May the 22nd, 1767, aged 51 years. Here also lies ye Body of John Highmore, Husband to ye above-named Mary Highmore, who departed this life Oct. 22, 1783, aged 66 years."

(8.) " Here also lieth the body of John Highmore, son of John and Mary Highmore, who departed this life July the 17th, 1781, aged 39 years.

" My parents dear, behold and see,
God hath prepared a place for *mee*,
To live with Christ and saints above,
For ever in eternal love."
(Below.)
" Farewell, my husband and children dear ;
I am not dead, but sleeping here.
My debt is paid, the —— you see ;
Wait but a little, you'll (?) *come to me.*"—C.H.
(On vase carved at top : " Reynolds 248.")

(9.) " Sacred to the memory of Edmund Sherring, who died December 31, 1834, aged 76 years.

" Also Mary, his wife, who died February 28th, 1815, aged 41 years."
" Also Catherine, their daughter, who died January 17, 1810, aged 16 months.
" And John, their son, died April 26, 1813, aged 10 years.
" William, their son, died May 1, 1813, aged 3 years."
" And Edward died May 14, 1813, aged nine years.
" Also Mary, their daughter, died August 30, 1823, aged 17 years."

(10.) " Here lieth the body of Jane, ye wife of Samuel Gyles (daughter of Richard and Margaret Slade), who lived with him in the estate of matrimony 38 years six months and 10 daies. Died in the 63rd year of her age the 25th day of January, Ano. Dom. M.D.C.LXXXXVI.

" Although with dust this body hath repose,
Yet virtue ever lives and blossoms like the rose.
Her better part the soul shall never die,
But far transends the clouds above ;
And in that day when ye last trump doth sound,
Then shall this body rise united (?) and renound,
For evermore praises and haleluiahs sing
In everlasting bliss with Christ her Lord and King.
This was her faith and it was —— "
(Three lines illegible.)

(11.) " Here lieth the body of John Highmore, who departed this life the 8th day of March, 1763, aged 72 years.
" Also here lieth the body of Susannah, daughter of John and Julett Heighmore, who departed this life March ye 12th, 1794, aged ——

" Death sudden took my home from me,
With pious, loving words was she.
A faithful friend and aunt sencear here,
Alone my (?) friend lieth here."

Other side of stone illegible, except :
" Daughter ——— John and Julett Highmore, Jan. 3, 179.

This concludes the inscription upon the grave stones now inserted in the pavement outside the west door of the Church.

(1.)   (Upright tombstone in churchyard.)

" Sacred to the memory of William Highmore, who died March 3rd, in 1799, aged 73 (?) or 8 years.

> " This is my house, my home, my grave
> (Whose or which) narrow room is all I have
> Here ―――― until the great Assize,
> Then beautifully changed, I hope to rise."

(On opposite side.)

" Sacred to the memory of William Highmore, who died January 17, in 1807, aged 57 years.

(Verse commencing)

" Farewell, ye loving wife and children dear."

(2) [In middle of churchyard on west side, on what is sometimes called the Robber's tomb.   Upright, enclosed with rusty iron rails.)

" Underneath lies interred William Tanner, Gent., who departed this life on the 17th day of November, 1782, aged 70 years.

> " Farewell, vain world; I've had enough of thee,
> And now am careless what thou says of me ;
> Thy smiles I count not, nor thy frowns I fear ;
> My Days are past, my head lies quiet here ;
> What fault in me you've seen take care to shun,
> And look at Home, enough there's to be done."

" In grateful remembrance of a most affectionate Uncle.   His Nephew William Row, has caused this tomb to be erected.

" In a vault underneath are deposited the Remains of William Row, Esq., who departed this Life April 19, 1832, aged 87 years." On opposite side, a nearly obliterated inscription records the burial of Ann, the wife of William Row.

EXTRACTS FROM THE EARLIEST REGISTER BOOK IN BARWICK CHURCH.

A Register Booke of all those persons that have been christened, marryed, or buryed w.hin the pishe of Barwecke, sythence the seconde yeare of the Raynge of our Soveraigne Ladye Queene Elizabethe :—

1560.

CHRISTENINGS.

January 20, Margaret Gardener, daughter to Rychard Gardener.
February 14, Jannet Tucke, daughter to Wm. Tucke.
February 22, Joanne Myller, daughter of John Myller.
June 7th, Edythe Clarke, daughter of Edwarde Clarke.
October 20, Henry Apsie, son of John Apsie.
October 29, John Ffry, son of Wm. Ffry.
November 8, Edythe Wyseman, daughter of William Wyseman.
December 31, Wm. Collins, son of Thomas Collins.

1561.

March 19, Henry Collins, son of John Collins.
March 23, Edythe Chrese, daughter of Richard or Ralph (?) Chrese.
April 10, Clement Donne, son of Wm. Donne.
May 3, Joanne Haryson, daughter of Wm. Haryson.

1562.

February 23, Joanne Gyllet, daughter of Richd. Gyllet.
March 20, John Myller, son of John Myller.
March 29, Agnes Wyseman, daughter of Wm. Wyseman.
Johanne Rawlings, Rector.

Thos. Ffry, } Gardiani
Wm. Done, }

April 4, James Ffry, son of William Ffry.
December 25, Leonard Haryson, son of William Haryson.
December 27, Thomas Chrese, son of Richd. Chrese.

1563.

January 26, Joanne Parsons, daughter of John Parsons.
April 15, Walter Burforde, son of James Burforde.
May 2, Matthew Gyllet, son to Richd. Gyllet.
May 17, John and Joanne Donne, children of Wm. Donne.
June 12, Lionell Chaplinge, son to Henry Chaplinge.
September 12, Wm. Collins, *daughter* (!) to John Collins.
October 13, Joanne Socke, daughter to Wm. Socke.
December 5, Geo. Collins, son to Thos. Collins.
December 11, Joseph Boole, son of John Boole.
December 15, Joanne Bartlett, daughter to George Bartlett.

1564.

January 2, Wm. Collins, son of Henry Collins.
February 6, Joanne Collins, daughter to Wm. Collins.
March 2, Richd. Parsons, son of John Parsons.
March 7, Dorowthie Chrese, daughter of Raphe Chrese.
March 21, John Sprage, son of Anthoine Sprage.
May 3, James Donne, son of Wm. Donne.
May 6, Maude Burford, daughter to Anthoine Burford.
May 13, Henry Russell, son of Thos. Russell.
May 20, Thos. Ffry, son to Wm. Ffry.
June 5, Alse Clarke, daughter of Edward Clarke.
June 10, Henry Holman, son of Wm. Holman.
June 17, Agnyes Myller, daughter of John Myller.
September 15, Thos, Grove, son of Mychaell Grove.
November 20, Tamflen Collins, daughter of John Collins.
December 25, Joanne Smyth, daughter of Lambert Smyth.

1565.

February 3, Elizth. Burford, daughter of James Burford.
March 14, Benedicte Gyllett, son of Richard Gyllett.
June 18, Agnes Harryson, daughter of Wm. Harryson.
November 17, Anthonie Myller, son of Thomas Myller.
December 8, Joanne Coxhole (?), daughter of John Coxhole.
December 16, James Collins, son to John Collins.

1566.

June 14, John Ffry, son of Wm. Ffry.
June 14, Alce Wiggott, daughter of Agnes Wiggott.
September 14, John Russell, son of Thomas Russell.
November 3, Geo. Clarke, son of Edward Clarke.
November 9, Joanne Gaynge, daughter of Walter Gaynge.

PISCINA IN THE SOUTH AISLE.
(See page 13.)

CHAPTER II.

CHILTON CANTELO.

THERE is not much to add to Collinson's account of this place. He considers it to be one of the Chiltons of the Domesday Survey of Somersetshire, but it is to be observed that only one Chilton can be found in the Survey, and that certainly was Chilton Polden, near Bridgwater. Mr. Eyton, in his "Domesday Studies," conceives Chilton to be included with Barwick in the old Hundred of "Givelea." That may be true as regards Barwick, which is contiguous to, and was not improbably part of, the Domesday Manor of Yeovil; but no such argument applies to Chilton, which is five miles distant from Yeovil. There can be no doubt that before A.D. 1201 Chilton was in the hands of the same lord as Barwick, who held that Manor of the King by the service of half a knight's fee, which half fee and also the advowson of the Church of Chilton were in the hands of the Crown. At the commencement of King John's reign, Walter de Cantilupe granted "the whole ville of Childeton" to Robert de Cantilupe, subject to the service of one knight's fee[1], which Robert was probably Robert the son of Roger de Cantelo, to whom Gilbert de Cantilupe granted lands in Camel by charter contemporary with the above fine[2]. Robert was succeeded by his son Richard. In the subsidy roll 31 Edw. I., Richard le Venour (who had married Alice, a daughter of Richard de Cantilupe)[3] and Wm. de Cantilupe are said to hold the Manor

---

[1] Somt. Fines, 3 John, No. 47.   [2] Harl. Charters 47, G. 33.
[3] Ass. Rolls, Div. Cos., 31 Edw. I., N. 2—12, 4.

of Chilton of John de Hastings by one knight's fee.[4] Le Venour was probably lessee.[5] William de Cantelo settled his lands in Chilton, subject to life interests to himself and his wife Margaret (who survived him and married Geoffrey de Pupelpenne), upon his sons John and Richard successively in tail, both of whom died s.p., and the ultimate heir of William was his nephew John de Cantelo, son of his brother Richard.[6] This was the John de Cantelo mentioned by Collinson. He died in 1350, his property in Chilton consisting of a messuage, curtilage, garden and dovehouse, 76 acres of land, a water-mill, and £4 16s. 8d. rent of Assize; and his heirs were his two daughters, Emma and Margaret.[7] Between these two a partition was made by the Escheator, 30 Edw. III.,[8] but Chilton appears not to have been included in it, for one undivided moiety (apparently Margaret's) vested by purchase or otherwise in Sir John Cary, Chief Baron of the Exchequer in the reign of Richard II. Upon his impeachment and attainder he was (upon slender grounds) found guilty, with the other judges, of attempting to subvert the constitution by his advice to the King; his estates were forfeited, and soon after the Manor of Chilton (nominally the entirety, but in fact only a moiety), and also the Manor of Hardington, were granted to John Wadham, of Edge, ancestor of the Wadhams of Merifield,[9] and by fine, 20 Rich. II., he settled both manors on himself and Joan his wife and their issue in tail, with remainder to his right heirs.[10] John Wadham (then Sir John Wadham, Knight) died in 1412, and his moiety of Chilton descended to his son and heir, Wm. Wadham,[11] and Robert Cary, son of the Chief Baron, released all his right in Chilton to him.[12] As regards the moiety of Emma, the other daughter of John de Cantelo, she was married twice. Her first husband was Thomas Chastelyn, of Trent, by whom she had a daughter, Joan; her second husband was Walter Parker, who survived her and died in 1362, holding her moiety as tenant by the courtesy.[13]

---

[4] Lay Subs. Somt., 169—3.
[5] Esch. 23, Edw. III., No. 47.
[6] Ass. Rolls, Div. Cos., 20 Edw. III., N. 2—22, 3.
[7] Esch. 23 Edw. III., No. 47.
[8] County Placita Som., 30 Edw. III., No. 82.
[9] Rob. Pat., 13 Rich. II., 3 Henry IV.
[10] Somt. Fines, 20 Rich. II., No. 93.
[11] Esch. 13 Henry IV., No. 39.
[12] Close Rolls, 3 Henry V., No. 7.
[13] Esch. 35 Edw. III., Pt. 2, No. 34.

It does not appear how this moiety passed to the Wadhams, but according to the Inquisitions, John Wadham (apparently grandson of the above William) had acquired the entirety before his death in 1473,[14] and ultimately it vested in his descendant, Lawrence Wadham, who died seized of the manor in 1523.[15] After the death of his only son, Nicholas Wadham, who left no issue, it must have been sold to John Parham, Esq., for by settlement dated 29th January, 17 James I., he settled the manor on his son, Sir Edward Parham, and Dame Bridget, his wife, and the heirs of Sir Edward,[16] from whom it passed into the hands of Sir George Strode, as mentioned by Collinson.

The advowson of the Church of Chilton was not included in the grant of the ville by Walter de Cantilupe in 1202, already noticed ; and, not many years after, King John bestowed on Hubert de Burgh, Justiciar of England and Earl of Kent, amongst many other valuable gifts, the manor of Camel,[17] which adjoins Chilton, and he and his son acquired, possibly from the Crown also, the advowson of Chilton and the over-Lordship both of Barwick and Chilton.[18] Hubert de Burgh died in 1243, leaving John de Burgh his son and heir, and Margaret, daughter of William King of Scotland, his widow, surviving him. Three years after, an arrangement was made between the Countess and John de Burgh whereby, in consideration of her releasing her dower out of the Manor of Camel and other manors, John de Burgh granted to her (inter alia) the advowson of the Church of Chilton and two knights' fees which William de Cantilupe held in Berwyk and Chilton, for her life only, " as after her decease the whole will revert to John."[19] This fine explains the Inquisition of George de Cantilupe, 2 Edw. I. (ante p. 3), which finds that he held the Manor of Berewyk of John de Burgh by the service of half a knight's fee, which John was the son of John the party to the fine. He died in 1279, s.p. m., and it is presumed that the advowson of Chilton with the fees reverted to the Crown by escheat or remainder, as it was held by Joan, daughter of Edward Plantaganet, son of Edw. I., the wife first of Sir Thomas Holand, Earl of Kent, and secondly of Edward the Black Prince. By the Inquisition taken after her death in 1385 (in which she is styled Joan the King's mother, late Princess of Wales), it was found that

[14] Esch. 14 Edw. IV., No. 19.
[15] Esch. 14 Henry VIII., No.
[16] Coker Court MS.
[17] Test. de Nevill, p. 160.
[18] Test. de Nev., p. 172.
[19] Fin. Div. Cos., 31 Hen. III., No. 219.

she held one curtilage in Chilton juxta Modiford, with the advowson
of the church, and that Thomas Holand, Earl of Kent (her son by
her first husband), was her heir.[20] He died seized thereof in 1397,
leaving another Thomas his son and heir,[21] who was beheaded as a
traitor in 1399, and the advowson became forfeited to the Crown.
From that time it remained in possession of the Crown until the
reign of Elizabeth, when it passed into private hands.

In 1864 the Church was restored, and on the walls were found
interesting mural paintings, illustrating the legend of the Assumption
of the Virgin, a particular account of which is to be found in the
Proceedings of the Somerset Archæological Society, vol. xx., p. 69.

---

[20] Esch. 9 Rich. II., No. 54.
[21] Esch. 20-22 Rich. II., No.

SUTTON BINGHAM.

T HE railways have introduced us to many attractive novelties, of which we previously knew little or nothing. We do not allude now to the acquaintances we make with sociable fellow travellers; they are all very well as long as they last; but they are gone like a shadow at our journey's end, leaving nothing behind them, except occasionally—an umbrella. We are thinking of the unknown regions which are discovered —the choice bits of scenery even in one's own district that never struck us before; the picturesque valleys, whose solitary charms we had always overlooked; and the trim stations in them, from which we catch a glimpse of an inviting village, whose "Hampden," perhaps, sleeps in yonder churchyard; but we turn in vain to our guide book to tell us anything of either. How few, for instance, know the existence, much more the history, of the little place to which we propose to dedicate this chapter. Buried in obscurity, unvisited except by the explorers of the wilds beyond—with its pleasant site, its wonderful little church, and its quaint mansion house, so it would have remained, had it not been launched into the world by the South Western Railway, and enrolled as a station in the lively pages of Bradshaw.

Sutton or South-ton, which lies south of the ridge which divides it from East Coker, and has the affix of Bingham from the De Binghams, its ancient lords, is a small parish 549 acres in extent, and a population of only 52. Towards the east it is separated from Closworth by the tributary to the Yeo, which descends from the Corscombe hills, and on which there is a small mill. The village stands at the extremity of a spur of land sloping gradually down to the valley and stream. The church, which is said to be dedicated to All Saints, is peculiarly interesting, and demands our first attention. It consists only of a nave and chancel, all on the same level, and though of small dimensions—the entire length being 50 × 15—it exhibits three distinct styles, Norman, Early English, and Decorated.

Referring to the exterior, the western end is very simple, but of good proportion. It is strengthened by two small buttresses of plain but effective outline, and in the centre is a Decorated two-light window with tracery of the ordinary type, but the unusual length of the lights gives it an elegant appearance. Above, near the apex of the gable, are two small but boldly treated Decorated arches, forming the belfry, and containing two bells, on one of which is inscribed " W. Compton, Ann. Dom. 1685."

Proceeding on the north side we come first to a small Norman window, deeply splayed ; and there is a corresponding one of similar design in the south wall opposite.

Next, on the same side, is a small modern porch. The circular arch of the internal doorway is of Norman work—portions of the label with flat dogtooth ornament remaining; but there are evidences of the whole of the arch having been rebuilt, which renders it difficult to describe its original design accurately.

Immediately opposite, on the south side of the nave, are traces of another Norman doorway, the lower part of which at some time has been walled up, and the upper part converted into a small window. It is perfectly plain in design, without any moulding or other ornament.

Eastward of the porch we come to a window which may be considered either late Early English or Early Decorated, and there is a corresponding window on the other side.

Following round the building we next come to the chancel, which is of the same height as the nave, the slight difference in the ridges being occasioned by the thick stone covering of the latter. The only noticeable feature on the north side is a boldly treated small Early English window, with wide internal splays, and an unusually effective trefoil-headed internal arch. On the south side of the nave are two more windows, precisely similar in design, but slightly varied in size. The eastern end is solidly built—of very early work —the angles having bold dwarf buttresses or spurs about three feet out of the ground, and, judging from the masonry, may be Norman.

The eastern window is a very interesting example of Early English plate tracery. It is a two - light window, with a small

SUTTON BINGHAM CHURCH.

To face pag. 34

quatrefoil in the circle. The massive mullion is relieved on the outside by a bold sunk moulding down the centre, and a simply-moulded label. Internally the window is treated with a very broad splay and a chamfered drop arch.

On entering the church the striking feature is the fine Norman chancel arch, of bold but simple design, which tradition says was brought from some religious house in the neighbourhood. The inside jambs are formed of half-circular columns with double jambs beyond, the outer one being chamfered and the angles filled with two small circular columns, with the bases simply moulded. The caps are elaborately carved, of various designs, and finished with a boldly-moulded abacus. The arch consists of three rows of members, the two outside ones being bold bead or roll mouldings, and the centre one formed of an elaborate zigzag ornament. Outside these is a bold label with a flat dogtooth, very similar in character to the label over the north door. This chancel arch, although so small (being only six feet in width), suits the simple character of the church, and throws a quiet shade over the chancel which adds to the interest of its appearance.

In the south-east angle of the chancel is an Early English piscina, the bowl being corbelled over the face of the wall with moulded edges; and in the nave is a circular font, fashioned with a cable moulding of undeniable Norman character.

The church was repaired, but fortunately not restored, in the year 1868, and in the course of the work several interesting discoveries were made.

On the walls of the chancel were found mural paintings, rude in execution, which extended down to about three feet from the floor. Though now confined to the chancel, they were probably continued in the nave also, as we found, on taking off the external coats of whitewash, traces of similar design underneath, and under that again were remains of still older work. They are outlines in distemper of a reddish brown colour, laid on a light ochre ground, which is studded between the figures with quatrefoils resembling roses. The space over the chancel arch is divided into squares, with a rose branch in each, and are about four feet in height. The original work is not scrupulously preserved, having been restored by an amateur artist, with a free pencil, but no alterations, we are assured, were made in the design. They were probably executed by a travelling painter (a mendicant friar it may be), who, in olden days of symbolism and superstition, combined painting with piety, and decorated the walls of churches to the taste of his employers.

Beginning at the west end of the south wall, the figures represent our Saviour crowning the Virgin, who is seated, with St. John standing near. Coming then to the single window on the north side, there stands on the west splay a mitred bishop, with his right hand raised, in the act of benediction, and holding a pastoral staff or banner in his left. On the palm of the raised hand is a lozenge within a quatrefoil, and on his breast two crosses patée, with an indication of jewellery between them, and the like on the mitre. It has been surmised that this figure was intended for Robert de Bingham, Bishop of Salisbury, brother of Sir William de Bingham, Knight, who was lord of Sutton in the reign of Edward III., and that the repetition of the crosses on his figure refer to the arms of the Bingham family—*az, a bend cotized between six crosses patée*—but there is nothing uncommon in the representation of bishops by such designs as these ; and as to the arms, the De Binghams of Sutton bore quite a different coat.

On the east splay of the same window is a female nimbed figure standing erect, her head-dress or whimple being encircled with a wreath of small cinquefoil roses of the pattern of those on the walls. Her right hand is extended across her breast, and there is a slight resemblance to the Annunciation. The paintings are continued on the eastern and south walls, but the figures are so much defaced that only a fragment (it may be a head or a foot) is here and there visible. With the exception of the Coronation of the Virgin there does not appear to be any representation of a miracle or legend, but the designs are confined to single figures, mostly crowned or nimbed, and as the church is dedicated to All Saints, they may have been those of favourite saints whose virtues the faithful were invited to imitate. Under the floor of the chancel were found some fragments of heraldic tiles, but only one perfect enough to be identified. The arms on it were *vaire*, which was the coat of Beauchamp of Somerset, and, with a canton, the coat of Filliol of Dorset. No canton is visible in the tile, as the dexter chief of the shield is broken off ; but we may venture to supply it, as the mother of Mary, wife of Thomas de Bingham, Lord of Sutton, who died in the reign of Henry IV., was Alice, daughter of Sir William Filliol.

Several broken sepulchral slabs or stone coffin lids were found buried in different parts of the church and churchyard, nearly all of them inscribed with crosses. Sunk in the centre of the nave was a massive stone coffin, six feet six inches in length, but without any cover, containing the disturbed bones of two bodies, said by a medical authority to be male and female. The cover, seven inches in thickness, was laid as pavement, with a Greek cross inscribed on it, in another part of the church. The cover of a small stone coffin was also found, only five feet in length, with ogee moulding round the edge, and slight remains of a rich foliated cross, carved in relief. Another of Purbeck stone, with a moulded edge, and on it the matrix of a metal cross.

On the floor of the chancel are several memorials of the Compton family, who resided here, and held the Manor for many years as leaseholders. The first is to the memory of Ann, daughter of Thomas and Maud Compton, who died 9th December, 1627. Another, in memory of Maud, the wife of Thomas Compton the younger, who died in 1628, with this couplet :—

> " Here lyeth a constant, wise, chast, pious wife,
> O Pitty 'twas—her Pitty cost her life."

The writer was perhaps inspired by the jingle in Shakespeare :—

> " 'Tis true, 'tis pity,
> And pity 'tis 'tis true."

There is a tradition that the death of this lady was occasioned by nursing her husband in the smallpox or some other infectious disease. He solaced himself with a second partner, and died 4th February, 1650, his gravestone being inscribed :—" Ecce quid eris." Elizabeth, his second wife, died in 1671. His father, Thomas Compton, died, as another stone tells us, 19th December, 1645.

In the churchyard, west of the church, are the remains of an interesting cross, which, judging from the moulding, is probably 15th century work, and it appears to have been combined with a somewhat elaborate tomb, on the western end of which it rests. The tomb is nearly eight feet in length and four in width, and stands about two feet out of the ground, and the base of the cross is cut out of the massive stone covering, which is of the unusual thickness of twelve inches. Underneath this slab a moulded decorated string is carried round, and no doubt a moulded base would be found below the surface, although now hid by the rising of the ground. The shaft of the cross is octagonal, about seven feet in height, tapering very much, and finished with a moulded octagon cap, with four plain shields on the cardinal sides. Traces remain on the cap of what may have been the base of a canopy for a sculptured figure, surmounted by a cross, but time or the spoiler has destroyed the crowning point of this interesting and almost unique relic.

The old registers are lost. Of those remaining the register of baptisms commence in 1742, the marriage register in 1766, and the burial register in 1777. The following list of rectors was taken from a transcript at the British Museum of the Diocesan Registers (Add. MSS., 32709-80), and since published in "Somersetshire Incumbents," by the Rev. F. W. Weaver.

Rectors.	*Patrons.*
1314 John de Bristol resigned the church of Sutton Cauvel. John de Petrestre succeeded him by exchange for vicarage of Chyweton.	
1348 John de Bingham, acolyte ...	William de Bingham.
1394 Adam Hill	Rector of Sutton Bingham, instituted to Compton Abbas, Dorset, on presentation of Abbot of Milton.
John Blanker	
1410 Thos. Gerveys	John Peny, domicellus.
1412 John Sheyle	Thos. Kayleway, arm.
1417 John Richard	The same.
1422 Reginald Peyt	Roger Wyke, arm.
1427 Wm. Maryet	The same.
1429 Thomas Vele	The same.
1433 William Clerc	The same.
1437 John Brome	Roger Wyke, arm.
William William	
1448 William Somerset, monk of Eynesham	The same.
1453 Hugh Wylkyns	The same.
1467 Gerard Rendyll	The same.
1478 John Yate	John Devyoke, arm.
1500 Hen. Fayeman	Wm. Kaylwey, arm.
1505 Wm. Tanner	Wm. Kaylwey, Kt.
1541 John Stone	Lionel Williams, hac. vice by grant of John Kalewey, of Rokeborn, Hants.
1559 Rawlin Radnor	John Chetell.
1561 Thos. Maister	George Sydenham, arm.
1586 John Morgan	George Sydenham, of Combe Sydenham, Kt.
1592 Thos. Jones	
1609 Wm. Gollop, A.B., on deprivation of T.J.	John Sydenham, Kt.
1625 Gibbes Gollop, A.M., rector of Odcombe	The same.
1645 Nicholas Stone, A.M.	Wm. Hanley, of Melbury Bubb hac vice.
1654 Saml. Thompson, A.B.	John Sydenham, Bart.
1676 Edwd. Burge, A.M. *	The same.
1708 Saml. Seward, A.B.	Thos. Compton.

* The name should be Birch or Burche. He married a daughter of Sir Humphry Sydenham, Knight. In the marriage allegations in the Registry of the Archbishop of Canterbury is this entry: "1682 May 16, Edward Birch, of Sutton Bingham, Clerk, Bachelor, about 37, and Mrs. Mary Sydenham, of Chilworthy, county Somerset, Spinster, about 22, with consent of her father, Sir Humphry Sydenham, Knight, at St. Bride's, London."

The Manor House is a moderate-sized, unpretending building of the Jacobean style, and was probably erected by some member of the Compton family. The first settler here was Thos. Compton, second son of James Compton, of Wigborough, in the parish of South Petherton, who removed from that place to Sutton in the reign of Queen Elizabeth (see Pedigree Somerset Visitation, 1623), and we may fairly presume that he built it. It is rather remarkable that there are no remains of an older mansion, as the De Binghams doubtless resided here. We can only suppose that after the family became extinct, the house gradually was deserted, and at last removed to make way for a more suitable one.

We will now endeavour to trace the descent of the Manor from the earliest times.

Sutton is not mentioned in the Inq. Gheldi but it was, no doubt, comprised in the Hundred of Givela (Yeovil), as the non-geldable virgate in that Hundred held by Roger Calvus. It has been suggested that this person may have been the Roger Boisell who was Roger Arundel's tenant of Sutton in the Domesday Survey, where the name of Roger Calvus does not occur, and that Calvus may have been a nickname, subsequently changed to Calvel. In the Exeter Domesday (fo. 414), Roger Arundel is said to hold the manor of Suton, which Wluuard held in the time of King Edward, and it gelded for five hides, of which five carucates were arable. " Roger Bissell holds this of Roger Arundel, whereof Roger Boiscell holds 4 hides and half and one ferting in demesne, and ' villeins ' hold the other land [the remainder]. Roger has there 6 bordars, 4 cottagers, and one mill, worth 16s. a year rent. There is a wood three furlongs in length, and two in width, and 12 acres of meadow, and it is worth per annum 30s., and when Roger Arundel received it, it was worth 100s."

Roger Arundel held also the adjoining manors of East Chelborough and Melbury, and Roger Bissell or Boisell was sub-tenant of the wife of Hugh Fitz Grip of lands in Poxwell and Chiselborne.[1]

Collinson says that this Roger Buissel was progenitor of the De Binghams, and in the 3rd edition of Hutchins' History of Dorset it is suggested that the De Binghams sprang from Bingham, in the county of Nottingham, a manor held at the Domesday Survey by Roger de Busli, and that he may have been the same person as Roger Buissel. But we doubt this theory. Roger de Busli was one of the most important of the Conqueror's grantees, deriving his name, probably, from one of the two places called Busli, near Eu, in

---

[1] Exon Dom., pp. 35—47.

Normandy. He held no less than 46 manors in Nottingham, 49 in Yorkshire, 5 in Leicestershire, and one at Sanford, in Devon, the last given to him by Queen Matilda. He resided at the Castle of Tickhill in Yorkshire; and at Blyth, in that county, where he had another castle, he and his wife Muriel founded a Priory A.D. 1083. It is most improbable, therefore, that this great lord could have been a sub-tenant of Roger Arundel of a single manor in Somerset.

Besides this, we have direct evidence of the early failure of his issue. He was dead in 1098, leaving a son, who died childless in 1102, and the issue of his only brother, Ewald, terminated in the reign of Henry III. with Idonea, the wife of Robert de Vipont. These facts appear in the pleadings of an action between Robert and Idonea and Alice Countess of Eu, descended from Beatrix, sister of Roger de Busli.[2] It is probable, therefore, that Buissel and de Busli were distinct families.

All the knights' fees held by Roger Arundel were, in the reign of Henry II., held by Gerbert de Percy, in right of his wife, Matilda, to whom they had descended. In the return made by the Barons, 12 Henry II., 1162, of the knights' fees they held of the king,[3] Gerbert de Percy certifies that he held thirty in Dorset, of which Robert Calvel held one, which we presume to be Sutton, although the return is classed under the head of Dorset. After De Percy's time his fees were divided between Robert de Newburgh and Robert Fitzpayn, and Sutton afterwards held of the Fitzpayn family was, it may be presumed, the Percy fee held by Robert Calvel in 1162. This presumption is very materially strengthened by a document in the Cartulary of Montacute Priory, preserved in Trin. Coll., Oxford.

The Priory were the owners of the Manor of Closworth (adjoining Sutton), which had been bestowed on them by William, Earl of Morton, son of the Domesday Earl; and amongst the charters in the Cartulary is one whereby Baldwin, Earl of Devon, gives to the Priory a mill-dam, "unam esclusaille," for a mill in Closworth, lying between the land of William Calvel (not Robert, as in Lib. Nig.), of Sutton and the bridge; and another charter, whereby William Calvel releases to the Priory all his right to the mill-dam adjoining his land of Sutton, for which Guido the Prior gives him one mark. There is no date to either charter, but we can fix it with tolerable accuracy, as Baldwin the Earl died A.D. 1155, and Guido had ceased to be Prior before A.D. 1174. By what title Earl Baldwin held this

---

[2] Hunter's South Yorkshire, I., p. 223.

[3] Lib. Nig.

mill-dam does not appear; perhaps as Overlord of the Hundred of Coker, in which Closworth was situated.

During the Calvel ownership Sutton acquired the distinctive title of Sutton Calvel (corrupted by scribes into Canvel and Chanvel), which it preserved for some time after it came into the possession of the De Binghams, the next owners. They were the elder branch of that ancient family which has flourished for so many centuries at Bingham's Melcombe, Dorset, and which, since the recent failure of the male line of the house of Frampton of Moreton, is, perhaps, the only Dorsetshire family which can show an unbroken male descent from the time of the Plantagenets. Some of the extravagant pedigrees of the Elizabethan age trace back this family at Sutton to the reign of Henry I. and II., but their earliest connection with it appears in the reign of Henry III., when William de Bingham, Lord of Sutton (elder brother of Robert de Bingham, the founder of the Melcombe branch), married Cecilia, daughter of Geoffry de Mandeville, Lord of Hardington and Coker. This marriage is proved by letters patent, dated at Westminster 20th December, 11th Edw. III., whereby the King confirmed to John de Bingham the gift made by a charter of Geoffry de Mandeville to William de Bingham in free marriage with Cecilia his daughter of the land in Sarpeham* which Master William, sometime Parson of East Coker, had of Peter Hokedyw, reserving only to Geoffry and his heirs eight feet in width of the land adjoining his pasture for digging a ditch, such land to be held in severalty, quit of all suits of Court and Hundred, gelds and customs to the tithing and liberty of Kocre pertaining, saving to Geoffry and his heirs two suits at the Hundred of Kocre for the Tithing of Sutton ; and the King also confirmed to the said John de Bingham the concession which John de Mandeville, son of Geoffrey, by his writing, made to the said William and Cecilia, of the land in Sarpeham, to be held in severalty as aforesaid, all which the King granted and confirmed to John de Bingham, cousin and heir of the said William and Cecilia, and to the heirs of his body, according to the terms of the said charter and writing.[4]

It is not known when William de Bingham died, but probably before 1243 (27 Hen. III.), as in the Assize Rolls[5] it is said that

---

* The old barn which stands about 100 yards *west* of Sutton station is still called " Sharpham Barn."

[4] Pat. Roll 11 Edw. III., m. 8.

[5] Div. Co., 27 Hen. III., m. $\frac{5}{13}$

Cecilia, Lady (Domina) of Sutton, in the Hundred of Coker, made default in her suit and service before the Justices Itinerant. We conclude that it was his son, whose name was also William, who held Sutton about 1204,[6] and was assessed to a subsidy in 1303.[7] He died about 1314, and on an inquisition, taken at Montacute 6th September in that year, the jury found that William de Bingham held for his life certain lands in Hardington, by lease of John de Mandeville senior, who held the same of the King in capite by the service of half a knight's fee; and further that the said William held in his demesne as of fee of his own inheritance the ville of " Sutton Channel," of Robert Fitzpayne, by the service of one knight's fee, worth by the year £15.[8]

We find no record of the death of John de Bingham, "cousin and heir" of William and Cecilia, but it occurred before 1357, as in that year William de Bingham (his son, it is presumed) held the manor of Sutton Bingham and the advowson of the church, by the service of one knight's fee and 20s. rent, of Robert Fitzpayn, as of his manor of Chelborough, and that Robert, with the King's license, commuted such service for a yearly rent of one penny.[9]

This William de Bingham held by Royal Grant, 29 Edward III.,[10] the custody of lands in Yeovil, in West Mersh, and Kingston-juxta-Yeovil, late of William Carent, deceased, until his heirs were of full age ; and amongst the ancient charters relating to the Yeovil alms-house, now unfortunately lost, was one dated at Yevele, 26 Edward III., whereby William de Bingham, described as " Dominus de Sutton Bingham," granted to William de Welde all the land which he had by the grant of Richard de Anne and Johanna his sister, situate on the fields of Kyngeston and West Marsh juxta Yevele, The seal to this charter discloses the important heraldic fact that the arms borne by the Melcombe branch down to the present time—*Az a bend cotised between six crosses patee or*—was not the original coat of the elder house, for the arms on this seal are *Ermine three lions rampant in chief*, with the legend : " Sigillum Willielmi de Bingham."*

---

[6] Kirby's Quest.

[7] Lay Sub., 31 Edw. I., Som. $\frac{18}{52}$

[8] Esch. 7 Edw. II., No. 15.

[9] Esch. 30 Edw. III., No. 60 (2d Nos.)

[10] Rot. Orig. 29 Edw. III., Ro. I.

* The writer communicated this discovery to the late Mr. Charles Bingham, and it is noticed in the third edition of Hutchins.

The same arms are quartered with those of Byset and Romesey on the tomb in Milton Abbey of Sir John Tregonwell, who married the heiress of Kelway. William de Bingham is mentioned as Lord of East and West Hascumb in or near Odcome, and he was the owner also of the manor of Binghams Worth, in the parish of Netherbury, Dorset, and 43 Ed. III. (1370) he and Margery his wife were possessed of other lands in that neighbourhood.[11] Indeed the De Binghams had an early connection with this part of Dorsetshire, for 8 Edward I. Justices were appointed to take the assize mort d'ancestor arraigned by William, son of "Robert de Bingham Lodres," against "Richard de Bingham Lodres," touching possessions in Bingham Lodres, Eggardon and Askerwell.[12]

In 1381 William de Bingham sold the advowson of the church and 15 acres of land in Sutton to Sir John Chideok, Knight, for 100 marks in silver, but this must have been only a temporary severance, as we find the advowson afterwards restored as appendant to the manor.

We do not know when he died, but we do know that, in 1382, he made a settlement entailing Sutton on his three sons, John, Thomas, and Richard, none of whom appear to have had any male issue. By a fine,[13] between John de Bingham (the son) and Joan his wife, plts., and William de Bingham, deft., Sutton was settled on John de Bingham and Joan his wife in special tail, remainder to John in tail male, remainder to Thomas in tail male, remainder to Richard in tail male, remainder to the right heirs of John. As the daughters of Thomas succeeded to the estate, it is clear that neither of the sons left any male issue, and it is equally clear that John died without any issue by Joan in the lifetime of Thomas, who having thereby the reversion in fee as John's heir-at-law, as well as his own estate tail, was practically the absolute owner. He married Mary, daughter and ultimate heiress of Sir Walter de Romesey, of Rockborne, Hants, one of the co-heirs of the great Barony of Byset,[14] and on his marriage Sutton was resettled upon him and his wife and their issue with remainder to Sir Walter in fee. The wife survived, and after her second marriage the following deed was made with no very apparent object.

[11] Hutch. Dors. II. 112.

[12] Pat. Rolls.

[13] Somt. Fines, 5 Ric. III., No. 37.

[14] Madox Bar., p. 51.

By a charter dated Friday before the feast of Trinity, 4 Hen. IV. (1403), reciting that Adam Hill, late rector of Sutton Bingham, and another, had granted to Thomas Bingham and Mary his wife (daughter of Walter de Romesey) and the heirs of their bodies, the Manor of Sutton Bingham, and the advowson of the church thereof, and one carucate of land called Shappenham (probably Sharpham) in East Coker [Sutton], and, in default of such issue, to Thomas and the heirs of his body, with remainder to Walter de Romesey in fee ; and reciting that Thomas and Mary had issue, Elizabeth, Johanna, and Alianor, their daughters and heirs ; that Thomas had died, and the said Mary had married John Peny, then her husband ; the said Sir Walter Romesey granted and confirmed the premises to the said John and Mary and the heirs of her body by Thomas [Bingham], remainder to Walter de Romesey in fee. The arms on the seal to this charter are a *fesse and in chief a label of three points.* Legend : " Sigillum Walteri de Romesey." Mary kept possession of the title deeds, but after her death her second husband, John Peny, handed them over in solemn form to her two surviving daughters, Alianor and Johanna (Elizabeth having, we may conclude, died unmarried). This appears by an indenture made at Sutton Bingham Wednesday after the feast of Trinity, 3 Henry V. (1416), between John Peny, surviving husband of Mary, late wife of Thomas Bingham, Lord of Sutton, of the one part, and Henry Horsey, husband of Alianor, daughter and one of the heirs of the said Thomas Bingham, and Thomas Cayleway, husband of Johanna, daughter and another heir of the said Thomas Bingham, of the other part, whereby it is recorded that John Peny had delivered to Henry Horsey and Thomas Cayleway, in the presence of John Wynford, John Warde (parson of Clowesworth), John Sheyl (parson of Sutton), Michael Otesford, John Beyvyn, John Passeware, William Godelegh, and others, divers chests, hampers, and " Pixides," and 84 Charters, Rolls of Court and other muniments, to the inheritance of the said Johanna and Alianor relating. (Originals at Montacute House.)

Besides the Manor of Sutton acquired from their father, these two daughters inherited the large estates in South Wilts and Hants of their maternal grandfather, Sir Walter Romesey, and Sutton by partition it is presumed became the sole property of Johanna, who survived Thomas Cayleway, and after her marriage with her second husband Roger Wyke, settled Sutton on her son John Kayleway. This was done by fine in 1448, between Nicholas Radeford and William Lytelwyke, plts., and Roger Wyke and Joan his wife, defts., whereby the Manor of Sutton Bingham and the advowson of the Church, and lands in East Coker and Sutton Bingham, were limited to Roger and Joan for their lives; remainder to John (son and heir of Thomas [John by mistake in the fine] Kayleway), and Joan his wife and the heirs of their bodies, remainder to the right heirs of Joan, the wife of Roger.[15] From this John Kayleway, Sutton descended to Sir William Kayleway, of Rockborne, who sold it to George Sydenham, Esq., of Cleve, Somerset, to whom by indenture dated 27 November, 3d Eliz. (1561) it was conveyed by the said Sir William Kayleway and Francis, his son and heir apparent. The deed is sealed with the arms of Kelway, quartering Ramsey, Byset, and Bohun. (Original at Coker Court.)

The purchaser, then Sir George Sydenham, of Combe Sydenham, Kt., died in 1596, and under his will Sutton passed, after the death, without issue, of his only daughter Elizabeth (the wife, first, of the famous Sir Francis Drake, and, secondly, of Sir William Courtenay of Powderham), to the eldest son of his brother, Sir John Sydenham, of Brympton, from whom it descended with Brympton to Sir Philip Sydenham, Bart. On the breaking up of the Sydenham estates, occasioned by the unfortunate extravagance of Sir Philip, he was compelled to sell Sutton in 1707, for £2,550, to Thomas Compton, who, as already mentioned, held the greater part on lease for lives.

Mr. Compton having no children, his estates (including Sutton) descended, on his death, to his sister and heiress, Isabella, wife of Charles Abingdon; but she also died childless, and, the family of Compton being apparently extinct, she gave Sutton by her will to her husband, and under his will in 1724 it passed to his nephew and heir, George Abingdon, of Over Compton. From him it descended to Barbara, his only daughter and heiress by his wife, Barbara Wyndham, of Dinton, who became the wife of Swayne Harbin, of Newton Surmaville. His eldest son, Wyndham Harbin, sold Sutton in 1815 to William Helyar, of Coker Court, whose great grandson, Mr. Horace Augustus Helyar, is the present owner.

---

[15] Somt. Fines, 26 Hen. VI., No. 82.

CHAPTER IV.

BRYMPTON.

THE forced sale of Sutton Bingham by Sir Philip Sydenham in the year 1706 cannot be dissociated from the misfortunes which compelled him to part with the whole of his ancestral estates, including—sad to say—the fair Manor of Brympton, which had come down to him from his ancestor, John Stourton, of Preston, who flourished in the reign of Henry VI.

Sir Philip Sydenham was the last of the Brympton branch of the most ancient and honourable family of Sydenham, the earliest recorded member of which was Robert de Sydenham, Lord of Sydenham or Sydeham, near Bridgwater, in the reign of King John. Sir Philip was the only surviving son of Sir John Posthumus Sydenham, of Brympton, one of the representatives of the county of Somerset in Parliament, who had the honour of entertaining the unfortunate Duke of Monmouth in his semi-royal progress through the western counties in 1680, when he sought to gain the affections of the people as champion of the Protestant cause, and secure their assistance in his aspirations to the Crown. Sir Philip's mother (his father's second wife) was Lady Mary Herbert, daughter of Philip Earl of Pembroke, and he was born in or about 1676. He succeeded as third baronet on the death of his father in 1696, his elder brother John, who was captain in a regiment commanded by his grandfather the Earl of Pembroke, having died a bachelor in 1692. Sir Philip received his university education at Catherine

Hall, Cambridge, and proceeded to his degree of M.A. He was at one time M.P. for Ilchester, and in 1701 and in 1702 for the county of Somerset. The county must have been quite alive with bell-ringing on both occasions, as his bailiff's account book (in the writer's possession) shews that largesse was distributed to the ringers of Yeovil, East and West Coker, Preston, Montacute, East Chinnock, Merriott, Odcombe, and Tintinhull. He subsequently became F.R.S., and, although not an author himself, was evidently a man of literary tastes, and a great collector of the works of others. Among his friends was that eccentric antiquary, Thomas Hearne, who dedicated to him a version of the "Iter Antonini," and eulogized his ancestor—Simon Sydenham, Dean of Sarum, who died in 1437. The learned Humphrey Hody, of Wadham College, Oxford,—son of George Hody, Rector of Odcombe (adjoining to Brympton)—was another of his friends, and in the British Museum[1] is an original letter from Dr. Hody to Sir Philip, respecting his ancestor, the Dean. He was a correspondent also of the Oxford historian, Anthony à'Wood, to whom he pointed out some errors in his "Athenæ."[2]

In his copy of "Walker's Sufferings of the Clergy," now amongst the Rawlinson MSS., Bod. Lib., he made some notes of local interest. "Mr. Ford, B.D., was," he says, "turned out of East Coker as being a pluralist, being also Rector of West Coker. He was not turned out of West Coker because he complied. Mr. Gove had the vicarage of East Coker till a few years before his death. Limberley, curate [perpetual curate] of Stoke-under-Hamden, was sequestered of an estate of tenant [*i.e.*, copyhold] of about £20 per annum, in the same parish. He had a wife and child. Mr. Hugh Brown was sequestered of Poorstock, in Dorsetshire. He and his family were afterwards in Hardington, where he died in 1659, and lies buried in the chancel of which he had been rector. He was a learned good man."

Until he sold Brympton, Sir Philip made it his country residence, living, as appears by his bailiff's accounts, in a frugal inexpensive manner. Being for several years member of Parliament he spent part of his time in London, but still there is no trace of any such extravagance as could have stripped him of all his property. Besides Sutton and Brympton, he possessed Houndston Farm in Odcombe, lands in Yeovil, and estates at Monksilver and Preston Bowyer, in Milverton, but they all went, leaving the unfortunate

---

[1] Aysc. Cat., 4,275.
[2] Tanner MSS., Bodl. Lib.

man almost penniless. Brympton was sold in 1722 to Thomas Penny (who had been Receiver General of the county) for £15,492 10s. The conveyance is dated 9th March, 1722, the parties being Sir Philip Sydenham of the one part and Thomas Penny, described as of Keyford, parish of Yevell, gent, and Onesiphorus Penny, of Yevell, haberdasher of hats (his trustee) of the other part. By it, in consideration of the purchase money (of which £3150 only came into the hands of the poor Baronet, the remainder being paid to his mortgagees, of whom Penny himself was one), " the manor or reputed manor, capital messuage, Barton Farm and demesne lands of Brimpton, in the county of Somerset ; and the advowson of the Church of Brimpton ; and the manor of Alvington, and all other the manors and hereditaments of the said Sir Philip Sydenham, in or near Brimpton, Alvington, West Coker, Odcombe, and Tintinhull, or any of them," were conveyed to Thomas Penny in fee. Penny died in 1730, and the trustees of his will in 1731 mortgaged the manor of Brympton (but not the advowson), and afterwards conveyed the equity of redemption to Mr. Francis Fane, of Bristol, who, by extraordinary fatality, eventually became Earl of Westmoreland. From him Brympton descended to John the 10th Earl, who devised it to his daughter, Lady Cecily Georgiana Fane, and on her death in 1874 it passed by her will to her nephew and godson, the Honble. Spencer Cecil Brabazon Ponsonby, who in compliance with the terms of the will assumed the additional surname of Fane.

Besides Brympton, Sir Philip was also obliged to sell an estate at Hackness, in Yorkshire, which descended to him from his great grandmother, Alice, daughter and heiress of Sir William Hoby. It came to Sir Philip's father from Sir Thomas Hoby (also Posthumus), who died in 1640, and there is a momument to his memory in Hackness Church, erected by Sir John Sydenham, in 1662. The last bay of the north aisle of that church, now used as a vestry, was enclosed, and appropriated by Sir Philip as a parochial library, and it is recorded that it was " erected by Sir Philip Sydenham, Lord of the Manor, in 1700."

Of his own books he published a catalogue in 1727, with this quaint title, " Catalogue of the Library of Sir Philip Sydenham Bt., late of Brimpton D'Evercey, in the county of Somerset. (' We are but of yesterday and know nothing. Our days upon earth are a shadow.' Job vii., 9. ' Righteous art thou, O Lord, and just are Thy judgments.' Psalm cxix., 137.) London, printed by J. Science in the year 1727." On the frontispiece are the Sydenham arms—*arg a chevron between three rams tripping sab*, and the name and title, "Sir Philip Sydenham, Bart., of ye Wannges, Yorkshire. 1727." At the end is a fantastic device, intended probably as a badge; it displays a tiger or wolf rampant on a cap of maintenance, bearing the Ulster badge on his shoulder, entwined with two serpents and surmounted with two doves volant. At the base are two storks holding a scroll, on which the name " Sir Philip Sydenham " is engraved.[15] There is no crest or motto, but from Harl. MS. 5915, he appears to have adopted a very commonplace one, " medius tutissimus."

There are also in the British Museum two engraved portraits of Sir Philip. One is a mezzotint from a painting from De Haese, on which is written in MS., " Sir Philip Sydenham, of Brympton, æt suæ, 24, 1700." The other is a small oval from a painting by N. Capana, in a furred dress, with the arms Sydenham and Stourton *(a bend between six fountains)*, quarterly, underneath.

A memoir of Sir Philip, penned by his contemporary and acquaintance, Mr. Hazelwood, and added in MS. to his copy of " Lloyd's Worthies," will be an appropriate conclusion to this rambling story. It appears in " Brydge's Restituta," vol. i., p. 471.

" SIR PHILIP SYDENHAM, BART., OF BRIMPTON, SOMERSET.

"Born, I believe, between 1680 and 1690, for when I first knew him in 1726 he seemed between 40 and 50. Died a bachelor about 1744. His estate of £4,000 a year he much wasted by expensive living and freakish generosity. Being disappointed in love with a lady after the match was agreed on affected his brain. Sold the remains of his estate to his cousin, Humphrey Sydenham, M.P. for Exeter in several Parliaments, only reserving £400 a year for his life. Drank very freely; loved books of English antiquities, collected a large library of such and of divinity, of which last he gave away many to private clergymen. Most of his books remained many years packed in boxes, and were so when he died, he having no house to put them in, living in lodgings in various places in Holborn, Hadley, Whetstone, Friar Barnet. Superstitious; died a Roman Catholic. Never did any one considerable deed of charity as I heard, but gave away many half-crowns to the poor and to drawers and taverns where he generally dined. His brain unsettled; I never heard he was confined. He was not like me, for he had no terror on his mind or lost his limbs. I was much trusted by him, and I never imposed upon him, or I might have got much from him by asking at proper times, but others I believe did."

---

[15] Brit. Mus. Aysc. Cat., ub sup.

Sir Philip was never married. He died in 1739, and was buried at Barnes, Surrey.

To come now to Brympton itself, Collinson's account ("Hist. Som.," vol. iii., page 214) is very meagre and imperfect, and was not derived from personal inspection. All his information, except a few extracts from Inquisitions, is copied (without acknowledgment) from a MS. volume called "Parochial Histories," in the library of the Society of Antiquaries (MS. 115), written by a Mr. Theobald in 1757, who certainly did visit Brympton, and made notes of what he saw.

Brympton—bright, sunny Brympton—has been a favourite resort of our Archæological Society, and the late Mr. Freeman, in vol. iv. of the Proceedings, noticed some of its attractive features.

As the Sydenhams were for many generations the owners, it will be convenient to present an epitome of the descent of this branch of that ancient Somersetshire family. Those who wish to consult a complete pedigree of the family and its various branches will find it in Burke's "Extinct Baronetcies," and more fully in a chart compiled by the late Rev. Frederick Brown and Mrs. Everett Green, called "Extracts from Pedigree of Sydenham Family."

The earliest member of the family connected with Brympton was :

(a.) John Sydenham I, who acquired it in the reign of Henry VI by his marriage with the co-heiress of John Stourton of Preston, and died in 1468, having been M.P. for the county.

(b.) Walter, his son, married Margaret, daughter of Sir Robert Harcourt, Kt., but survived his father only one year.

(c.) John Sydenham II, son of Walter, three years old at his father's death; married first, Elizabeth, daughter of Sir Humphrey Audley, Kt., and Elizabeth his wife, daughter of Sir Philip Courtenay; and 2ndly, Joan, a daughter of the house of Arundel, of Lanherne, Cornwall—possibly Joan, daughter of Roger Arundel, and widow of William Pentier, who died 1529, when she was only 19. John II died 6th December, 1543, and was succeeded by his son.

(d.) John Sydenham III, who was knighted 1548; M.P. for Somersetshire 1554 ; married Ursula, daughter of Sir Giles Bridges, Kt., and died in 1557. He must have been a very wealthy landowner. By his will, made at Brympton 8th April, 1557, he directs "his body to be buried in the parish church of St. Androwe in Brympton," to which he bequeaths 6s. 8d. To his daughter Anne he bequeaths 400 marks towards her preferment in marriage, and after payment of his debts he gives his estates in Bouley, Mylstone,

Monkensale, Morestone, Sampford Peverele, Uplomen, Holiecombe Rogus, Burlescombe, Columpton, Teverton, Gambostone, Chyttlehampton, Thorverton, Upton Pyne, Langleigh, and Bollestone, in the county of Devon, to his son Henry in tail male, with remainder to his (the testator's) right heirs. His estates in Donyford, Hartrowe, Kings Brompton, Upton, Stokegummer, Bicknaller, Crocombe, Brompton-Raufe, Mylverton, West Stowey, West Leigh, Combe Florie, Kingstone juxta Yevyll, and the Borowe of Wachett, in the county of Somerset, " all of which I lately purchased together with Sir John Wyndham, Kt., and late were the inheritance of John Sidenham, of Orchard, Esq., deceased," he gives to John, his " younger son of that name," in tail male, with like remainder to his (the testator's) right heirs. His messuages and lands in the borough or elsewhere in the parish of Chard, which he had lately purchased of Thomas Cogan, of Mountague, he gives to his son Walter in tail male, with like remainder to his (the testator's) right heirs. He gives to Ursula, his wife, in fee, all his estates in the parishes of East Coker, West Coker, and in Keinsford, or elsewhere in the parish of St. Deacon [Decuman's], subject to the payment of an annuity to " Johanner, sometime the wyef of my brother John Sidenham, deceased," during his life. Then he directs that his estate of Combe Sidenham, in the parish of Stogummer, after the death of himself and his wife, shall remain to his son George in tail male, with remainder to his (the testator's) right heirs. His manor of Lopen, which he lately purchased of Sir Gyles Strayngewayes, Kt., he gives to John Sidenham, his eldest son and heir-apparent, in fee, subject to his confirmation of certain copyhold grants, in default of which he gives the said manor to his son William in tail male, with remainder to his (the testator's) right heirs ; and he gives the residue of his personal estate to his said wife " to dispose of for my soule helthe as she shall seme best," with legacies of 40s. to each of his " yeomen servinge-men being howshould servaunts," and 6s. 8d. to each of his " hynes laborers."[16]

(*e.*) His eldest son, John Sydenham IV, was 30 years old at his father's death, and no doubt Brympton came to him by settlement, as it is not mentioned in the will. He was knighted in 1574, and married, 1st, Grace, daughter of Sir William Godolphin, of Godolphin, Cornwall; and 2ndly, Mary Blount. The date of his death has not been ascertained. He was living in 1583, returning to the Musters of Horse in that year one demy lance and two light horsemen. In 1567 he had returned one billman, one gunner, and two pikemen, one

---

[16] Inq. p. m., 4 & 5 Ph. and Mar., pt. 3, No. 237.

great horse with a demy lance, three corslets and one gelding for a
light horseman. Mary, his widow, was afterwards married to
Walter Dennys, Esq.[17]

(*f.*) John Sydenham V, his son, knighted 1603, married, 1st,
Mary, daughter of John Buckland, Esq., of West Harptree, Somerset ; and 2ndly, Mary, daughter of Sir Thomas Guilford, Knight. Sir
John died 30th November, 1625, and was buried in the Church of
Brympton on the 15th December ; his relative, Humphry Sydenham
(called, from his eloquence, " Silver-tongued Sydenham,") preaching
a sermon at the funeral which was afterwards published. The
sumptuous tomb in the church was erected to his memory by his
son. His second wife survived him, and married, the third time,
Andrew Lord Gray ; her first husband was John Baker, Esq., of
Cranbrook, Kent. She forfeited two thirds of the manors of
Brympton and Alvington for recusancy, and the same were granted
to one Patrick Mawle, 10th June, 1629.[18]

(*g.*) John Sydenham VI, his son, married, in 1617, Alice,
daughter of William Hoby, Esq., and died 10th March, 1626. His
widow married Sir Francis Dodington the Royalist, and died in
1653.

(*h.*) John Sydenham VII, his son, born in 1621, and created a
baronet in 1641, married Anne, daughter of Sir John Hare, of Stow
Bardolf, Norfolk, where he was buried in 1643.

(*i.*) His son, Sir John Posthumus Sydenham, was the father of
Sir Philip Sydenham, and died in 1696.

The Lord of Brympton had a manorial residence there certainly
as early as the time of Edward II, in the 18th year of whose
reign Sir Peter D'Evercy died seized of " a certain capital
messuage there, with gardens and closes adjoining." As he
represented Somersetshire in Parliament he was at least an
occasional resident, and his widow, Dame Isabella, made it her
home after his death, as she is taxed at Brympton to the subsidy 1
Edwd. III (1327). It was still occupied by the owner in the
reign of Henry VI, and probably was not destroyed or (perhaps)
discarded until the erection of what may be called the Tudor House,
the principal remains of which now form the highly embellished
northern wing of the west front.

This wing carries with it the best evidence of its date. It is enriched with the insignia of Henry VIII, boldly carved in Ham Hill

---

[17] Cal. Proc. Canc., temp. Q. Eliz.
[18] Cal. Priv. Seals.

stone, having in the centre the Royal arms, France and England quarterly, encompassed with the Garter and Crown, and supported with a lion rampant (not crowned) on the right side, and a dragon on the left; and attached are his hereditary badges, the Ostrich feathers, Rose and Crown, Fleur de Lys, and Portcullis. The reasons for attributing this Achievement to Henry VIII are (1.) That, according to authorities, he was the first king who added the Garter and Crown to the Royal arms ; although it may be remarked that this is not quite consistent with the fact that these distinctions appear on the tomb of Henry VII, his father, in Westminster Abbey. (2.) That the supporters are those adopted by Henry VIII some time after the commencement of his reign. At first he used a dragon and a greyhound, as his father did, but afterwards he changed the greyhound for a lion rampant (not crowned), placing it on the right hand side and the dragon on the left. (3.) That the badges are those of Henry VIII, the hawthorn bush of Henry VII being absent. The Ostrich feather badge, as carved on this example, was used as the badge of the Reigning Monarch as well as of the Prince of Wales.[19] It may fairly be presumed therefore that the Tudor house was built by John Sydenham II, who was born in 1470 and died in 1543 (34 Henry VIII,) and who being, through Stourton, of the blood Royal, could, in his ostentatious display of loyalty, venture to set up the Royal arms.[20]

South of this wing stands the hall, which, apparently, is much altered from its original state. The front wall was at some period set forward so as to conceal the full beauty of the contiguous turret, and the dimensions of the interior were so much enlarged, both in height and in length, that it was necessary, in order to bring the fireplace into the centre, to shift it from its original position on the north side, where its remains, walled up, were recently discovered. Altogether, these alterations, coupled with the chambers over and the lofty windows—quite out of character with those of the north wing—stamp this hall as a " second edition enlarged and improved," but not in keeping with the adjoining Tudor building.

The rather clumsy-looking bay window on the ground floor (converted by Lady Georgiana Fane into the entrance) was an addition in 1720, that date being cut in the stonework. This refutes a floating notion that it was brought from Clifton Maybank, as the mansion there was not taken down until more than 50 years afterwards.

---

[19] Sandford's Genealogical History, by Stebbing, p. 479.
[20] Coll. Top. & Gen., I, 312.

According to the usual arrangement, the hall would have communicated on the south with the solar or withdrawing - room, occupying the site of those apartments at the end of the south front generally called Col. Fane's rooms ; but in attempting to finish the house in this direction one can only build a castle in the air, for, with the exception of a gable in the roof to the west and an angular buttress towards the south-west, nothing is left. It is reasonable to suppose that the western end of these rooms exhibited a south wing corresponding with that on the north side, but if ever it existed, it is now swept away, and replaced by a blank wall with a solitary Palladian window in the upper storey, corresponding with those in the south front ; and yet it is hard to suppose that Inigo Jones, or anyone inspired by him, would have destroyed the continuity of such a choice specimen of the Tudor style, unless it was absolutely necessary for the full development of his own plan; and if that plan extended to the western extremity, why were the Fane rooms left ?

Leland, in his Itinerary, writing in 1540-42, says " The oldest house of the Sidenhams is at Brimtoun by Montagu, and this Sidenham, a man of good yeres, lyeth now at a litle maner place of his withyn a mile of Orchard, caulled Combe."

This must refer to John Sydenham II, by whom the Tudor house was probably built, and his non-residence at Brympton may be accounted for by the fact that a few years before his death he had given it to his son John Sydenham III. This appears by a deed dated 26th May, 25 Hen. VIII (1534), preserved in the Augm. Office, whereby John Sydenham, senr., granted to his son and heir apparent, John Sydenham, jun., his manor of Brympton and all other his manors in the counties of Somerset and Dorset or elsewhere, " except one close called Brode Close in Brympton, the Nether orchard, the lower parlor with two chambers over, and the advowson of the church," subject to a yearly rent. Afterwards, by another deed, dated 7th July, 29 Hen. VIII (1538), John Sydenham, sen., settled all these excepted premises upon himself and Joan (his second wife) for their lives, and after their deaths upon Richard, Walter, and Thomas, their sons successively, with remainder to Elizabeth and Joan, their daughters. Judging from the subsequent title the settlement did not take effect, possibly owing to the discovery of a previous settlement on the eldest son.

The position of the turret in the west front is anomalous. Turrets usually project at the angles of buildings, whereas this stands in the face of the work. Internally there is a Tudor arched entrance from the hall, which, if it existed, as it probably did, before the hall was

TUDOR FRONT, BRYMPTON.

To face p. 54

enlarged, must have been an external one. At the foot of the stairs, there is walled up at right angles to it another doorway, communicating with the adjoining room, which gave access either up the staircase or to the outside. By such an arrangement this end of the house could have been converted into a separate residence, and may have been called the lower parlour and chambers over, as reserved in the deed.

The erection of the South Front has been generally but inaccurately attributed to Sir Philip Sydenham.

Horace Walpole, in his " Anecdotes of Painting,"[21] says, " The garden front of Hinton St. George, Earl Poulet's seat, and the front of Brympton, formerly the mansion of Sir Philip Sydenham, were erected from designs of Inigo Jones." As that great architect (who was born in 1571) died in 1651, these designs, if by him, must have been made for Sir Philip's grandfather, who died in 1642. Probably the work was commenced, if not completed, by the grandfather. It appears from other sources that he sold or mortgaged estates to the amount of nearly £50,000 (£48,248 in fact), part of which may have gone in house building. On the other hand, the front may be the work of Sir Philip's father, who was born in 1642, and who, as his first wife was a daughter of the house of Poulet, may have wished to possess a mansion more suitable to his dignity, and taking Hinton as a pattern, built Brympton in a similar style. He died in 1696, when Sir Philip came into possession, who lost no time in trying to sell the estate, and as the earliest particulars of sale are dated in 1697, *he* could not have been the builder. In these particulars (one of which is in the writer's possession), the house is said to be " A very large *new built* mansion house which cost £16,000 (in another paper £20,000), with gardens and orchards containing 20 acres ; " and as a suitable appendage to such a mansion there, was " the park, containing 120 acres and upwards, well stocked with deer."

The new work does not extend to the whole length of the south front, as Colonel Fane's rooms at the western end are much older, and may have been part of the Tudor house, afterwards modernised with new windows and fittings. The new design, whatever it may have been, was not carried out beyond the foot of the great staircase, the hall not being touched. Altogether, the appearance of this part of the house externally conveys a strong impression that the execution of the plan was arrested for want of funds, or some equally cogent

---

[21] 4to Ed., vol. iii, p. 275.

reason, and that the building was abruptly closed as simply and as inexpensively as possible.

Mr. Freeman, who first visited Brympton in 1855, does not, from his description, appear to have seen the south front. His observations are confined to the west front. After speaking of the church, he proceeds :—" The great house, to which the chantry house now forms a horticultural appendage, presents a west front of great splendour, which is throughout essentially of good Perpendicular architecture, though extensive portions have been altered in later styles. The north-west portion is untouched, and presents a magnificent display of oriels, turrets, chimneys, and open battlements. The central part, containing the hall, has been altered in Elizabethan times, but it retains its original basements, and a curious kind of oriel, which now at least acts also as a porch. The south part has been still more recently altered in an Italianizing style, in which also a grand southern porch has been added [this is a mistake], but the walls are original, as the chimney and some of the windows testify."

On that puzzling building which stands between the house and the church it would be hazardous to express any decided opinion. Down to a recent period it has been spoken of as the residence of a chantry priest. Mr. Freeman says : " The Chantry House is an oblong Perpendicular building of two stages, chiefly remarkable for the octagonal turret which gives access to the upper one, and which is so large as to have quite the air of an oriel. A good open roof and some fine plaster ceiling of later date will be found above."

There was at Brympton the Chantry of the B.V.M., founded by Sir Peter D'Evercy, who obtained, in 1307, the King's licence to give one messuage of the yearly value of 12d., and 40 acres of land of the yearly value of 13s. 4d., in " Brompton juxta villam de Montacute," to a certain chaplain to pray daily for the soul of Sir Peter and the souls of his ancestors for ever.[22] That the license was acted on and the chantry founded is clear, for in 1327 John de Putteford, who was rector of Brympton, recovered two rods of land in " Brympton juxta West Coker," in an action against Roger de Bor, chaplain of the chapel of the B.V.M. of Brympton ;[23] and subsequent documents show that the advowson or patronage both of the church and the chantry belonged to the Lord of the Manor — one inquisition in the reign of Edward IV speaking of the chantry of the B.V.M. *in* the church. Its

[22] Inq. q. d. 34 Ed. I., No. 186.
[23] Ass. Rolls Div. Cos. 1, Ed. III, n. 2, 18.

exact position will be discussed in a subsequent part of this chapter; suffice it to say here that if the expression "in" be correct, the idea that this building was the chantry chapel may be dismissed. Then it is said—and tradition steps in here—if not the chapel, it was the residence of the chaplain, and Mr. Freeman appears to have been of this opinion. He says, "Some benefactor, or some inhabitant of the adjoining mansion, founded a chantry for three priests [mistake for one], and built for their dwelling the house which still remains on the north side of the churchyard." But it seems much too large and important a house for a celibate chaplain; and if a priest's residence at all, why not rather that of the Rector, who may at some later period have exchanged it for the preferable site of the present Rectory? Unfortunately, in this case no assistance can be obtained from the Surveys of Chantries at the time of their suppression by Edward VI. Brympton is not mentioned in them; in fact, all trace of this chantry is lost after the reign of Henry VI, and it is possible that as the patronage of both church and chantry were in the same hands, the endowment of the latter was absorbed into the manorial demesnes, and the soul of the founder left to shift for itself.

The greater part of the ground floor of this building was at one time a stable, and the massive stall posts and other fixtures remained down to a recent period. Mr. Richardson, an architect of considerable authority, considered them to be part of the work of Inigo Jones, and he made drawings and sections of them, which were published in the *Builder*. May they not be of much earlier date, and is it very unreasonable to suppose that the whole building was stables and other offices attached to the Tudor house? In those days stables were not, as now, kept in the background, but often made prominent features. Whether the turret staircase now giving access to the upper storey forms part of the original work is doubtful. There is no trace of a junction in the masonry, but that may be accounted for. If an addition, it was probably made when the east portion of the upper storey was converted into domestic apartments, and the turret may have come from the west front. When or for what purpose the alteration was made is matter of tradition, but in the writer's boyhood, the old housekeeper, Mrs. Lucas, used to tell of an "unfortunate lady" shut up there, and showed her portrait, attired in cinnamon satin, at the head of the staircase in the great house, with outstretched arm and forefinger ominously pointing to the scene of some dark deed.

In all that has been said respecting this building, the

opinion of an architectural expert[24] that it was the original Manor House has not been overlooked. His arguments are of considerable weight. There are several examples of this kind ; one at Brooke, in Wiltshire, the seat of the Pavelys ; but no instance has been met with of an external *Turret* staircase to a mediæval house. It may also be observed that the position of this building, standing on the churchyard, does not seem a very likely or lively site for the lord's mansion ; but to the priest it would be convenient, especially with a doorway into the churchyard, which still remains, although walled up.

There are two early engravings of Brympton ; one from a drawing by James Fish, of Warwick, in 1699 ; and the other a formal bird's-eye view by Kyp. There is also in the house a small oil painting of it, ascribed to Wootton, an artist of some celebrity in the last century.

The church, dedicated to St. Andrew, stands south - west of the mansion, and forms with it and the old building a very picturesque group. It was concisely described by Mr. Freeman on the visit of the Somerset Archaelogical Society there in 1855.

He says :—" The church is small, and was originally a Decorated cross church, without aisles or tower. The south transept, with a beautiful Geometrical window to the south, and a foliated arch connecting it with the nave ; the foliated south door and a piscina in what was the north transept are all pleasing examples of that style, and enable us to form a good notion of a Somersetshire church of the earlier period. But some benefactor of Perpendicular times— some inhabitant doubtless of the adjoining mansion, whose name and exact date some local antiquary will, I doubt not, be able to supply—founded a chantry for three priests. He built for their dwelling the house which still remains on the north side of the churchyard, and modified the church to adapt it to his purpose. He made an eastern addition to the north transept, and altered the direction of its gable, so as to give it the external appearance of an aisle, while internally it makes two chapels, the south transept being doubtless the third. A stone rood screen, that uncommon feature in a parish church, must date from the same period ; so also must the western bell-cot of a very distinctive character—a wiser addition, I think, than either a meagre tower, which would have been of no beauty in itself, or a magnificent one, which would have destroyed

---

[24] Som. Arch. Soc. Proc., vol. xvii.

the beauty of the rest of the church. I cannot speak with equal praise of the addition of a flat-panelled ceiling, which, though very good in itself, cuts off the head of the beautiful south window."

The chantry was endowed for one priest only, not three ; and, with great deference, it is submitted that the eastern addition to the north transept was not built for the chantry, as it is Perpendicular work, whereas the chantry was founded in the reign of Edward II. The ancient endowment of the church is to be found in the Nona Roll, 14 Edward III. The jury, consisting of William Musket, Thomas atte Wiche, Robert Nyweman, and William atte Orchard, parishioners of Brympton, say on their oaths that the ninth of corn, wool, and lamb there is worth this year £4 and no more, and so doth not amount to the tax of the Church, because the rector there hath of the endowment of his said church a house, curtilage garden, 25 acres of arable land, and two acres (sic), which are worth by the year 33s., the tenth of hay, worth by the year 5s., oblations, and other small tithes, £6 1s. 3d., all of which are comprehended in the tax.

In a charter of Henry II[25] the King confirms to the Priory of Montacute the gift which Geoffry (Galfridus), chaplain to William Earl of Moretain, had made to it of the church of Brumeton—which has been supposed to mean Brympton. There is also another charter of the same King confirming to the Priory the chantry of Brumeton and Odcombe.[26] If Brumeton means Brympton there must have been an earlier church there, as the present one contains no features anterior to the Decorated style. It has, indeed, been doubted whether the charter does refer to the church of Brympton ; and certainly, if it ever did belong to the Priory, the monks must have parted with it before the reign of Henry III, when the manor came into the possession of the D'Evercy family, as Peter D'Evercy was patron of the church in 1321, and it was appendant to the manor from that time down to the time of Sir Philip Sydenham.

From the north transept an obtuse arch leads into the " eastern addition," which is open to the chancel. It is in the Perpendicular style, and lighted by two windows of rich tracery on the north and one in the east wall, with remains of painted glass in all three. On one of the bosses of the panelled oak roof are the arms of Stourton, and on others is a stag couchant,

---

[25] Dugdale's " Monasticon," 1, 670.

[26] Dugdale, *ib.*

possibly intended to show the connection of Sydenham through Dalyngrig with De la Lynde of Dorset, and the legendary White Hart of the Vale of Blackmore. This chapel was probably therefore built by John Sydenham I in the time of Henry VI or Edward IV, and is no doubt " the new Ile of the Parish Church of Brympton " which we shall find mentioned in the will of Walter Sydenham. There must have been an altar at the east window, as there still remains on either side a niche or tabernacle, with crocketed pinnacles, and a piscina on the south side.

As the D'Evercy chantry was founded long prior to the erection of this chapel, its altar could not have originally stood there ; but it may have been removed to that situation from some other part of the church—probably one of the transepts, in each of which a Decorated piscina is preserved.

The Decorated arch dividing the south transept from the nave is not in the centre, and on the east side of it are the stone jambs and head of an unaccountable internal window, about four feet from the floor, which are chased for holding the glass. Until recently there were windows only on the south and east sides, but recently, when this transept was repaired and partly reconstructed, Sir Spencer Ponsonby-Fane found the foliated head of a small Decorated window buried in the old eastern wall, and he judiciously substituted it for the existing east window, which he removed to the west side. At the same time he took down the panelled ceiling of which Mr. Freeman properly complained, and transferred it to the north transept, where it harmonizes well with the roof of the Sydenham Chapel. The door into this transept and that into the north one are comparatively modern. The only ancient entrance to the Church is through the Decorated arch on the south side, to which the porch was subsequently added.

The large tomb in the Sydenham chapel, described by Collinson, was erected by John Sydenham VI, in honour of his father John Sydenham V. It is steeply coped and covered with a rich canopy, each angle surmounted with the Sydenham ram supporting a shield of arms, and every available space of the whole monument covered with coats of arms, gaudily but not always correctly represented.

Fifty years ago the writer amused himself with endeavouring to blazon and identify the different coats, and the result, from his sketch book, is here presented. A reference to the foregoing pedigree will explain the introduction of many of the quarterings, but

SYDENHAM MONUMENT, BRYMPTON CHURCH

several remain to be identified, a task which is left for keener eyes and greater diligence.*

On the south side of the tomb are three shields, say D, E, and F.

D.—The first contains :—

1. Arg. three rams tripping sab, horned or (Sydenham).
2. Arg. a bend fusilly sab. (originally Kittisford, and afterwards borne by Sydenham of Combe).
3. Arg. a cross engrailed gu. (Dalingrig).
4. Sab. a bend or between six fountains az., on the bend a mullet for difference (Stourton),
   impaling
   (a) Erm a chevron gu. *(Touchet.)*
   (b) Gu. a fret or (Audley).
   (c) Gu. three lions pass arg. (Gifford.)
   (d) Checky az. and or a bend gu. *(Clifford.)*
   (e) Arg. two bars gu., each charged with three annulets, or. *(Martin.)*
   (f) Gu. two bars az. and ermine. *(Braose.)*

E.—The second contains :—

1. Sydenham.
2. Kittisford.
3. Per fesse gu. and erm.—a crescent for a difference. *(Hussey.)*
4. Stourton,
   impaling
   (a) Arg. on a cross sab. a leopard's face or (Brydges).
   (b) Arg. a fesse sab. between three Cornish choughs of the
   (c) last *(Barkley)*.
   (d) Or a Pile gu. (Chandos).
   (e) Or three piles in point vert. (De Bryan).
   (f) Gu. a fesse arg. between three crescents of the last. *(Holway)*.
   (g) Brydges.

F.—The third contains :—

1. Sydenham.
2. Kittisford.
3. Dalingrig.
4. *(Hussey)*.
5. Stourton.

---

* The task has in a great measure been accomplished by a writer in the *Miscellanea Genealogica et Heraldica*, 2nd series, Vol. III, p. 323, and the italics in the text show his additions, some of which must be adopted with reserve.

6. Vert. a crescent in fesse or between six billets of the last (Dummer),

impaling

(a) Gu. a double-headed eagle displayed—between three fleurs de lis arg. (Godolphin.)

(b) Arg. three bars indented gu. *(Balune.)*

(c) On a field arg. within a bordure sab. a double-headed eagle displayed of the last beaked and taloned, or *(Killegrew).*

(d) Arg. a fesse chevronelled counter changed sab. and arg. *(Trenouth.)*

(e) Arg. a fesse sab. between three fleurs de lis of the last. *(Bonython.)*

(f) Godolphin.

G.—A large shield at the foot of the tomb containing 18 quarters.

1. Sydenham.
2. Kittisford.
3. Dalingrig.
4. *Hussey.*
5. Stourton.
6. Godolphin.
7. *Balune.*
8. *Killegrew.*
9. *Trenouth,*

impaling

(a) Gu. three lions ramp. arg. In a canton sab. a fret or (Buckland).

(b) Vert [should be az] a Dolphin embowed arg. between three mullets or (Fitzjames).

(c) Sab a cross floriated between billets or *(Chamflorie).*

(d) Arg. a cross engr. sab. In a canton an eagle displayed gu. *(Draycot.)*

(e) Arg. a bend trick charged with (?) *(Whitinge.)*

(f) Az. three leopards' heads erased or. *(Proudham.)*

(g) Arg. three escallops gu. (Clyvedon.)

(h) Per fesse az. and gu. three fleurs de lis or *(Pauncefoot.)*

(i) Per pale az. and gu. three lions rampant erm. (Herbert.)

At the top of the canopy in the centre is a richly mantled shield with Sydenham impaling Buckland.

At the eastern end of the canopy is the Sydenham ram supporting a shield with Sydenham imp. on a bend gu. two mullets arg. (Bampfyde?) At the west end the ram supporting a shield with Sydenham imp. Harcourt. Around the cornice are shields repeating the arms already described.

There are three shields on the north side corresponding to D, E, and F. 1. Sydenham imp. *(a)* a fesse between three hawks *(Hoby)*, *(b)* on 3 battle axes in pale arg. *(Bylmore)*, *(c)* an eagle displayed *(Gregerer)*, *(d)* a lion ramp. within a bordure indented *(Tewder)*. 2. Arg. six fleur de lis az. in pile, on a chief indented or, a mullet az. for a difference *(Paston)*, imp. Sydenham. 3. Sydenham with an impalement blank.

The shield corresponding to the centre one of the canopy on the south side contains Sydenham imp. or a saltire sab. between four cornish choughs of the last *(Guilford)* ; at the end of the tomb is sab. six swallows arg. Arundel imp. Sydenham. [This coat should be reversed.] Another shield contains Sydenham imp. gouttee a cross engrailed gu. *(Fitz.)* Under the canopy at the head of the tomb is the Sydenham shield with all the quarterings, viz. : (1) Sydenham, (2) Kittisford, (3) Dalingrig, (4) Hussey, (5) Stourton, (6) arg. a griffin segreant sab. langued gu., footed or *(Langland)* ; (7) arg. on a bend az. a square billet, or between six cross crosslets of the last *(Beaupre)* ; (8) gu. a bend or between six cross crosslets (Furneaux). This shield is surmounted with the Sydenham crest—a ram's head erased sab. horned or, langued gu.

Under the Canopy is this inscription :

" My founder Sydenham, matcht to Hobye's Heir,
Badde me informe the gentle Passenger
That what hee hath done in me is only meant
To memorise his Father and's discent
Without vayne Glorie, but he doth intreat
That if thou com'st his legende to repeate
Thou speake him truly as he was, and than
Report it (Sr) he dyed an Honest mane.
December, 1626."

A small slab close to the tomb states that " this monument was repaired at the expense of the Rev. John Williams, M.A., Patron of this church, and descended from a branch of the Sydenham family, 1827."

On another slab near is an inscription, evidently copied from a stone now lying outside the south transept door, which has been read as an elegiac verse :

" Si rogitis quam terra tegit Matris inspice nomen
Regis supremi et nominis instarerat
Ast plus Sydenhami Bucklandi filia Conjux
Armigeri vivens dum fuit ista fuit."

and translated thus : " If you ask whom this earth covers, behold the name of her Mother, which was the same as the mother of the

King Supreme (Mary), but further she was the daughter of Buckland the wife of Sydenham Esq., whilst she was alive,"† Underneath it is recorded that " Mary abovesaid was daughter and heiress of John Buckland, Esq., of West Harptree, in this c'y, and wife of John Sydm. Esq., afterwards knighted, by w. she had George, who died 1615 unmarried ; John, yt married Hoby, and died 1626-7 ; Ralph knighted, and master of ye Charter House, London, and died 1671 ; and Frances, married to Edward Paston, Esq., of Glostershire, and of Appleton in Norfolk, where she lies buried. Mary died 1596. Sir John was buried under the monument 15th December, 1625."

This account was evidently written many years afterwards, probably by Sir Philip Sydenham, who took care to preserve the Latin inscription, which was no doubt removed to make room for the memorial to his father and mother. Collinson professes to give copies of them, but with two gross mistakes—Elizabeth Poulett is called Pomfret, and her son John is said be buried at Binjo, instead of Hinton. Both these errors were copied from Theobald's MS.

The inscriptions correctly copied read thus : " Here lies my honoured father, a great lover of his Country, Sir John Posthumus Sydenham, bart., son of Sir John Sydenham, bart., and Anne, second daughter of Sir John Hare, of Stow, Norfolk. He died 1696, aged 54. Philip Sydenham."

" Here lyes Elizabeth, dter of the ancient and noble family of ye Pouletts, of Hinton St. George, first wife of Sr John Posths Sydenham, by w she had John, yt died and was buried at Hinton, 1664 ; she died 1669."

" Here lyes ye best of wifes and ye best of mothers ye Lady Mary, second dter of Philip, Earl of Pembroke, and 2nd wife of Sir John Posthumus Sydenham, by w. she had John, who died unmarried 1692, Philip liveing 1714, and Mary, who died 1698. She died to the great loss and greif of her family, 1686."

On the pavement of the north transept is an elegant incised floriated cross with an inscription at the base very difficult to decipher. It probably is

" ORATE : PRO : ANIA : ALICE. M.
JOHIS SIDE'HAM Q. O. A DNI. . . ."

The date is quite obliterated except the last figure, but in 1841 it was legible, and the writer copied it as 1525—but it may have been 1523—although Theobald, who saw it in 1757, proposes to read "15LI," whatever that may mean. The name is certainly Alice,

---

† The writer is indebted to the Rev. C. W. Penny, of Wellington College, for suggesting the above reading and translation.

although correctly it should have been " Aliciæ " or " Alicie," and the letter M may mean ' mater ; ' but John Sydenham II was living in 1525, and his son would hardly, in his lifetime or afterwards, in a memorial to his mother omit his father's name. May not M. mean Marita—the wife of John Sydenham? She may have been Audley's daughter, first wife of John Sydenham II, called by her synonymous name of Alice instead of Elizabeth or Eliza ; and John Sydenham III may have had a first wife named Alice, which would, perhaps, account for his having two sons named John, as mentioned in his will, it being more probable that they were the children of two marriages than of one. But either alternative should not be adopted without further investigation.

There is also on the floor of the same transept a slab of Purbeck marble (not noticed by Mr. Theobald) on which is the matrix of an elegant brass cross, and round the verge can be traced some isolated words in Lombardic characters, but nothing resembling a date.

A friend of Lady Georgiana Fane a few years ago thought he could discern these words :—

> " O Precor . . O . . . .
> . . . risu . . . vivat cum
> . . . . O tumulo Galfridus in Isto qui
> jacet in. cor . . . o"

but this reading is rather imaginary. Certainly, however, it was intended to commemorate the burial (in hoc tumulo) of a certain Galfridus, and, to hazard a very wild guess, he may have been the chaplain of that name who bestowed the church of Brumeton on the Priory of Montacute ; if so, its identity with Brympton is almost conclusively established.

When Mr. Theobald was at Brympton—now nearly one hundred and fifty years ago—there were in the churchyard four monumental effigies, of which he gives this account :—

" In the churchyard are the following figures, carved in stone, and raised but a very little way from the ground, and are the covers to stone coffins which seem to have been moved out of the church to make way for pews or other monuments of later date. The two first lye close together under the north wall of the chancel door ; the man on the left hand, who seems by his being cross-legged to have been a Knight Templar, or one at least engaged in some crusades, and not to belong to the lady, who appears to be some nun or religious. The third seems to have been some lady of distinction, in the habit of the times. This lies at the west end of the church, and by a part of the stones being broken, discover bones in a stone coffin.

On the north side of her, at a little distance, lies the fourth. This very plainly appears to have been a monk or priest, by his shaved crown, and having on his ecclesiastical habit used at the celebration of mass, and having a chalice in his hand. The figures are still pretty entire, though they have suffered by time. I could not learn from any of the present inhabitants anything relating to them, but imagine there must have been some religious foundation in that neighbourhood. They are all in alto relievo."

As Mr. Theobald could obtain no further information respecting them, it is to be presumed that these figures had lain for many generations where he found them, neglected and forgotten, and so they remained until a few years ago.

It is not to be supposed that they were originally placed in the churchyard, as sculptured effigies are almost universally found over the graves of persons buried in the church ; but whether in this case they were brought out of the church, as Mr. Theobald suggests, or whether they belonged to a chapel annexed to the church, which had been destroyed, it is impossible now to decide. The latter alternative is the more probable, as many years ago a richly sculptured arch, broken in two pieces, was dug up in the churchyard, the spandrils being carved in bas-relief—one representing the Annunciation and the other the Adoration of the Magi. These subjects are so appropriate to a chapel dedicated, as the D'Evercy chapel was, to the Virgin, that the arch may be looked upon as some evidence that the chapel stood within the churchyard, and that the figures were originally in it. At the same time, the scattered and irregular position in which Mr. Theobald found them, favours the notion that they had beeen brought from different places at different times.

Wherever the effigies came from, they have found a resting place at last within the church, into which Lady Georgiana Fane removed them, with the exception of the base of one which still lies at the north transept door. They were all, as might be expected, much mutilated, and Mr. Carew, the sculptor, who was commissioned by Lady Georgiana to repair and restore them, did his work, perhaps rather in the spirit of an artist than of an antiquary, adding a battlemented cornice to the old sculptured arch, and converting it into a canopy over the priest's effigy, " matching " it with another of his own design—our Lord bearing the cross and the crucifixion—over the " religious female." Theobald gives sepia sketches of the figures, and it is to be regretted that Mr. Carew did not see them. He would have observed, amongst other things, the peculiar attitude of the mailed knight, whose legs are not closely crossed in the usual manner, but the left leg is raised and gracefully bent over the right one, somewhat similar to the wooden effigy of Robert Curthose, in Gloucester Cathedral, with the rowelled spur prominently projecting. The dress of the religious female is confined at the waist by a rope girdle fastened with a buckle, and her feet rest on a greyhound; those of the lady of quality are laid on two smaller hounds sejant indorsed.

Fragments of painted glass are still left in the windows of both chapels, and a figure, possibly of St. Lawrence, holding a gridiron, was observed by a visitor in 1847. Theobald also mentions that in the east window was a scroll, with the words, " Cuis aie propiciet De omnipotens ame," showing that it was a memorial window, probably to a Sydenham.

The church has an unusual feature for a small parish church. The chancel is separated from the nave by a stone screen in the Perpendicular style, but very simple in execution, with a projection running the whole length on the nave side, forming a narrow bench or seat. Resting on the screen is the rood-beam, deeply moulded, the face of which is decorated with three shields of arms in colours :—

1. Sab. a bend or between six fountains.
2. Gu. three crescents or and a canton.
3. Sab. three pellets wavy or, on a chief of the first three crescents gu.

These arms, no doubt, commemorate the liberality of the persons at whose expense the whole chancel, or, it may be, the rood screen only, was built ; and it will be interesting, therefore, if possible, to identify them.

The first coat is certainly that of Stourton, which fact, coupled with the absence of the Sydenham coat, leaves little doubt that the rood screen was erected *after* Stourton was connected with Brympton, but *before* Sydenham succeeded to it. Now it will be seen by the subsequent part of this chapter, that early in the reign of Henry VI, John Stourton of Preston, whose daughter married John Sydenham I, purchased of John Wynford and Alice his wife the reversion of Brympton ; that is to say, he was not to come into possession until after their deaths, and then only provided John Wynford left no issue. At that time, therefore, Wynford and his wife and Stourton were the joint owners, and, as might be expected, the Stourton arms form one of the coats. Stourton deserves especial notice in the history of Brympton ; but as his seat was in the adjoining Manor of Preston Plucknet, which his daughter Cecily inherited, it will be more appropriate to defer the account until a subsequent chapter which treats immediately of Preston and its owners. Turning now to the second coat on the Rood-beam—three crescents and a canton—these arms were borne by the family of Le Veer, of Veers Wooton, Dorset, and the Isle of Wight; but the question is whether they are intended for Le Veer in this instance. Prefixed to the pedigree of Battiscomb in the Visitation of Dorset, 1623, is one of Le Veer, accompanied by two documents, (1) an extract from a deed (in Latin) of Walter Le Veer, Esq., son and heir of John Le Veer, dated 1st April, 13 Hen. VI, to which the seal of his arms is attached—three crescents and a canton ; (2) a confused abstract of another deed (in English), which is as follows :—

"This indenture witnesseth that I, Walter Veer, Squyer, have delivered to Alyce Winford, some time the wife of John Winford, my cosen, a Boxe, with their evidences underwritten, &c. [Itm. in the said Boxe is a Byll without seal that I found in a Coffer of my Father's within the Isle of Wight in my Maunor of Stanton, that maketh mention of all my ancestors from the tyme of King Hen. the 3 to the will of John, my brother, that was elder than I, and died without heir of his body begotten] and upon condition that if John Battiscombe doe pay to the said Alyce 20li in gold that I may have it in a good purse when I com hidder again and for divers other causes for my Maunor of *Brimpton,* and if the said John Battiscombe pay out the 20li. in gold and a right good purse, then I will that the said Alyce make deliverance of the said box of evidences to you, &c. In witness, &c., dated at Brimpton, in Somersetshire, Monday next before St. Valentine's day, the 13th of Henry VI." The passage within brackets is evidently no part of the deed, but only a note by Le Veer respecting his family. Who "you" was does not appear.[27] No relationship is shown by the Visitation to exist between Le Veer and Battiscombe, the only connection between them being that Battiscombe, temp. Henry VI, purchased Le Veer's estate in Dorsetshire; and as Alice, the wife of John Battiscombe the purchaser, was the daughter of Thomas Beauchin, whose arms are those of the third coat on the Rood-screen, it is probable there was some connection between the three families which has not yet been found out.

But although it must be admitted that Walter le Veer bore the second coat, John Wynford, his cousin, was equally entitled to do so, the arms having descended to them from common ancestors, who rightly or wrongly assumed them. Three crescents and a

---

[27] Harl. MS., 1166 (Dorset Visit., 1623).

canton was the seal of Gracia de Lisle (called Maude by Dugdale), wife of Bryan de Lisle, Lord of Bryanston, Dorset, temp. Hen. III, and daughter and heiress of Thomas Saleby, of Saleby, in the county of Lincoln, who held that manor under the family of Blanchard, bearing for their ancient arms three crescents. Bryan de Lisle died about 19 Hen. III, without issue it is believed,[28] for in that year Thomas de Brito and Alice his wife, William de Glamorgan and Ralph de Stopham succeeded to his estates as his heirs;[29] and as some generations after these arms are used by the heiress of De Stopham and the co-heirs of De Glamorgan, it is concluded that the two families derived them from Gracia de Lisle, although their right to bear them, according to the laws of heraldry, may be doubtful. That they were used by De Stopham appears from the seal of William De Echingham, who married Eva De Stopham; and although they are not found borne by any of the name of De Glamorgan, they were adopted by the co-heirs of John de Glamorgan in the reign of Edward III, and, therefore, it is to be assumed that he used the arms in his life-time. The descent of the De Lisle coat is given in an article on "Derivative Arms" in volume xxx. of the Sussex Archæological Society's Collections, which is noticed in the Genealogist (N.S., vol. 7), but several statements in it require verification.

Sir John de Glamorgan, who, as will be seen, became the owner of Brympton, died early in the reign of Edward III, and left several daughters, who, after the deaths of their brothers Peter and Nicholas without issue, became his co-heiresses. A contemporary document tells us[30] that John Wynford was the son of one; William Lewston, of Lewston, near Sherborne, of a second; . . . Veer (said to be illegitimate) of a third; and John Urry of a fourth; all of whom, except perhaps Veer, were competent to quarter three crescents and a canton with their own arms, if they had any, or to adopt them if they had not. We know nothing of Urry; but as to Veer we have seen that Walter de Veer, whether his ancestor was legitimate or not, used these arms in legal documents; as to Lewston, there was in the old Mansion House at Lewston, in 1600, a shield bearing three crescents and a canton, quartered with three battle axes, for Lewston;[31] and as to Wynford, the conclusion

[28] Nicolas Historic Peerage.
[29] Extr. Rot. and Fin., vol. i., p. 265.
[30] See Harl. MS., 4120.
[31] Harl. MS., 1427.

is that the second coat on the rood screen refers to John Wynford— simply because he—and not Le Veer—was the owner of Brympton. That Wynford used it, is proved by an independent piece of evidence still preserved in an oak shield with these arms carved on it, formerly one of the bosses of the roof of the old chantry chapel which stood at the west end of Yeovil Church, in which, after John Wynford's death, Alice, his widow, with others, founded a chantry to pray for his soul.[32]

It may be said that, admitting that Walter Le Veer (assuming the legitimacy of his ancestor) was entitled to these arms, and as in the deed quoted he speaks of *his Manor of Brimpton*, why should not the second coat refer to him? Probably the word "Brimpton" in the deed is a clerical error of the copyist, and should, from the context, have been "Stanton." The records show that previous to the sale to Stourton, Brympton belonged to the Wynfords only, and they alone conveyed it to him. Beyond this, John Wynford presented to the church of Brympton, 5 Henry VI, and Alice, his widow, did so 23 Henry VI, being styled "Domina de Brympton," whereas if Le Veer had been the owner he would have been the patron. The deed, in fact, had nothing to do with Brympton ; it only happened to be executed there.

Coming now to the third coat, this is undoubtedly Beauchin, an ancient family seated at Beauchinhays, in the parish of Whitchurch Canonicorum, Dorset, temp. Edw. III, but afterwards at Cottels, near Bradford, Wilts.[33] Allusion has already been made to the marriage of Alice Beauchin with Battiscombe, and Alice Wynford may have been a Beauchin ; but from a charter quoted in Hutchins' Dorset (iv., 318) she appears to have been a sister of William Lambrook, Treasurer of Wells Cathedral, and one of the co-founders with her of the Chantry at Yeovil already mentioned, which she endowed with lands at Galhampton, Somerset. John Wynford was her second husband. By her first, John de la Bere, she had three daughters co-heiresses, (1) Edith, the wife first of Richard Becot, and second of William Alisander ; (2) Alice, wife first of Roger Stourton, a brother of John Stourton of Preston, and secondly of William Warr ; and (3) Elizabeth, who, as far as is known, was never married. (Hutch., ub. sup.) If the charter quoted means that Alice Wynford was only sister-in-law of William Lambrook, she may have been a Beauchin, but if she

---

[32] Pat. Rolls, 11 Henry VI.

[33] Wilts Visitation, 1623, Harl. MS., 1111.

was his sister in blood, no near relationship can be suggested between her and the Beauchins, and so, confessing our inability to identify the third coat satisfactorily, we step out into the churchyard, where we see the circular base of an old cross, noticed by Mr. Pooley, in his "Old Crosses of Somerset," as fifteenth century work. Besides this there are several massive altar tombs of very striking and venerable appearance. The sides of one are filled with carved quatrefoils; another, more recent, is a memorial to "John Whyt," in 1575; and a third is to the memory of John Nowis, of Alvington, in 1645. He must have been the father or grandfather of John Nowis or Nowes, of Romsey, Hants, who, by his will, in 1718, endowed the Charity School of Yeovil for the education of poor boys of Alvington, where he was born.

And here in the "last resting-place" we close our imperfect description of dear old Brympton. Although a task of pleasure, it has been mingled with melancholy. It was begun 50 years ago in the sunshine of trysted life; it has been finished in solitary gloom and declining days. The contrast is depressing :

> "Shades of departed joys around me rise,
> With many a face that smiles on me no more,
> With many a voice that thrills of transport gave,
> Now silent as the grass that tufts their grave."

It is now proposed to trace briefly the descent of Brympton from the earliest owners on record down to the Sydenhams, and illustrate it with documentary evidence. But it is only fair to warn the readers—if perchance there are any left—that unless they have acquired a taste for such "musteries," they will find what follows very dry and dull.

Brympton and the neighbouring manors of Ashington and Limington, and also the manor of Kilve on the Bristol Channel, were parts of the large possessions in Somersetshire conferred by the Conqueror on Roger de Corcelle (Dom. Book), after whose death they passed (by inheritance, it is believed) to the knightly family of Malet, and so continued until the reign of King John, when they were forfeited for the treason of William Malet, one of the rebellious barons. The tenancy in chief under the Crown belonged to the Abbots of Glastonbury, who had been lords of these manors in Saxon times;

the same being probably part of the eight hides in de la Stane, which King Edmund had bestowed on the abbey; and Malet's forfeiture was so far condoned that the mesne lordship under the abbey was granted to his daughter Mabel, and her husband William de Vivonia[84] from whom it descended, temp. Edw. I, to Cecilia, wife of John de Beauchamp of Somerset.

Another mesne fee or sub-tenancy was created in these manors by Malet or his successor, by a grant to a family named Fitzwilliam, of which there were several connected with Somersetshire. It is probable that these Fitzwilliams were allied by marriage, if not related in blood, to the Malets, as Lucy Malet, daughter of Ralph Fitzwilliam, confirmed a grant of land to the Priory of Taunton,[85] which Ralph flourished temp. Ric. I and John (Pipe Rolls). In the Pipe Roll for Dors. and Som., 31 Hen. I (1131), the death of Robert Fitzwilliam is recorded, who left his wife Emma entitled to dower, and in the aid granted 12 Hen. II (1166) for marrying the King's daughter, Richard Fitzwilliam is certified to hold ten fees of Moreton, in Somerset. Another Robert Fitzwilliam, probably son and heir to Richard, died in 1186, leaving a son Reginald, a minor, upon which the Crown, as his guardian, took possession of his estates, and the Sheriff accounts for the rents of Ashington and Kilve down to 1202, when Reginald came of age.[36] He must have died soon after without issue, as, in 1214, Joan, one of the daughters and co-heirs of Robert, had married Henry de Furnell or Furneaux, and in the partition of her father's estates Ashington and Kilve fell to her share.[37] The Sheriff did not account for the rents of Brympton and Limington, because an additional sub-tenancy in those manors—*i.e.*, the actual right to the land and the income therefrom—had been created before the death of Robert Fitzwilliam, and consequently there were no rents to be accounted for. But that the over-lordship of Brympton passed from Fitzwilliam to Furneaux is clear from " Kirby's Quest," made about 12 Edward I, by which it was found that Thomas D'Evercy, the then owner of Brympton, held it of Matthew De Furneaux (the descendant of Henry and Joan), who held it of Cecilia de Beauchamp, and she of the Abbey of Glastonbury, and the Abbey of the Crown; whereas Matthew De Furneaux, in the same record, is returned as the

[84] Coll. Som., iii., 462.
[85] Som. Soc. Proc., ix., 32.
[36] Pipe Rolls.
[37] Pipe Roll, D. and S., 15 John, and Coll. Som., iii., 213, 532.

terre-tenant of Ashington, thereby showing that no sub-tenancy had been created of that manor. It should not, however, be overlooked that according to the Beauchamp Cartulary, compiled in the reign of Edward III,[38] the heirs of William Avenel are said to hold eight fees of the Barony of Fortibus, appertaining to the manor of Dunden, three of which were Brympton, Ashington, and Kilve, and the then tenant was Symon de Furneaux, who was the son of Matthew de Furneaux. Now Matthew was the heir of William Avenel,[39] and therefore it may be presumed that Avenel acquired these manors in free marriage with a daughter of De Furneaux, but dying in 1254 without issue,[40] they reverted to that family again, who, though not perhaps the heirs general, became as regards the tenure under Beauchamp " the heirs of Avenel." The sub-grant of Brympton was made to the family of de Cilterne, who took their name from the neighbouring parish of Chilthorne or Cilterne.

In 1166 William de Cilterne held one knight's fee of Moreton, of Richard Fitzwilliam;[41] and in 1191 William, son of Robert de Cilterne, gave to the Priory of Bermondsey 10 acres of land in Cilterne, and his son, "Richard Fitz William Fitz Robert de Cilterna," made a donation of the tithes of 16 acres of land in the same place.[42] The Priory had a previous connection with Brympton itself, for according to the annals Odo de Tiron [Pirou], who was a Knight of Wynebald Balun (another donor), bestowed on them the Tithes of Estinton [Ashington] and Alvineton, which gift William Rufus confirmed by his charter, and in 1199 Richard de Cilterne paid five marks for a writ from the King's Court against Hawise de Pirou for one knight's fee in Brumeton, *i.e.*, Brympton.[43] The two families of Fitzwilliam and Pirou must have been related, as in a charter made to Wells Cathedral, temp. Richard I, Ralf Fitzwilliam is said to be the heir of Robert de Pirou.[44] Richard de Cilterne probably succeeded in his action, as, in 1202, he paid two marks for having a record of the judgment. Brympton continued in possession of De Cilterne until 1220, when Thomas de Cilterne (a son probably of William)

[38] Augm. Miscell. Books, 58, P.R.O.
[39] Ass. Rolls Div. Cos., 5 Edward I.
[40] Roberts Cal. Gen., p. 61.
[41] Lib. Nig.
[42] Berm. Ann. Rolls series.
[43] Pipe Rolls, Dor. and Som.
[44] Wells Index, p. 29.

sold it to Thomas D'Evercy, and by fine released to him all his right to one knight's fee in Brimtun and Allwinton (Alvington).[45]

There is not much material for a history of the house of D'Evercy, but it may be fairly presumed that the family sprang originally from Evrecy—a ville in Normandy situated a few miles south-west of Caen. Several of the name occur as benefactors to the Cistercian Abbey of Alnay or Aunay, founded by Jordan de Say about 1131. In 1222, Thomas D'Evrecy Kt., by charter gave to that abbey certain lands and rents at Evrecy. The seal to this charter displays a female figure with her right hand extended holding a branch of palm, with the legend " SIGILLUM THOME DE EVRICIE." Attached to another charter is the seal of Graveran D'Evrecy, Abbot of Aunay—an eagle displayed, standing on one leg, with the legend " SIGILLUM GRAVERAN DE EBRECIO."[46]

The family is found in England at a very early date. They seem to have been particularly connected with the Isle of Wight, and were probably in the retinue of the Earls of Devon, lords of the island. In the reign of Henry II " Grffard de Everci " was one of the witnesses to a grant (sans date) of the ville of Techmul, in Ireland, to Peter Giffard, of Chillington, by Earl Richard FitzGilbert, progenitor of the great family of Clare, and husband of Rohesia Giffard,[47] and the same " Giffard de Evreci " was also witness to a charter (sans date) of William de Vernon, afterwards 6th Earl of Devon, granting land at Piddletown, Dorset, to the Abbey of Quarr, in the Isle of Wight.[48] Of the same family was Robert D'Evercy, who, in 1206, obtained confirmation from the Crown of a grant made by him of lands in Yate, in the county of Gloucester, to Ralph de Wilington and his issue by his wife Olympiad, who, it may be conjectured, was a daughter of D'Evercy;[49] and who by another charter (sans date) granted land at Bishopshall, in Yate, to William FitzHarold in free marriage with Margaret, his cousin, daughter of Robert de Meysey.[50]

---

[45] Somt. Fines, 4 Henry III, No. 44.
[46] D'anisy Cart da Calv., ii., 55.
[47] Proc. Brit. Arch. Assoc., vol. iii., 347.
[48] Harl. Charters 55, D., 22.
[49] Index to Chart. Rolls, p. 158.
[50] The Rev. George Harbin's MSS.

Another D'Evercy married Annora de Albemarle, daughter of Robert de Albemarle of Gloucestershire, and in 1226 her son, Thomas D'Evercy (probably the purchaser of Brympton), succeeded in her right as one of the heirs of William de Albemarle, of Ruardyn, Gloucestershire (brother of Robert), to one fourth-part of land in Stintescombe in the same county.[51] From this there can be no doubt that the Gloucestershire and Brympton D'Evercys were one family, as both Stintescombe and Brympton were held by the same individual. In 1280 Thomas D'Evercy, with Robert de Glamorgan, claimed wreck of the sea bordering on his lands in the Isle of Wight, against Isabella de Fortibus, Countess of Devon, the owner of the Island, and he was one of the witnesses to a charter (sans date) granted by the Countess to the borough of Newport, I.W. He also held of her one fee in chief, of which the Manor of Standon or Stanton was part. Sir Thomas D'Evercy, Kt., died at Ruardyn before 1293, and it was found by Inquisition that he held certain lands in Ruardyn of the King, in chief by serjeanty, and that his grandson, Thomas, son of Thomas D'Evercy, aged 23, was his heir.[52]

Contemporary with Thomas D'Evercy was Peter D'Evercy, also a knight, probably the son of Thomas, but as he did not die until 1325 he must have been preceded by one, if not more, of the same name, as Peter D'Evercy was witness to a charter granted to Newport not later, according to Worsley, than 1246, and was charged with scutage for his land in the Isle of Wight in 1255. Brympton had been, as appears by Harl. MS. 4120, entailed on this Peter (supposed son of Thomas) and his issue. To guard against the contingency of his leaving no issue a further settlement was made in 1282 by indentures of fine between " Peter de Evercy," plt., and " Thomas de Evercy," deft., whereby one messuage and one carucate of land in Stintescombe, and one messuage and two carucates of land in Brympton, were settled on Thomas for life, and, failing the issue of Peter, to Anselm, brother of Peter, in tail, remainder to Joan, Mabil, Marista, Nichola and Aleysia, sisters of Anselm, for their lives, and after their deaths to the heirs of the body of Joan, with remainder to the right heirs of Thomas.[53] This settlement did not, however, take effect, as Peter left issue an only daughter. As tenant for life, Thomas de Evercy

---

[51] Inq. p.m., 40 Hen. III., No. 34. ; Ext. Rot. Fin., ii., 228.
[52] Inq. p.m., 21 Edw. I., No. 10.
[53] Fin. Div. Cos., 10 Edw. I., No. 33.

is returned in Kirby's Quest as feudal tenant of Brympton, under Matthew de Furneaux, but in the Inquisition of knights' fees, 31 Ed. I., Peter de Evercy is returned as the tenant both of Brympton and Alvington,[54] which change was probably made in consequence of the death of Thomas. Peter is also returned by the Sheriff as Lord of Brympton in the Nomina Villarum, temp. Edw. II, but in the copy of that record just issued by "The Somerset Record Society," the Christian name, by a clerical error, is unfortunately printed "Johannes," instead of "Petrus."

Sir Peter D'Evercy must have been an important personage both in Somersetshire and the Isle of Wight, as he represented the former county in Parliament in 1307 and 1315, and was member for the county of Southampton in 1319. In 1325 he was witness, with his son-in-law, John de Glamorgan, to a grant by the Abbey of Quarr,[55] but died shortly afterwards.

An inquisition after his death was held at Yeovil. The jury found that "Peter de Everci" held the hamlet of Brumpton, co. Somerset, of Simon de Furneaux, as of his Manor of Ashington, by knight service, in which hamlet was a certain capital messuage, with gardens and closes adjoining, worth by the year 5s.; and in demesne 100 acres of arable, worth by the year 33s. 4d.; each acre 4d. and five acres of meadow, worth by the year 5s.; three free tenants, rendering by the year 5s. 8d.; seven "nativi," each holding one furlong of land, and paying yearly 21s. 6d.; 10 "cotarii," each holding one messuage and curtilage, rendering yearly 10s.; and pleas and perquisites of court; that the said Peter, and Isabella his wife, who still survived, held a messuage and dove house in the ville of Montacute of the Priory of Montacute by the service of 2s. a year; and that Amice, his daughter, aged 24 years, and wife of John de Glamorgan, was his heir.[56] Although only Brympton and Montacute are mentioned in the Inquisition, the D'Evercys had other property in Somersetshire, there being an entry on the Beauchamp Cartulary that the heir of D'Everci held of the Lord de Beauchamp of Somerset one-fifth part of a fee pertaining to the manor of Shepton Malet, afterwards purchased by Robert Martyn.

The family De Glamorgan was one of considerable influence in the Isle of Wight, residing at their Manor of Brooke, and they were also landowners in Surrey and Sussex, for which counties Robert de

---

[54] Lay Sub., 31 Ed. I, 169-3.
[55] Madox Form Angl., p. 165.
[56] Esch. 18 Edw. II, No. 54.

Glamorgan was Sheriff in 1293. Ralph de Glamorgan was witness with Peter D'Evercy and others to a charter said to be granted to the borough of Newport in the reign of Henry II, and he is found at a very early period interested in property in the neighbourhood of Yeovil. In the first year of King John, Robert de Glamorgan was in litigation with Robert de Mandeville respecting five hides of land in Hardington,[57] and the following year Ralph de Glamorgan was engaged before the Justices Itinerant against Robert de Mandeville for a moiety of one knight's fee, also in Hardington ;[58] and Ralph de Glamorgan and Philip de Glamorgan were witnesses to a charter (sans date) whereby William de Oglander granted lands to Quarr Abbey.[59] This Philip had the custody of the lands and heir of Baldwin de L'isle, 7th Earl of Devon, and died in 1247, when William de Glamorgan was proved to be his heir.[60] He is supposed by the writer in "Early Sussex Armoury," already mentioned, to have married the daughter of De L'isle, but the evidence only shows that he was one of de L'isle's heirs. In 1280 Robert de Glamorgan was chief lord under the Countess Isabella de Fortibus, of the Manor of Broke, Isle of Wight,[61] half a knight's fee in which was held of him by John Passelewe.[62] Sir John de Glamorgan, the husband of D'Evercy's daughter, was, in the reign of Edw. II, one of the representatives in Parliament for the county of Southampton, but nothing is heard of him in connection with Brympton ; the cause of which probably was that Dame Isabella D'Evercy, who held it for her life, outlived him, for according to Harl. MS, 4120, Peter, son and heir of John de Glamorgan, took possession after her death, which did not occur until after 1327, as she was taxed at 40d. to a subsidy at Brympton made in that year.

The title to Brympton after the death of Dame Isabella is obscure and intricate, and gave rise to much litigation. Some early antiquary, who had access to documents no longer in existence, has left, in Harl. MS, 4120, extracts from charters and other deeds connected with families and estates in Somerset and Dorset, and

---

[57] Rot. Cur. Reg. i., 245.

[58] Rot. de Obl. Fin., p. 59, Pipe Roll, Dor. and Som., 3 John.

[59] Worsley Appx., No. lxxiv.

[60] Esch., 31 Hen. III, No. 9.

[61] Worsley's Isle of Wight App., No. xxx.

[62] Test. de Nev., Hants.

amongst them are two relating to Brympton. The first, which is in Latin, runs thus :—

" IN CHARTA ANTIQUA SIC REPERIO. JOHANNES DEVERSEY MILES FUIT SEISITUS DE MANEIRO DE BRIMPTON ET DEDIT DICTUM MANERIUM PETRO DE EVERSEY ET HŒRED DE CORPORE SUO EXEUNTIBUS QUI HABUIT EXITUM QUANDAM FILIAM ET HERED DISPONSAT JOHANNI GLAMORGAN CHEV QUI HABUENT INTER EOS QUINQUE FILIAS JOHANNES WYNFORD PATER JOHANNIS WYNFORD EXIT DE UNA WILL LEWESTON EX 2NDA . . . . VEERE BASTARD DE TERTIA ET JOHES UVRY DE IUSUL VECT DE QUARTA."

The second is in English :—

" OUT OF AN OLD WRITING IN FRENCH, ABOUT EDWARD II. OR III., I FIND THAT DAME ISABEL DEVERSEY WAS SEIZED OF THE MANOR OF BRIMPTON, AND DIED ; AFTER WHOSE DETH ENTERED PIERS GLAMORGAN, SON AND HEIRE TO AMYE, WHO WAS DAUGHTER TO THE SAID ISABELL. AFTER [AFTERWARDS] THE SAID PIERS [GLAMORGAN] ENTAYLED THE SAID MANOR TO HIS AND HIS WIFE'S [ISSUE], AND FOR DEFAULT OF ISSUE TO JOAN GLAMORGAN, HIS SISTER."

Probably the name of *John* D'Evercy, Kt., in the first extract is an error for *Thomas*. No member of the family called John is to be found in any record or document except this ; whereas *Thomas* D'Evercy, Kt., is mentioned in several, and he *was* the owner of Brympton, and competent, therefore, to make a settlement of it. There is another similar mistake in stating that there were five daughters (quinque), but enumerating only four (quatuor). Four is believed to be correct. The reader cannot fail to notice also an inconsistency between the two extracts, for according to the first there was issue of the marriage of Sir John De Glamorgan with the D'Evercy heiress four daughters only, whereas, according to the second, there was also a son, Peter ; and, in fact, there was another son, Nicholas. The discrepancy can only be reconciled by supposing that the charter referred to in the first extract was not made until after the death, without issue, of both Peter de Glamorgan and Nicholas his brother *(i.e.,* after 1363), when their four sisters, daughters of their mother, or their issue, would be the heirs of the body of the original settlor, and consequently, if the D'Evercy settlement was still in force, entitled to Brympton in co-parcenary. But they could not be so entitled if the second extract was correct, for, according to that, Peter de Glamorgan made a settlement of Brympton after he came into possession, which superseded the D'Evercy one, and cut off all his sisters but one ; and we believe that he had perfect right to do so. It is clear from the Fine, 10 Edw. I, already quoted, that the settlement on Peter D'Evercy and the heirs of his body had been then previously made, and consequently, not being affected by the Statute De Donis, Peter D'Evercy had a conditional fee in Brympton, which, on the birth of his daughter Amice, or Amye, enabled him to acquire the fee simple. On his death the property would descend to such daughter, and after her, as the second extract says, to her son and heir, Peter de Glamorgan. Peter then married, and, as absolute owner, settled it on his issue, and, if none, on his sister Joan de Glamorgan. The ownership of Peter de Glamorgan is corroborated by his having, in 1342, granted Brympton an the advowson of the church and chapel to Thomas Hacket and Annie his wife for her life, which he could not have done unless he had been full owner.[63]

Peter de Glamorgan died before 1344,[64] but left no issue; and Nicholas, his brother, was found to be his heir—that is, his heir at the common law; Joan, his sister, being entitled to Brympton under the settlement. But the existence of it seems to have been concealed, for the Crown, after holding an inquisition (26 Edw. III), which found his death and that his brother Nicholas was an idiot, took possession of Brympton (jure coronæ), the only counter-claimants being Hacket and his wife, under the grant of 1342. They petitioned Parliament 22 Ed. III for restitution (2 Rot. Parl. 180), and the litigation was still pending 27 Ed. III,[65] but the Crown must have successfully resisted the claim, as five years afterwards the lessee under the Crown was in possession, and accused of oppressing the tenants at Brympton with great hardness and extortion.[66] The grievance, however, was ended by the death of Nicholas, which happened in 1363. Soon after an inquisition was taken (the settlement on Joan being still suppressed), by which the jury found that Nicholas held the Manor of Brympton juxta Yevele, and the advowson of the church of Isabella Blount, as of her Manor of Ashyngton by knight service, and that Isabella, Petronilla, Margaret, the wife of Walter Rose, Nichola, Alianor, the wife of Peter Veer, sisters of the said Nicholas, and John Wynford, aged 14 years, son of Joan, another sister, were his heirs.[67] The consequence was that, apart from the settlement, Brympton would be the property of these

---

[63] Inq. p.m., 26 Ed. III.
[64] Plac. Cor. Reg. 17 Ed. 3, No. 147.
[65] Plac. Cor. Rege. Ro., 64.
[66] Inq. 33 Ed. III, Nos. 45 and 46.
[67] Esch. 36, Ed. III, No. 82.

heirs of Nicholas in six equal shares ; but Isabella, who died unmarried, had sold her share in her lifetime, and it was afterwards
purchased by Walter and Margaret Rose, who by that means had
two-sixths.[68]　Soon after the death of Nicholas the settlement
must have come to light, for in 1365, John Wynford, son
of Joan de Glamorgan, in whose favour it had been made, set up
his claim under it, and an assize was held to try whether Roger
Rose and Margaret his wife, Wm. Urry, Petronilla Urry, Peter de
Veer and Alianor his wife, and Peter son of Peter de Veer, Nichola
Glamorgan, Johanna De L'Isle (in the Isle of Wight), John de Doo
and Robert Atteyard had disseised him of five sixth parts of the
Manor of Brympton (the remaining one-sixth being admitted to be
his), and the jury found a verdict in his favour, thereby establishing
his title to the estate.[69]

From him Brympton descended to John Wynford, his grandson,
and in an inquisition taken in 1431 he is returned as the owner of
lands in Somersetshire worth £20 per annum.　In the same year he
sold the reversion, contingent on his death without issue, to John
Stourton, of Preston, and by a fine, levied Easter Term 9 Hen. VI,
between John Passeware and William Bochell (trustees), plts., and
John Wynford and Alice his wife, defts., the manor of Brympton,
with the appurtenances and the advowson of the church and chantry
of Brympton, were limited to the said John Wynford and Alice his
wife and the heirs of the body of the said John Wynford, with
remainder to John Stourton, of Preston Plucknet, Master Richard
Stourton, William Carent, William Powlet, John Hody, John
Fauntleroy, John Wilke, John Smythe, and John Dyker, and the
heirs of the said John Stourton.[70] John Wynford died very soon after
without issue, otherwise Stourton would not have succeeded to the
estate, but his wife Alice survived for many years, and was living
1356. Three years after his purchase John Stourton settled Brympton
on his daughter Joan.　By indenture of fine (Michas. Term, 12 Hen.
VI) between John Sydenham and Joan his wife, plts., and John
Sydenham, of Preston Pludknet, John Hody, and John Smyth,
defts., the Manor of Brympton and the advowson of the church and
chantry (then held by William Lambroke, clerk, William Alisandre,
and other trustees therein named, for the life of Alice, late wife of

---

[68] Close Rolls, 39 Ed. III., m. 29.

[69] Ass. Roll Somt., 38 Ed. III, No. 2-27 7.

[70] Somt. Fines, 9 Hen. VI, No 56.

John Wynford, Esq.), were limited after the decease of the said Alice to the said John Sydenham and Joan his wife, and the heirs of their bodies, with remainder to the said John Stourton, John Hody, and John Smyth, and the heirs of the said John Stourton.[71] John Sydenham died 4th April, 1460, leaving his wife Joan surviving. The inquisition after his death (8 Edward IV, No. 22) does not mention Brympton, as it passed to his wife by survivorship, but it details many manors held by him in the counties of Somerset and Devon, and finds that Walter Sydenham, aged twenty-five years, was his son and heir.

Walter soon followed his father, and died 1st May, 1469, jointly seized with his wife Margaret of the manor of Chilthorne Domer, leaving John, his son and heir, aged two years.[72]

The premature death of this young man, leaving his wife and infant son, must have been a distressing event. His will, made about a month before his death, has been found. Mediæval wills are nearly all of the same type—seldom dealing with real estate, which was the subject of more technical procedure—but confined to directions for superstitious works of merit in aid of the testator's salvation, and to bequests of his personal effects.

Some preliminary notes on this will may be useful. It is difficult to explain the expression " xxs of peise grots." " Peise " is said to mean " weight," and grots were silver coins of the value of 4d. Amongst the accessories for the services of the Romish Church was the pyx, a small vessel or chalice, generally made of silver or gold, and sometimes studded with jewels, for containing the Host; and it is probable that the testator intended that one should be made of twenty shillings worth of silver peise grots, which would have to be beaten out or melted down for the purpose, and he afterwards adds the silver harness—that is, the mountings of his sword—to make up any deficiency.

The will shews that he had land in Montacute and Tintinhull, and that the tenant of the former was John Smith, of Gofford— which is Gosford, the name of a farm or hamlet in the parish of Odcombe. The lamp at the altar was put out by the Reformation extinguisher, and the church left for some centuries in Protestant darkness, but during the incumbency of a late Rector a gloomy glimmer was kept suspended over the chancel screen; whether fed with the 11s. 8d. is uncertain, but it did not appear to the spectator

---

[71] Somt. Fines, 12 Hen. VI, no. 1.

[72] Inq. 9 and 10 Edward IV, no. 18.

calculated to enlighten the parishioners. The horse allotted to the parson for his mortuary was in discharge of a customary right, resembling a heriot in modern times, and the gift to his servants affords an example of the equipments of a young country gentleman of the period.

The following is the text of the will :—

" In the name of God, Amen, the second day of the month of April, the yer of our Lord MXXXXLXIX.

" I, Walter Sidenham, esquier, sone and heire of John Sidenham the elder, esquier, hole of mynde and of memorie, make my testament in this wise.

" First, I bequeth my soul to Almighty God and to o^r Lady seint Mary and to alle the companye of heven ; my body to be buryed in the Newe Ile of the parisshe church of Brympton. Item, I bequeth to the High Aulter of the said parisshe church one paire of Aulter Clothes of crimesyn Damask with a frontall of blak velvet embrawded. Itm, I bequeth xx^s of peise grotes to make a boxe to put in o^r Lordes body and to hange over the said Aulter. Item, I bequeth to the mayntenance of a lampe to brenne afore o^r Lordes body at the said Aulter xi^s viii^d, to be taking perpetually by the yer, whereof vi^s viii^d going out of the londes yat John Smyth, of Gofford, holdeth nowe of me in Hidefield, in ye parisshe of Montagu, and v^s, a yere going oute of the londes which I purchased late of Browning in Tintenhull. Itm, I will that the parson of Brympton have for me to his mortuarie a donne hors of myne. Itm, I will yat my servant William Wilson have a sorell hakeney of myne with a sadill and a bridele and alle other my ryding harness, yat is to say my doubelet of fustian, a short blak goune, and a short crymesyn gowne, my bots, my sporis, my bowes and arrowes, my swerd, except the silver harness on the same swerd, which I bequeth to the making of the said boxe. The residue of my goodes I bequeth to Margaret my wife and to John my son to dispose the said goodes for the welth of my soule as they thinke best, and the said Margaret and John I make and ordeyn myn executors and to pay my detts, yat is to say, to Walter Pauncefoot, esquier, xli. Itm, to Parker, Draper, of London, x marks. Itm, to oon Richard, Tailor, Flete Strete, in London, 1^s. Itm, there remayneth withe the saide Draper iii. yerdes of brode cloth, violet, price vi^s viii^d a yerd, in plegge of payments of part of ye said 1^s. Itm, I owe to Barnabie ys wife, of London, for ij pair of hosis, price, I suppose, viii^s. Itm, I owe to Nicholas Forest, Taillor, of London, vi^s for the making of a dowblet of silk of myn, and iiij^s for a dowbelet of fustain to my child.

" Proved at Lambeth, xxii January, 1469, by Margaret the relict."

Joan, the mother of Walter and widow of John Sydenham I, died 21 April, 1472; and an inquisition respecting her property was held at Crewkerne 31 Oct. in the same year, before " Thomas Phelipp," escheator, but it does not give much information, its main object being to show how her husband and herself had divested themselves of the legal ownership of their property, with the loyal intention, it may be, of escaping from feudal obligations attached to the actual possession of it. The jury found that Joan and her husband were at one time jointly seized in fee of *(inter alia)* the Manors of Brympton and Alvington, and the advowson of the church and chantry, as well as of lands in Chilthorne Domer and at Streme in St. Decumans, but that by certain assurances therein recited the said manors had become vested in the said Joan in fee by right of survivorship; that she had enfeoffed John Chayney, John Byconyll, Robert Hymerford, Thomas Phelipp, John Lyte, Esqrs., Master Thomas Bertelott, clerk ; Simon Sydenham, Bachelor of Arts; and Henry Frank, of the said Manors of Brympton and Alvington, and the advowson of said church and chantry, upon trust to perform her will. It winds up by finding that John Sydenham, son of Walter Sydenham, Esq., was the next heir of the said Joan, viz., son of Walter, son of the said Joan, and aged three years.[73]

Whether Joan Sydenham devised Brympton by her will is not known. Probably she allowed it to pass to her grandson and heir, John II, from whom it came down to his descendants, as already shown.

---

[73] Inq. p. m., 12 Edward IV, no. 45.

INCUMBENTS OF BRYMPTON.

[*From Weaver's " Somersetshire Incumbents."*]

Date of Institution.	Incumbent.	Patron.
1321	...Joh. de Putford	Petr. D'Evercy, Mil.
1344	...Joh. Pulle	Rex.
1352	..Phil. le Doo.	
1353	.. Rob. Douslond	Edw. III Rex. ratione terrarum et tenementorum Nich. fil. Joh. Glamorgan idiotæ in manu sua existentium.
1427	...Tho. Ford	Joh. Wynford, arm.
1445	...Tho. Wayte	Alic. Wynford dna de Brimpton.
1449	...Will Cayrus	Alic. Wynford.
1459	...Tho. Shortrigge	Joh. Sydenham, arm.
	Rob. Wodeford	J. Sydenham, arm.
	Rob. Genys.	
1472	...Joh. Touker	Joh. Cheyney, Joh. Byconel, Rob. Hymerford, Tho. Philipps, Joh. Lyte, Tho. Bertelot, Simon Sydenham, et Hen. Franke ratione feoffamenti man. et advocationis per Johannam nuper uxorem Joh. Sydenham.
1475	..Simon Sydenham, A.M.	Alex. Sydenham et Ric. Sydenham arm.
1477	...Clemens Winterbourne	,, ,,
1480	...Tho. Hawkyn	,, ,,
	Wil. Russel	,, ,,
1519	...Joh. Hacket	Joh. Sydenham, arm. ,,
1547	...Hugo Sydenham, arm	,,
1571	...Joh. Cossyns	,,
1580	...Tho. Pinfold	,,
1597	...Joh. Willes, A.M.	,,
1613	...Will. Arden, A.M.	Joh. Sydenham, mil.
	Nich. Templeman	,,
1639	...Will. Cuthbert, A.M.	Carolus Rex. ratione minoris ætatis Joh. Sydenham wardi sui.
1660	...Brian Congall, A.M.	Joh. Sydenham, Bart.
1673	...Ric. Hody, A.M.	,,
1701	...Jac. Upton, A.M.	Phil. Sydenham, Bart.
1711	...Will Baker, A.M.	,,
1723	.. Sydenham Burgh, A.M.	,,

CHAPTER V.

HOUNDSTON.

ONTIGUOUS to Brympton, but situated in the parish of Odcombe, although quite isolated from it, is Houndston Farm, and as it was for many generations part of the Sydenham estate, it may conveniently be noticed here.

According to Collinson,[1] Houndston is identical with a ville called Hunesberge which a Saxon king gave by charter to the Abbey of Glastonbury A.D. 757,[2] but as the charter speaks of it as " lying on the eastern ripe of Parret," it can hardly be Houndston, which is at least five miles distant. Then he says that William the Conqueror took Hunesberge from the Abbey and gave it to Robert Earl of Moretain, and that his son William conferred both the church and manor of Hunesberge on the monastery he had founded at Montacute. On reference, however, to the foundation charters of that Priory, it is clear that the grant was of the hundred of Hunesberge only, the church and manor being Chinnock. In fact there is no satisfactory evidence that there ever was any ville called Hunesberge except the Saxon charter quoted, and that comes from too doubtful a source to be implicitly relied on.

There was, however, certainly a Hundred of Hunesberge, which exists to this day under the name of Houndsborough. It is not noticed in the Inquisitio Gheldi, and it probably therefore was a post-Domesday Hundred, carved out of the Hundred of Givelea or Ivle.

---

[1] Hist. Som. II. 323.

[2] John de Glaston. Hist.

At the time of the Domesday Survey Ansger Brito held Houndston as sub-tenant of the Earl of Moretain, and it no doubt formed part of his Barony, which passed, in the reign of Henry III, to the daughters and co-heiresses of William Briwere, one of whom was Alice, wife of Reginald de Mohun of Dunster.[3]

In the partition made of the Barony of Brito between these co-heiresses, Houndston must have fallen to the lot of Alice de Mohun, for it is mentioned in Kirby's Quest as held under the Mohuns, and in 1279, amongst the fees assigned to Alianor, widow of John de Mohun, great grandson of Reginald, for her dower, was half a fee in Houndston held by Roger de Putford.[4] In 1331 Thomas West held the " Hamlet of Hundston " of John de Mohun by the service of one knight's fee; and in 1346 John West was rated to the subsidy for half a fee in Houndston which John de Kykely formerly held. In the reign of Richard II the manor of Houndston was the property of Sir John Cary, of Cary, Devon, Lord Chief Baron of the Exchequer; but in 1390 he had the misfortune to be impeached and convicted with four other judges for unconstitutional advice to the King, and Houndston and all his possessions were forfeited to the Crown. Soon after it was, with other lands in Yeovil and Kingston juxta Yeovil, granted by the Crown to Sir John Hulle, or Hill, of Kitton, Holcombe Rogus, Devon, one of the Judges of the King's Bench.[5]

Sir John settled the manor and lands upon himself and his second wife, Matilda (daughter of Sir Giles Daubeny, of Barington) and their issue male, with remainder to his own right heirs. He died in 1400, leaving his wife surviving, and in 1411 she had married again to Sir Robert Latimer, of Duntishe, Dorset, for in that year they were defendants in an assize brought by John Murydon to recover the manor of " Hundeston " and lands in Sok and Thorn Coffin, to which they pleaded the said Crown grant, and that in right of the said Matilda Sir Robert then held the said manor.[6]

After the death of Lady Latimer, which occurred in 1416, we find no record of Houndston until 1454, when by Fine between Wm. Bonevyle, Kt., John Cheyne, of Pyne, and John Hill, clerk, plts., and Robert Hymerford, Esq., and Alianor his

---

[3] Som. Arch. Soc. Proceedings, vol. xx, p. 113.

[4] Esch., 7 Edw. I, no. 13.

[5] Pat. Rolls, 15 Ric. II.

[6] Addl. MSS., Br. Mus., no. 25174, p. 56.

wife, defts., the Manor of Houndston and 2 messuages, 172 acres of land and 12 acres of meadow in Houndston, Thorn Coffyn, Chestermede, and Sok were, in consideration of £300, limited to the plts. and the heirs of the said John Hill, with a warranty against Nicholas, Abbot of Glastonbury, and his successors.[7]

John Hill, clerk, to whom the manor was limited, was John, the eldest son of Sir John Hill by his second wife. Being in holy orders he was never married, and on his death was succeeded by his brother Ralph, who died in 1475,[8] leaving a son, Robert. He married Alice, one of the three daughters and co-heiresses of John Stourton of Preston, and widow of Wm. Daubeny, of Barington ; and it is singular that John Hill, jun., grandson of Sir John Hill by his first marriage, married Cecily, another of John Stourton's daughters. Robert Hill died in 1493, seized of this manor and of the lands in Yeovil, still said to be held under the Mohuns as " part of the Honor and Castle of Dunster,"[9] and it may be presumed that he was buried at Dunster, as his arms, impaling those of Stourton, were set up in Dunster Church,[10] and Margaret, his sister, was the wife of Sir Hugh Luttrell.

The descendants of Robert Hill enjoyed Houndston until 1567, when Robert Hill, of Heligan, Cornwall, exchanged it with his kinsman John Sydenham, of Brympton (both being descended from John Stourton), for the manor of Timberscombe, in the western part of Somersetshire. It remained annexed to Brympton until 1703, when Sir Philip Sydenham sold it to Elizabeth Hawker, of Vagg, widow, for £3,200. From her it passed to her daughter Elizabeth, wife of Joseph Clarke, of Chipley, near Milverton, and so to the Sanfords of Nynehead, who sold it, in 1797, to Elias Hawkins, of Brympton.

---

[7] Somt. Fines, 30 Hen. VI, no. 119.

[8] Esch., 15 Edw. IV, no. 2.

[9] Esch., 9 Hen. VII, no. 3.

[10] Harl. MS., 1559, p. 235.

Chapter VI.

PRESTON.

THE parish, of Preston lies between Brympton and Yeovil, and that portion of it comprising the manor or reputed manor of Preston Plucknet was purchased by Mr. Fane soon after he bought Brympton, and still forms part of the Fane estate.

At the time of the Conquest it was in the manor of Ivle, held by Hugh Maltravers under William de Ou, with the exception of two hides, which were granted by the King as a separate manor to Ansger Brito. This led to the division of Preston into two tithings of the Hundred of Stone, which acquired the names of Preston Bermondsey and Preston Plucknet, the latter name in modern times being applied to the whole parish. Collinson[1] considered that these two tithings represented two distinct manors in the Domesday Survey, one held by Ansger, and the other by Hugh (not Maltravers) under Alured de Hispania.

A very competent authority[2] has already questioned Collinson's conclusion, for although there is no difficulty in identifying Ansger's manor as Preston Bermondsey, there is nothing to show that Hugh's manor was Preston Plucknet.

"Presteton," which gelded for three hides wanting one virgate, was held by Hugh under Alured de Hispania, together with several

---

[1] Hist. Som. iii., 223.

[2] Eyton Dom. Stud. Som.

other manors in and about Milverton, and there is a manor in that parish called Preston Bowyer. It seems a strong measure to transfer it to a distant part of the county, especially as it is tolerably clear that Preston Bowyer subsequently became part of the possessions of the Priory of Athelney, and was held by it at the dissolution of monasteries[3]. We conclude therefore that the only Domesday manor at Preston was that granted by the Conqueror to Ansger.

Ansger, called Brito, or le Breton, from the country of his origin, but sometimes Ansger de Montagud or Montacute, was one of several Ansgers who followed William in his invasion of England. He was tenant in chief of several manors in Devonshire, and in Somerset he held Trent, Odcombe, Houndston, and many other manors under the Earl of Moretain. In Dorset he held two manors at Cerne and one at Up-Sydling. All these manors were constituted a land barony, called the Barony of Brito, the head of which ("caput Baroniæ") was Odcombe, where Ansger resided, and from this circumstance the Barony was sometimes designated "The Honor of Odcombe."[4]

Ansger did not retain Preston long, for in 1092 he bestowed it on the Priory of Bermondsey, Surrey, probably in gratitude to his patron, William Earl of Moretain, who after his disgrace retired to it as a monk. The deed of gift is to be found amongst the extracts made by Glover, Somerset Herald, from an ancient Cartulary of the Priory (now unfortunately lost) and said to be compiled by one of the monks, Wm. de Preston, a native of Preston, who lived about 1363. It runs thus :—

"Ego Ansgerus Brito concedo ecclesiæ Sancti Salvatoris de Bermondseye et Monachis de Cluniaco ibidem Deo servientibus totam terram meam de Prestitona Test Waltero filio, meo, Roberto de Bello campo."[5]

There is no date to the charter, but it is ascertained from an entry in the Annals[6] of the monastery of Bermondsey, which says : " A.D. 1092 Ansgerus Brito dedit prædictis monachis manerium de Preston scilicet duas hides,"—from which it follows that the grant included the whole of Ansger's Manor. Henry I, by a charter addressed to " J. Bishop, of Bath " *(i.e.,* John de Villula) and " R," the Chamberlain, and all his Barons, French and English, confirms the gift

---

[3] Val. Eccl. I., 207.

[4] Som. Ant. Soc. Proc., vol. xx, p. 113 ; xxi, p. 29.

[5] Glover's Misc. Collections, Coll. Arm B, fo. 111.

[6] Rolls Series. Annales, Monastici, vol. ii.

and testifies that he had granted to God and the Holy Trinity and the monks of Cluny that land of Presteton which Ansger Brito gave to them. Test. Walter, son of Ansger, and R. Chamberlain, at Chigebergam, and R. de Bellocampo.[7]

In 1095, Walter Brito, son of Ansger, gave to the Priory two hides of land de la Stane,[8] and by charter, tested at Windsor, addressed to W. Capre and all his faithful people, French and English, of Somerset, William [Rufus], King of England, grants to God and the monks of Bermondsey two hides of land which Walter Fitz Ansger gave to them, T. Ansell de Parrantun and W. Pevrel.[9]

Stane, or de la Stane, gelded for two hides, could not have formed part of Ansger's manor of Preston, as it was in Mudford, and held at the date of the survey by the Earl of Moretain in capite with Sock and Draycott. It may be presumed that the Earl gave it to Ansger, and that it descended after his death to Walter his son, who conferred it on the Priory. Stane is now represented by an isolated farm, about one mile from Yeovil, called Stone Farm, surrounded by the parishes of Yeovil and Mudford, although legally within the parish of Preston. It derives its name from an ancient stone standing on the most elevated part of it, on the spot where the Courts for the Hundred of Stone used to be held. The identity of the Abbey lands is easily to be traced. For example, one part of it, lying west of Stone Lane, was, in 1650, conveyed as "a Close of Pasture called Longstone, containing 29 acres, together with the herbage of Brodemead Waye leading to Longstone, situate at Stone, in the county of Somerset, and parcel of the manor of Preston, now commonly called Preston Bermondsey, and reputed to be parcel of the manor or farm of Stone, heretofore parcel of the possessions of the late dissolved Abbey of Bermondsey."

In the early part of the reign of King John, the Barony of Brito passed from the family of Brito to Richard Briewere, son of Wm. Lord Briewere, a baron of great wealth and influence in the west, and not long after, Hugh, the Prior of Bermondsey, paid him, as the representative of the Britos, forty marks for a confirmation of the gifts of the land of Preston and de la Stane.[10]

---

[7] Cott. MSS., Br. Mus., Claud. A viii, p. 115.

[8] Glover, *ub sup.*

[9] Cott. MSS., *ub sup.*, p. 119.

[10] Cott. MSS., *ub sup.*

In addition to Preston and Stone, the Priory also possessed the Manor of Kinewardeston (now Kingweston), in Somersetshire, which was given to them about the year 1114 by Mary, wife of Eustace, Earl of Bolonia, when on her death-bed; and the gift was confirmed by her husband after her death.[11]

Altogether the Priory had considerable property in the county of Somerset, and according to Pope Nicholas' Taxation, 1291, it possessed lands in Preston, Gevele, and Stone of the aggregate value of £14 8s. 4d. per annum, and in Kynewardeston of the value of £10 per annum.

In the reign of Henry IV the Crown made a claim on these manors, as forfeited, on the ground that they had been given to the Priory (then Abbey) upon certain trusts which had long been neglected. By an Inquisition taken at Yevele, 6th of July, 4 Hen. IV (1403), it was found " that a certain progenitor of the now King, whose name was unknown to the Jurors, gave to the Prior of Bermondeshey and his successors for ever the manor of Kynwardestone Preston, near Yevele, with members pensions and portions to and the same manors of old time appertaining, to find two monks, chaplains, to be resident on the site of the manor of Preston, and to celebrate Divine service in the chapel of St. Mary, within the said manor, every day in the year for ever, for the souls of the King's progenitors, formerly Kings of England, and of all the faithful departed, which said services have been withdrawn for forty years and more," and that the said manors were worth by the year beyond reprises fifty marks.[12]

No further proceedings appear to have been taken on this Inquisition, but fourteen years after another was taken at Yeovil, 30th July, 5 Hen. V (1417), whereby the jury found " that John, Abbot of Bermondesey, and the convent there, held the manor (manerium) of Preston Bermondsey and Stone of the King as of the gift of his progenitors formerly made to their predecessors in pure almaign for ever, to find two fit chaplains for ever to celebrate daily in the Chapel of Preston Bermondesey and to pray for the souls of the said King, his progenitors and heirs, and all the faithful departed." That the said John was Abbot, and his predecessors and convent had withdrawn the services of the said two chaplains for twelve years past and more, and found or supported

---

[11] Cott. MSS., *ub sup.*

[12] Inq. ad. q d 4 Hen. IV, no. 15.

no chaplain, to the prejudice of the King's right. The manor was worth beyond reprises £20 by the year, and was so let to farm.[13]

A trial followed upon this Inquisition, the record of which has not been found; but according to the Abbey annals they came off victorious, as in the year 1417 is this entry :—" This year there was an action in the King's Chancery between our Lord the King and Thomas Thetford, Abbot of Bermondesey, respecting the manor of Preston Bermondesey and Stone, in the county of Somerset, and it was recovered by the said Abbot.[14]

Natwithstanding this, many years after the claim was revived, and by a third Inquisition, taken at Yeovil 16th October, 7 Edw. IV (1468), it was found that there was a cell (sella) at Preston Bermensey, near Yevell, appertaining to the Abbey of Bermensey, founded by the King's progenitors and of the King's patronage, in which there used to be of old time two monks to celebrate divine service; that the Abbot received the rents of the lands, but neglected to find the two monks or any other priest or clerk, as customary of old time, and permitted the cell to fall as if utterly destroyed, and so the divine services had been for a long time withdrawn, contrary to the form of the foundation.[15] Whether any steps were taken on this Inquisition does not appear, but it is to be presumed the claim was abandoned (possibly in consequence of the decision in 1417), as the manor continued in the possession of the Abbey.

The whole proceeding on the part of the Crown authorities was evidently a fishing enquiry. They were in such ignorance of the facts that they had not learnt even who the donors were, or what lands were given. At first their claim extended to Kingweston as well as Preston, but failing in that they confined it to Preston and Stone, where they failed also.

At the same time the Inquisition shows that the Abbey had a cell on their manor at Preston, in which two monks resided, that there was a chapel standing within the manor, dedicated to St. Mary, in which these monks celebrated divine service; and that in 1467 it had been neglected and allowed to fall down. This cell and chapel stood, it may be presumed, on or near the site of the present farmhouse, but there is no trace or tradition of their existence.

---

[13] Inq. ad. 9 d., 5 Hen. V, no. 9.

[14] Ann. Berm., ub. sup.

[15] Esch. Inq., Som. and Dor., Series 1, file 1666.

After this litigation we hear no more of these manors until the year 1557, when by letters patent, dated 31st May, 3 & 4 Phil. and Mary, in consideration of the good services to the Crown performed by Thomas White, gentleman, in the late conspiracy of Henry Dudley, the King and Queen granted unto him and his wife Agnes, and to the heirs of his body, "all those our manors of Preston, Stone, and Kynwardeston, in the county of Somerset, parcel of the possessions of the late dissolved monastery of Bermondsey."[16]

The property was afterwards divided and sold, and Preston Bermondsey (generally called Preston Farm) passed through various hands until the year 1709, when it was conveyed by Henry Moore, of West Coker, to Philip Freke, of Bristol, in whose family it remained until the latter part of the last century.

Recurring now to the remainder of Preston (afterwards called Preston Plucknet), if, as we suppose, it formed part of Wm. de Ou's manor of Ivle, it afterwards was created a post-Domesday manor distinct from the manor of Preston Bermondsey. Ecclesiastically, the whole of Preston had no separate existence from the parish of Yeovil, of which it was part and parcel. Preston is a parochial chapelry, and the so-called church is only a chapel-of-ease to Yeovil, the chaplain of which in early times took an oath on his appointment not to subtract or receive anything to the prejudice of the Rector of Yeovil or his Vicar in the way of tithes or otherwise.[17] To this day the incumbent of Yeovil is instituted to the Vicarage of Yeovil with the Chapel of Preston Plucknet annexed. It may here be observed that the patronage of the Rectory of Yeovil, which embraced also the Lordship of the Borough, belonged, previous to the reign of Hen. VI, to the Maltravers family as lords of the manor of Hendford ; and at Yeovil, as in some other parishes, there were both a Rector (sometimes a layman), who enjoyed all the profits, and a stipendiary Vicar, who performed all the duties. Hen. VI, having purchased the rectory, appropriated it to the Abbess and Convent of Syon, who held it until the dissolution of monasteries. In 1610 Sir Edward Phelipps and his son Sir Robert purchased it of the grantees from the Crown, and in 1637 Sir Robert sold the rectorial tithes of Preston to John Hodges, of Lufton.

In 1675 his granddaughter Jane, on her marriage with Wm. Phelipps of Preston (her second husband) settled them on her kinswoman

---

[16] Pat. Roll., 3 and 4 Phil. and Mary, pt. 10.

[17] Cart. Miscell., Aug. off., vol. iii, no. 179.

Elizabeth, the wife of William Hooper of Montacute, ancestor of Judge Hooper, the present owner.

It is impossible to say when the chapel of Preston was built. Our impression is that the existing building is the original one, and that the date of it may be approximately fixed at the latter end of the reign of Edw. III, perhaps during the incumbency of Robert de Sambourne, Rector of Yeovil, who was an energetic and, apparently, a wealthy man, contributing liberally to the enlargement of the parish church.

In 1402 there was some question whether the Vicar was bound to provide daily service in the chapel; and in proof of the usage, solemn depositions were publicly made in the church of Yeovil before certain of the inhabitants, by John Botor and William Smyth, two of the Vicar's chaplains who served the chapel, to the effect that Divine service was only performed there three days a week, viz., Sundays, Wednesdays, and Fridays, and on certain fasts and festivals,[18] and that the Preston people were quite contented.

In the subsidy 1 Edward III, "Preston" is assessed as one Tithing only in the Hundred of Stone, John de Preston being rated at 3s. Later on, in a muster roll for the Hundred, temp. Hen. VIII, the entry as to Preston is as follows :—

The Tything of Preston Bermondsey.
Raynold Harrison, 1 hole harness, 1 bowe, 1 sheff, ar.
Lionell Harrison, 1 hole harness, 1 bill.
John Whitbye, 1 bowe.

The Tything of Preston Plucknet.
Thomas Whitbye, 1 pair of splynts, 1 byll, 1 sakett.
Leonell Whitbye, 1 bowe.

Able Byllmén finding Harness.
John Sely, vi. ar.
William Houper, vi. ar.
Thomas Atwyllo, sen., 1 byll.
Vins Alyngs.
George Garrett.

Able Archers.
Thomas Beaton }
William Farr } 1 bowe.

Men not Able.
John Pawly, 1 byll.
William Pawly, vi. ar.
Thos. Gaylerd, di sheff ar.

The existence of the chapel at Preston did not convert it into a separate civil parish. Lay or civil parishes were the

---

[18] Cart Miscell., aug. off., vol. 12, no. 31.

outcome of the Statute of Elizabeth relating to the relief of the poor, but even in the reign of Chas. II lands are described in deeds as situated in Preston Plucknet, within the parish of Yeovil. Previous to the reign of Elizabeth, the civil division of the country for fiscal and departmental purposes was that of Hundreds and Tithings, and subsidies and military services were all raised and levied by the Constable of the Hundred and the Tithing men. The Constable was a great man in those days, and James I is said to have " commended that condition of man as a happy mean who is between a Justice of the Peace and a Constable of the Hundred."

There was no parochial system ; the Manor Court (or Court Baron) was practically the parish vestry, for although these courts were originally constituted for the protection of the Lord's rights, by degrees they took cognizance of rights and wrongs, such as highways, nuisances, &c., as between the tenants, and looked after the interests of the inhabitants generally.

In the reign of King Stephen, Preston Plucknet was held by William Fitz Walter as part of the Barony of Haselbere.[19] This Wm. Fitz Walter bestowed the Church of Haselbere as a Prebend on the Cathedral Church of Wells, and his son, " William Fitz William of Haselbere," was assessed in 1166 for three knights' fees to the aid for marrying the daughter of Henry II. That Preston formed part of the Barony is proved by the fact that " Richard of Haselbere, son of Wm. Fitz William," held in capite two hides in the ville of Preston appertaining to the Barony of Haselbere,[20] which Barony he held of the King by knight service.[21] Being convicted of treason against King John he was hanged at Sherborne, and his lands forfeited. He left a widow, Isabella, who recovered as her dower one-third of a virgate in Haselbere, and one-third of three virgates and a half in Preston.[22]

About this time Walter de Bruges must have acquired some interest in Preston. The Monastery of Abbotsbury received an annual quit rent of 15s. from Preston, which had been granted to them prior to 1269 (54 Hen. III) by Walter de Bruges and Alice his wife, out of his lands there held of the fee of William Quarrel,[23] and

[19] Lel. Coll. II, 445.

[20] Wells MSS. Index, p. 34 ; Test. de Nev., p. 161.

[21] Test. de Nev., 163.

[22] Somt. Fines, 3 Hen. III, Nos. 31, 39, 41.

[23] Inq. 54 Hen. III.

the rent continued to be received by the Abbey down to the time of the dissolution.

Little is known of Walter de Bruges. He was under sheriff (sub vice-comes) of Dorset and Somerset 38 Hen. III, and probably had some official connection with the Castle of Sherborne, as in 1258 (42 Hen. III) he was ordered to deliver it to Stephen Longspee, agreeably to the provision made at Oxford under the Barons.[24]

In 1306 Walter Bruges and Alice his wife presented to the Church of East Kennet, Wilts.[25] In 1260-1 (45 Hen. III) a fine was levied between Ralph Daubeny Qu. and Nicholas Quarrel and Alice his wife, defts., of 2 virgates of land in South Petherton, formerly of Thomas de Bruges, grandfather of Alice, and the Prior of Montacute, and Alisia de Bruges and Joan her daughter, put in their claim. In 1277-8 (6 Edw. I) another fine was levied between Walter de Bruges, Qu., and Peter de Bruges, deft., of lands in North Cheryton and Holton, which were limited to Peter for life, rem^r to Walter and the heirs of his body, rem^r to right heirs of Peter.

The Barony or Manor of Haselbere, after its confiscation by Richard of Haselbere, was granted to John Marshal, nephew of the Earl of Pembroke, then constable of the Castle of Sherborne. His son William took part in the rebellion against Hen. III, and being attainted, his estates were forfeited, and Haselbere came again into the hands of the Crown. In 1270 (54 Hen. III) it was granted to Alan de Plugenet, who in "Kirby's Quest" (circ. 12 Edw. I) and in the Nomina Villarum, (9 Ed. II) is enrolled as Lord of Haselbere, and he also held Preston Plucknet, in the Hundred of Stone, of the King in chief by military service.

Sir Alan de Plugenet, or Plukenet, said to be a Breton, was nephew of Robert Walerand, and, as his ultimate heir inherited the Castle and Manor of Kilpek, co. Hereford. He was first summoned to Parliament 23 Edw. I, and died in 1299. His arms were Erm. a bend fusilly gu.[26] He was succeeded by his son Alan, also summoned to Parliament (5 Edw. II), who died s.p. before 1326, leaving his sister Joan his heir. On her death, a claim was set up by the Crown to his estates, including the Barony of Haselbury, on the ground that Alan (the father) was illegitimate; but on a trial his legitimacy was apparently established.[27] Alan, the son, must have been a very violent

---

[24] Hutch. Hist. Dorst. iv., 267.   D'Ewes Extracts Harl. MSS. 30.

[25] Phillipps Wilts Institutions.

[26] Esch. 27 Edw. I.

[27] Plac de Banco Q.B. Tim. T., Edw. III, Ro. 21, Somst.

and lawless character, defying even the authority of his Bishop. It is recorded of him that in the year 1315, contrary to the expressed wish of his late mother, the " Lady H. de Plukenet," who had requested to be buried in Sherborne Minster, he, failing in all duty and reverence, interred her remains elsewhere. Complaint of his conduct being made to the Bishop of Bath and Wells (J. de Drokensford) a letter of monition was sent, under the Bishop's seal, requiring Sir Alan to re-inter his mother's body in the place she had selected, and the Rural Dean was directed to serve it personally at Haselbury. Sir Alan on seeing him seized the poor Rural Dean by the throat, and forced him to eat and swallow the letter and the wax of the seal, and otherwise assaulted and ill-treated him. For this offence he was excommunicated, but afterwards appearing before the Bishop and expressing his contrition, the Bishop granted him pardon and absolution.[28]

The family of de Preston were the tenants of Preston under de Plukenet. In 1326 John de Preston, sen., by fine entailed divers lands in Preston Plukenet and in Chestermede, at Ilchester, on his son John and Matilda his wife and the heirs of their bodies ;[29] and in 1329 he died seized of 3 messuages, 60 acres of land, and 7/4 rent in Preston Plukenet, held of the King in chief by service of one sixth of a knight's fee, which he acquired of Alan Plukenet without licence.[30] From this we think that by this purchase the over-lordship became united with the feudal tenancy of the land, and that de Preston afterwards compounded for the want of license, although the pardon is not extant. This would account for the fact that we hear nothing of the over-lordship after de Plukenet.

John, the son, held the same lands (27 Edw. III),[31] and on his death (35 Edw. III) was succeeded by his daughter and heir, Elizabeth, wife of William de Pappeworthe, who survived her father only ten days, and, leaving no issue, the estate vested in her six aunts (sisters of John de Preston) or their children.[32]

Wm. de Pappeworthe was tenant by the curtesy, and he appears to have bought up several of the sisters' shares,[33] and then sold

---

[28] Bp. Drok. Reg. for 77 a 78 a.

[29] Somst. Fines, 19 Edw. II, no. 70.

[30] Esch. 2 Edw. III, pt. 2, no. 1.

[31] Inq. ad. qd., 27 Edw. III, pt. 2, no. 14.

[32] Esch. 35 Edw. III, pt. 2, no. 22 ; Ib., no. 40.

[33] Inq., 41 Ed. III, 2nd, no. 28.

them, for in 1380 he obtained license to grant one-third part of six messuages, one carucate, and 92 acres of land, eight acres of meadow, and 9d. rent in Preston Plucknet, and one-third of a messuage and 12 acres of land in the same place, all held of the King in chief, to John de Stourton and Alice his wife and the heirs of their bodies, remainder to William, son of the said John in tail, remainder to the right heirs of the said John.[34]

John de Stourton was a member of the ancient family of Stourton, of Stourton, Wilts. By his second wife, Alice, he had a son John, sometimes called Jenkyn or little John. He was generally known as John Stourton of Preston, the prefix "de" being dropped. In his will, dated 10th November, 1438, he tells us precisely that he is "John Stourton of Preston, senior, son of John Stourton some time Lord of Stourton, and brother of William son and heir of the said John;" he speaks also of his wife, Katherine, and his nephew, Sir John Stourton—who was afterwards created Baron Stourton. He allied himself by marriage with several leading Somersetshire families, and could boast of large estates in the immediate neighbourhood of Yeovil, holding the manors of Brympton, Pendomer, and Preston Plucknet (where he resided), and perhaps part of Thorn Coffyn, and he must have been a person of considerable influence in Somersetshire, as he represented the county in six Parliaments, from 1420 to 1435. He died in 1438, and was buried in the Priory of Stavordale, near the remains of his father.

The Stourton family were great benefactors to that Priory, and in the act appropriating the Church of Wincanton to the Priory, about 1374, the prayers of the Prior and Canons are enjoined for John de Stourton [Father of John of Preston] and Alice his wife, and for William de Stourton [his grandfather] and Johanna his wife.[35] John Stourton of Preston probably rebuilt the Priory Church, as there is a commission of Bishop Stafford in 1443 appointing a suffragan to consecrate the "nave with the choir and chancel of the Conventual Church of Stavordale which John Stourton in his lifetime ('dum inhumanis agebat') had rebuilt and made the place of his burial." (?) [36] He was no doubt also the donor to the Priory of three parts of the Manor of Thorn Coffyn, and the advowson of the church,[37] which he vested in trustees upon trust, it is to be pre-

---

[34] Inq., ad. q.d., 3 Ric. II, no. 148.

[35] Index to Wells Cath. MSS., 172.

[36] Bishop Stafford's Register.

[37] Weaver's Somerset Incumbents.

sumed, for the Priory, as after his death, in 1442, they obtained the Royal license to alienate it to the Prior and canons, and their successors for ever.[38]

According to a collection of ancient pedigrees compiled soon after 1505,[39] John Stourton of Preston was married three times, and by each marriage had an only daughter. His first wife was said to be ". . . . daughter and heir of . . . Payne "—by whom he had a daughter "Joan, wedded to John Sidenham." By his second wife, whose name was unknown, he had a daughter "Cecily, wedded to John Hill, of Spaxton," and his third wife was " . . . daughter and heir of . . . Peny," by whom he had a daughter, "Alice, married first to William Daubeny," Lord of Barington, Somerset, son and heir of Sir Giles Daubeny, Kt. ; and secondly, to Robert Hill, of Houndston. Stourton's will shows that the Christian name of the third wife was Katherine, but her surname was Payne and not Peny, as we learn from Sir William Pole that "Thomas Payne, of Paynshay, Devon, by his wife Margery, daughter and heir of Peter de Yeovilton, left issue Katherine, first married unto John Stourton, of Preston, and secondly unto William Carrant (Carent), and by Stourton's daughter Alice, married unto William Daubeny," Paynshay came to that family.[40] Wm. Carent was her third husband in fact, her second being John Beynton, of Hampreston, Dorset, Kt.[41]

There is conclusive evidence that the first wife of John Stourton was Joan, daughter of William Banastre, who, either as the son or husband of the heiress of Philip Wellesleigh, held the manors of Wheathill, Radstock, and perhaps East Lydford.[42] At her father's death in 1395, she was the wife of Robert Affeton,[43] who must have died a few years after, as she was married to John Stourton before 1403, when they presented to the church of East Lydford,[44] and

---

[38] Pat. 20 Hen. VI, pt. 1, m. 21.

[39] Harl. MSS., Br. Mus., no. 1074, Coll. Top. and Gen. I., 312, 409.

[40] Collections, p. 127.

[41] Close Rolls, 8 Edw. IV, m. 5.

[42] Coll. Somt. iii., 450.

[43] Esch., 19 Ric. II, no. 6.

[44] Som. Incumbents.

she died before 1416, when license was granted to the Priory of Whitehall, Ilchester, to endow a chaplain with lands to pray for (amongst others) " the soul of Joan, sometime the wife of John Stourton."[45]   By this Joan, John Stourton had one daughter, Cecily, the wife first of John Hill of Spaxton, and secondly of Sir Thomas Kuriel, Kt.[46]   John Hill died in 1435,[47] and a few years before, in an assize to try whether the Dean and Chapter of Wells had disseized him and Cecilia his wife of a messuage in Wells, it was proved that William Banastre, Lord of Wellesleigh, grandfather of Cecily (whose heir she was), viz., father of Joan, mother of Cecilia, by deed dated 12 Ric. II, gave the messuage to a Canon of Wells.[48] No clue has been found to the second wife, but the third, as shewn above, was Katherine Payne.

By the Inquisition taken at Yeovil, 17 Hen. VI, 1439, after the death of John Stourton, it was found that Cecily, the wife of Thomas Kuriel, Kt., aged 34, Johanna, the wife of John Sydenham, Esq., aged 21, and Alice Stourton, aged seven, were his daughters and co-heirs.[49] It was also found that he held no lands in the county of Somerset, the fact being that he had in his lifetime settled his estates on his three daughters, viz., Preston on Cecily, Brympton on Joan, and Pendomer on Alice. Preston, on Cecily's death in 1472, was inherited by John Hill, her son by her first marriage, whose son (also John Hill) died in 1474 (13 Edw. IV), seized in fee of the manor, leaving Genosefa (Genevieve), his daughter and heiress, then aged 14 years.

It is probable that the King's Escheator took possession of this infant's lands during her minority as her guardian, since two bailiff's accounts have been discovered embracing the period from the 14th to the 17th of Edward IV. They are nearly similar, and the following is an abstract of the earliest, which is for two years from the 14th to the 16th Edward IV.[50]

45 Inq. ad. q. d. 3 Hen. V. no. 14.

46 Esch., 12 Edw. IV, no. 51.

47 Esch., 13 Hen. VI, no. 31.

48 Ass. Rolls, Div. Co., 2—7, Hen. VI, no. 2, 41 — 1.

49 Esch. 17 Hen. VI, no. 6.

50 Ministers' Accounts P.R.O., Bundle 977, no. 19.

The Account of John Wylley, Bailiff there.

Arrears.—The same renders account of £40 0 10 upon the same account remaining for the year next preceding, as appears in the foot there.

Sum, £4 0 10

Rents of Assize.—And he answers for 2s. received of John Ettemete for free rent of his tenement which he inhabits. Sum, 2 0

Ferm of Demesne Lands.—And for £20 received of John Wylley and Richard Pawley Fermors there for the whole rent of all the demesne lands there for two years. Sum, £20 0 0

Ferm of Tenements.—And 28/8 received of John Wegge for the ferm of one tenement in which he dwells for two years at 13/4 per annum.

14/- of John Ettemete, junr., for two years at 7/-

s.	d.			s.	d.	
26	8	of John Brystowe for 2 years at		13	4	per annum.
18		of John Edmunds for	do.			do.
14		of William Taylor, Clerk,	do.			do.
4 0	0	of John Gaylard	do.	£7		do.
38	4	of William Gaylard	do.	19	2	do.
28		of Richard Pawley	do.	14		do.
10	8	of John Alford	at	5	4	do.
20		of John Clerke	at	10		do.
16		of do.	at	8		do.
24		of Henry Carter	at	12		do.

Sum, £15 16 4

				s.	d.	
Ferm of Cottages.—6	8	of William Thorneford	at	3	4	do.
3	4	of William Shepherd	at	1	8	do.
8		of Richard Wyget	at	4		do.
4		of Walter Bristow	at	2		do.
10		of { the same Walter for / cottage with 3 acres }	at	5		do.
3	4	of { William Gaylard for / a little close }	at	1	8	do.
3	4	of Agnes Hayward	at	1	8	do.
8	0	of John Blyth	at	4		do.

For cottage called Clyth's Cottage, nothing, because it is totally waste.

Perquisites of Court.—Nothing here. Sum, 52 8

Sum total received with the arrears, £42 11 10

Rents resolute.—Thereout the same accounts in rents resolute paid to the hundred of Stone for the term of this account 10/-, that is to say 5/- per annum, and paid at the town of Hampden for the time of this account 10/-, that is to say for each year 5/- and the expenses of the Steward there holding 2 Courts during the time of this account 2/6. And in expenses of James Martall remaining in account &c., 16/- Sum, 20/10

Decay of rent.—And in decay of rent of a certain cottage late in the tenure of Richad Wyget &c., nothing received therefrom for the time of this account 8/- that is to say 4/- per annum. Sum 8/-

Payment of money Sum £34 6 8

Sum of all allowances and deliveries £35 15 6

And he owes £6 16 4

The Lady Genosefa was married in her minority to William Say, Esq., afterwards Sir William Say, Kt., of Sawbridgeworth, Herts, but died without issue in 1480, leaving her husband surviving. In 1529 Sir William Say died, and the Inquisition held on his death stated that Thomas Hussey, William Clopton the younger, Eleanor, wife of George Babington, and John Walgrave were cousins and next heirs of the said Genosefa, namely, Thomas Hussey was son and heir of Ann, daughter and heir of Joan, one of the daughters and heirs of John Cheyney, of Pynno, son and heir of Elizabeth sister of John Hill, of Spaxton, father of the said Genosefa ; that William Clopton the younger was son and heir of Elizabeth, another of the daughters and heirs of the said Joan ; John Walgrave was son and heir of Isabella, another of the daughters and heirs of the said Joan ; and Eleanor was daughter and heir of Elizabeth, another of the daughters and heirs of the said John Cheyney, and the same was worth in all issues per annum beyond re-prizes £18.   Edward, son and heir of John Walgrave, was the ancestor of the Lords Waldegrave, and before 1599 the entirety had centred in Charles Waldegrave, who settled it on the marriage of his eldest son Edward with Elinor Lovell.   It continued in the Walde-grave family until the year 1725, when the manor was sold by trustees, under a private Act (12 Geo. I, cap. 20), to Mr. Fane, the purchaser of Brympton.

Preston Church stands in Preston Plucknet, and is said, on questionable authority, to be dedicated to St. James.   It is a simple structure, of the late Decorated style of architecture, and consists of a nave and chancel, with two small chapels at the east end of the nave, which externally are magnified into transepts, thereby making the building more important.   At the western end is a handsome tower, apparently of later date than the body of the church, if the Perpendicular window is original.   In the interior the restoration renders it difficult to distinguish old from new work, but the original roof is probably preserved, and is of the circular west country type.   The restored chancel is very ornate, and dismally dark.   If the new east window is a copy of its predecessor, it stamps the date of the original building distinctly.   The chapel on the south side is said to be appurtenant to the manor house of Preston Plucknet.   It is entered through a pointed, chamfered arch springing from two corbelled heads, one a man with flowing locks, the other a female with her face bound with a whimple.   Next to the south window of this chapel is a piscina with a Decorated arch, and there is a hagioscope, and close to it two stone brackets—

statuettes of saints, perhaps—but one of them seems misplaced. The piscina suggests a chantry, but there is no trace on any records, to which the public has access, indicating the foundation of one in the church. Such a record, if any exists, would probably be found in the Bishop's Registers, but they, for the sake of a pittance, payable to the official in charge of them, are sealed books. On the north side is another rather larger chapel, which stands one step above the floor of the nave. It is entered by a similar arch to that of the south chapel, and was evidently supported by two columns, the capitals of which only remain. On one of them is carved a hare and on the other a hound, with decorated foliage round them. They are probably only devices, but if this chapel is coeval with the church the hare may be in honour of Bishop Harewell, who occupied the see of Bath and Wells from 1366 to 1386, and bore three hares for his arms. The window in the north end is the only one in the church which does not appear to have been patched or restored, and is therefore a valuable relic of Decorated work. As this chapel is reputed to belong to the owner of Preston Bermondsey Manor, a presumption might be raised that it was the Chapel belonging to the Cell of the Abbey of Bermondsey, but the documentary evidence already quoted clearly shows that this could not have been the case, as the Bermondsey chapel stood within that manor, and was dedicated to St. Mary.

The Manor house of Preston Plucknet (now a farm-house) stands on high ground near the centre of the village, and forms, with the grand barn at right angles to it, a picturesque group of mediæval buildings. It is called the Abbey, there being a general impression that it was a grange or farm belonging to the Abbey of Bermondsey, but there is no foundation for this. Neither the house, the farm, nor the lands in Preston Plucknet ever belonged to any monastic body, but were always in lay hands; excepting, of course, the glebe belonging to the Rectory of Yeovil. The house was probably built by John Stourton of Preston ; we have evidence that he resided in it from Camden's " Brittania " (Holland's additions), which says, "And here I must not forget Preston, sometime the seat of John Sturton, younger son to the first Lord Sturton, one of whose heirs was married to Sidenham, of Brimpton thereby." He was not, however, a son of the first Lord Stourton, but his uncle.

The house is a long parallelogram in the Perpendicular style, probably of the time of Hen. VI, running north and south, and divided into two compartments, with a modern annexe to the north.

It faces the west, and the entrance is through a lofty porch with a groined arch roof, the ribs, which terminate in a centre boss, carved as a rose; over the porch is a chamber, lighted by a pointed arch window with traceried head. An inner arch opens from the porch into a passage running across the house, and is enriched with a square labelled moulding and spandrels filled in with blank shields and clusters of roses. To the right of this passage is the hall (converted into a cider cellar with a loft over), separated now by a stone wall, but originally, no doubt, by an oak screen supporting the minstrel gallery.

Left of the passage, opposite the hall, is a pointed archway, leading to the other part of the house, with a buttery doorway on either side, now walled up. The only noticeable feature in it is the large hall or room at the end, the fire-place of which extends the whole width of the building, and is so deep and capacious that it contains a closet and a cupboard, and a small, well-concealed hiding place, entered only by a trap-door, which served as a refuge in time of trouble. The chimney itself—amounting almost to a turret—is remarkable, resembling the lantern or louvre often found in mediæval halls. It consists of an octagonal shaft divided into two tiers, and resting on a massive square base, round which are trefoiled-headed vertical openings for the escape of the smoke. These outlets are now blocked up with brickwork, which, from its contrasting colour, disturbs the harmony of the structure.

The barn is a very fine specimen of fifteenth century masonry, but beyond the richly-carved finials on the gables there is nothing particular to be noticed in it.

In the *Gentleman's Magazine* (Nov. 1841) there is a view of the house, engraved from a drawing made by Mr. John Buckler in 1811. Comparing it with the present house it is evident that a gable which flanked the porch on the north side has been altogether removed, and it is pretty clear that the original hall roof—an ornamental one, it may be presumed—has been taken down and replaced with another at a lower level, thereby destroying the traceried arched head of the oriel, and reducing the window to a square-headed one, as it stands now. The south end wall must also have been rebuilt, but without the hall fire-place, the chimney of which is shown in the engraving as the finial of the gable. We can only regret, with Mr. Buckler, that these alterations have deprived the house of some of its interesting features.

CHAPTER VII.

COKER.

THE principal design of this chapter is to trace, as far as the scanty materials which are available will allow, the early history of East Coker and its owners ; but as East Coker and West Coker were originally included under the general name of Coker, and, with Hardington, were for many generations held by the same lords, they have to some extent a common history, and will therefore be all noticed in the present inquiry.

Coker* is a large tract of land adjoining to Yeovil on the south, and about 3,400 acres in extent. The soil for the most part is a light sandy loam, fairly fertile and easy of cultivation. In the southern slope of the parish of East Coker the red ochre colour of the earth indicates ferruginous matter in the composition of the soil, and in a meadow in the Moor called "Blackwells" a very copious chalybeate spring bursts up to the surface, and sometimes rises several inches above it, the qualities of which are not unknown to the villagers, who occasionally resort to it for medicinal purposes.

The variety of soils in Coker is particularly pointed out by Captain William Dampier, the circumnavigator—a native of East Coker—in a passage of "Dampier's Voyages."[1]   Alluding to the

---

* No satisfactory derivation of the word "Coker" has yet been discovered, and a very high authority in Anglo-Saxon literature, consulted by the writer, expresses himself quite unable to explain it. The point must therefore be left for future solution.

[1] Vol. i, p. 123, ed. 1699.

soil of one of the islands he visited, he goes on to say :—" But to be very particular in these things, especially in all my travels, is more than I can pretend to, though it may be I took as much notice of the difference of soil I met with as most travellers have done, having been bred in my youth in Somersetshire, at a place called East Coker, near Yeovil or Evil, in which parish there is as great variety of soil as I have ordinarily met with anywhere—viz., black, red, yellow, sandy, stony, clay, morass or swampy, etc. I had the more reason to take notice of this because this village in a great measure is let out in small leases for lives of twenty, thirty, forty, or fifty pound per annum, under Col. Helliar, the lord of the manor; and most, if not all, these tenants had their own land scattered in small pieces up and down several sorts of land in the parish, so that every one had some piece of every sort of land—his black ground, his sandy, clay, etc.— some of 20, 30, or 40 shillings an acre for some uses, and other not worth ten groats an acre. My brothers being possessed of one of the leases, and having of all these sorts of land, I came acquainted with them all, and knew what each sort would produce—viz., wheat, barley, maslin, rice, beans, peas, oats, vetches, flax or hemp— in all which I had a more than usual knowledge for one so young, taking a particular delight in observing it. But enough of this matter."

These advantages, combined with a running stream, several springs, and a southern aspect, no doubt led the aborigines of these parts to settle here. The Roman invaders naturally followed in their footsteps, and accordingly we find in both parishes traces of occupation by Roman colonists.

In the year 1753 the remains of a bath-room in a Roman villa were discovered in a field called "Chesells," or "Chesil," in East Coker, on the east side of the road leading to Yeovil (now allotment ground), close to a good spring of water, and within a short distance of the vicinal way from Ilchester to Dorchester. In the *Yeovil Evening Post* of June 23rd, 1753, it is thus described :—

" The mosiac work lately discovered about a mile and a-half south of Yeovil, in Dorsetshire, and in the way to East Coker, appears to be a floor of a Roman sudatory or sweating house. The cavity below, by its divided walls, burnt stones, &c., very plainly shows itself to be the fire-place ; but one flue remains to convey the warm air to the room above. This floor is composed of burnt bricks, blue, red, and white, none more than an inch square, most less. The outmost border has in it a greyhound pursuing a hare, a buck pursued by some dogs, and a Mercury's head, as it seems by the wings, in each corner. Within a beautiful square containing a circle are the figures :—A woman, dressed, 'tis thought, in a Roman stola with its purple laticlave or border; another, much damaged, which, with the former, each gives a hand to fix the cloathes round another woman laid on a couch, naked down to below her waist, and on whom the physician hard by prepares to do some operation by the fire, either cupping or burning. This piece suits the use of the room." See also Collinson's History of Somerset.[2]

From a letter of Dr. Andrew Ducarel, the secretary of the Society of Antiquaries, to Dr. Ward, Professor of Rhetoric at Gresham College,[3] we learn that fine drawings of the pavement were exhibited at a meeting of that learned body July 18th, 1753, but no notice of it appears on the Society's minutes, nor is it known whether the drawings are still in existence. It is said in Phelps' History of Somerset[4] that the account was drawn up by Dr. Denham, a physician then living at Yeovil, and that the tenant of the field ploughed up the pavement, under the pretence that the visitors injured the land.

In 1820 another excavation was made in the same or the adjoining field, under the superintendence of Mr. John Moore, of West Coker (a great lover of antiquities, and always eager to investigate them), in the presence of those learned antiquaries, Sir Richard Colt Hoare and the Rev. Mr. Skinner, and they were rewarded by the discovery of a tesselated pavement representing the " Return from the Chase." It was carefully taken up and set in plaster, and for many years kept at Coker Court by Mr. Helyar, in whose land it had been found ; but on the establishment of a County Museum at Taunton he kindly deposited it there, and there it is hoped it will remain until the foundation of a museum at Yeovil.

Mr. Moore being the owner of a field in West Coker, also called " Chesells," Mr. Skinner expressed an opinion to him in conversation that the word " Chesells " referred not only to the sandy nature of the soil, but meant also the great house, or place, and he said " Search in your field, and it is my opinion you will find Roman remains."

It was not, however, until 1861 that Mr. Moore followed Mr. Skinner's advice, and then on examining the spot and excavating

---

[2] Vol. ii, p. 340.

[3] Add. MSS., Br. Mu., no. 6,210, fo. 50.

[4] Vol. ii, General Introduction, p. 167.

about two feet into the soil he found a dark rich earth, beneath
which was the *débris* of unmistakable Roman remains, a foot or
more in depth, consisting of fragments of masonry and loose
stones, tesseræ, plaster, tiles, and pottery, and a few articles in
bronze (one of which was a statuette of a nude figure, supposed to be
the god Mars), several coins from the second to the fourth century,
bones, flints, and personal ornaments. As some of the articles were
of the kind generally found in Celtic interments, Mr. Moore conjectured that the villa was erected on the site of a British village, but
it is more probable that it was the work of a Romanized Briton,
which may explain the absence of any tesselated pavement. A
detailed account of this discovery was communicated by Mr. Moore
to the British Archæological Association.[5]

The most important Roman relic found was a votive tablet by
Juventius Sabinus to Mars Rigidus, formed of a thin plate of bronze
about 3in. by 2in., with this inscription on it in punched letters :—

> "DEO MARTI
> RIGISAMO
> IVENTIUS
> SABINUS
> V[OTUM] S[OLVIT] L[IBENS] M[ERITO]."

The fact of Roman occupation of the Cokers was confirmed by
the discovery, not many years ago, in an ancient trackway leading
from East Coker towards Coker Wood, and still called the Roman
Road, of a quantity of brass coins of Tetricus and other so-called
British Emperors of the third century.

In addition to these remains a small plantation in East Coker
parish, on the road between Yeovil and West Coker, called Furzy
Knaps, was supposed by Mr. Moore to have been a military out-
post to the Roman fortress on Hamdon Hill, about three miles
distant. As he knew it many years before it was planted he had no
doubt seen indications justifying his opinion, but at present no
artificial work can be traced beyond great irregularities in the surface
of the ground. It may also be mentioned that within a few hundred
yards of this spot is a farm in West Coker called Fee Barrow, and
some cottages to the west of it known as " Camp."

No express reference to Coker has been found in Anglo-Saxon
times, but it may be surmised that it was part of the large domain
called "That land at Gifle and Crucerne," which King Alfred by his
will gave to his younger son Ethelward.[6]

---

[5] Proc., vol. 19, p. 322.

[6] Cartularium Saxonicum ii., 176.

If there is any foundation for this conjecture, it is possible that out of this land was taken a Hundred, comprising the two Cokers, Hardington, Pendomer, Sutton Bingham, and Closworth. Coker is not, however, enrolled as a Hundred in the " Inquisitio Gheldi," the earliest territorial record extant, and there are reasons for believing that in præ-Domesday times the hundred composed of the above six manors was called " Liet or Lieget." In the entry of Yeovil or Givelea Hundred, Inq. Gheldi,[7] it is said " of this Hundred Osbern holds of the Bishop of St. Lo two hides and two virgates, the Geld for which he renders in the Hundred of Liet." In one of the Indices the Hundred is called " Lieget," and in the other[8] the name was originally written " Cocker," but altered to " Liet." The name still survives in a farm called " Lyats," situated at the junction of the three parishes of East Coker, Hardington, and Pendomer, and parts of the farm lie in each of those parishes.

Mr. Eyton suggests[9] that " Liet " was only an alternative name for Coker, but as " Cocker " is erased from the Index there was probably some other reason for the alteration.

Both Coker and Hardington were part of the possessions of Earl Harold's family. In the time of Edward the Confessor Coker belonged to Gytha, the widow of Earl Godwin and mother of Harold ; and Hardington (which may have been the " Hortnegtune" given by King Alfred's will to his eldest son Edmund[10]) belonged to Gunnilda, Harold's sister. They came, therefore, to William " jure conquesti," and were Royal Manors at the time of the Domesday Survey.

The description of Coker in the Exeter Domesday is as follows :—
" The king holds one manor which is called *Cochra.* Guida the Countess held it on the day that King Edward was living and dead. In it are 15 hides, and it paid gild for 7 hides. Of these, 15 carucates can be ploughed. Thereof the king has 5 hides and a half and three carucates in demesne, and villeins the other land and 12 carucates. The king has there 35 villeins and 4 coliberts and 42 bordars and 7 serfs† and one swineherd, who pays 10 porkers and

---

[7] Exon. Dom., p. 71.

[8] Ib., pp. 57—58.

[9] Somt. Domesday, vol. i., p. 168.

[10] Cart. Sax., *ub. sup.*

† *Villeins* (villani) were tenants who farmed the lands held by them of the lord, subject to certain personal and other services, originally at the mere will of the lord, but afterwards regulated by the custom of the vill or manor, which ultimately converted the lands into modern copyholds. *Coliberts* were enfranchised

1 colt and 4 horses and 20 swine and 150 sheep and 48 goats, and 1 mill which pays five shillings, and wood 8 furlongs in length and 6 in breadth, and 100 acres of meadow and pasture, 1 mile long and half in breadth. It renders 19 pounds and 12 pence of white money, which William the sheriff receives."

We now arrive at a perplexing stage in the history of Coker, relating to its connection with the Abbey of St. Stephen, at Caen, in Normandy. That abbey was founded about the year 1064, by William the Conqueror, then only Duke of Normandy, and endowed (inter alia) with the manors of Northam, Devon, Frampton and Bincombe, Dorset, and "ten hides of land in a territory in the county of Somerset called Crucre [*i.e.*, Crewkerne], with the church and all the tithes of the same territory."[11] Collinson, in his account of Crewkerne,[12] speaking of the Abbey, says, "To this Abbey William was extravagantly munificent; for besides the immense bounties which he in his lifetime conferred thereon, he, on his death, was fain to give it all his favourite trinkets, the crown which he used to wear at high festivals, his sceptre and rod, his cup set with precious stones, his golden candlesticks, and all his other regalia; nay, even the bugle horn which he used to carry at his back, went to pot ! It seems it was some difficulty to recover these matters from the Abbey; for it is evident that it cost King William the Second the manor of Coker, in this county, and a large parcel of exemptions, to redeem what had been so foolishly squandered." Again, under the head of *East* Coker[13] he observes, " King William Rufus granted the manor of Coker to the Abbey of St. Stephen at Caen," and further on, speaking of *West* Coker only, he says,[14] " Upon the grant of King William Rufus of part of his demesne lands in Coker to the Abbey of St. Stephen at Caen, in Normandy, the Abbot and Convent thought fit to transmit hither a certain number of monks to superintend their estates. These in process of time established a cell here, and the convent enjoyed other property in this place till the despoliation of alien priories in the time of Henry V, when they were given to the priory of Montacute." Collinson's authority for

---

serfs. *Bordars* (bordarii) were the same as cottagers who occupied small holdings of the lord's, who stocked the lands for them, and received in return a part of the produce for his table. *Serfs*, sometimes called nativi, were of the lowest grade.

[11] Dugdale's Monasticon ii., 956.

[12] His. Som., vol. ii, p. 162.

[13] Ib., p. 341.

[14] Ib., p. 344.

the leading part of this story was " Gough's Account of Alien Priories,[15] but for the part ascribing to the abbey the establishment of a cell at West Coker he quotes no authority whatever. It was probably nothing more than traditionary gossip.

Death-bed gifts to the Church are always open to suspicion, and it is difficult to believe that the Conqueror, if in possession of his faculties, would give these Royal insignia away from his son and successor—who was in attendance on him during his last illness— and bestow them on the monks of St. Stephen, to whom they could be of no real value, except for ornament or for conversion into money. Such a gift, if made, could hardly be kept a secret, and yet it is unnoticed by the chronicler, Ordericus Vitalis, who, not 30 years after, narrates in minute detail all the incidents of the King's last illness, and the disposition he made of his property. Knowing the artifices to which religious houses would stoop in order to increase their wealth, it is not improbable that the articles had been left by the King at the Abbey for safe custody, and that on his death the monks, calculating on the eagerness of William Rufus to recover them, did not scruple to claim them as the King's gift, and to make the best terms they could for their redemption.

But even admitting that the regalia were given, an examination of the records throws great doubt on the alleged exchange for Coker. The only ancient piece of evidence in support of it must be received with considerable caution, as it comes from the archives of the Abbey itself. It is an inspeximus or official copy, made in 1424, of an entry in the Abbey cartulary, under the date 1088, which, after relating the gift of the crown and other articles to the Abbey, professes to set out the contents of a charter, under the hand and seal of William Rufus, and witnessed by five bishops and many noble officers of state, whereby he granted to the Abbey, in exchange for the regalia, " a certain manor, by name *Cocre*, situate in the county of Somerset, with all its appurtenances and with Sac. Soc. Theol, Thean, and all other customs as freely and peaceably as he the King held his demesne manors."[16]

On the other hand there is strong evidence to show that it was not William Rufus, but his brother Henry I, who succeeded in getting back the treasures, and that it was not Coker, but Burton Bradstock in Dorset (anciently called Brideton), which was the price paid for the redemption.

---

[15] Vol. i, pp. 126, 127.
[16] Neustria Pia, p. 638.

By a charter, without date, to which John, Bishop of Bath, Geoffry de Magnavilla, and others were witnesses,[17] Henry I confirms to the Abbey his father's gifts of Frampton, Bincombe, and Northam, and also his own gift of the manor of Brideton, and he declares that he gives and confirms all the said manors for the redemption of the souls of himself, his parents and ancestors, and expressly (nominatim) in exchange for the crown and other ornaments which his father had bestowed on St. Stephen, *and which the monks delivered to him (Henry) at Caen.* This charter is corroborated by one of Henry II,[18] whereby, after confirming the original gifts of Frampton and Bincombe, and the ten hides of land in Cruke (*i.e.*, Crewkerne), with the church and tithes of the same, and the church of Corsham, he confirms also the grant of the manor of Brideton, which his grandfather King Henry had made, partly for the crown and other ornaments given by his father to the Abbey, and " partly for the exchange of the churches and lands of Crukerne and Corsham." Lastly, there is a charter of Richard I, dated at Rouen 1 Ric. I,[19] whereby he repeats his father's confirmation almost in the same words, but omitting any notice of the exchange of Crewkerne and Corsham.

It may well be questioned whether the alleged charter of Wm. Rufus was not a forgery, and it is remarkable that in none of the subsequent Royal charters is there any confirmation of the grant of Coker, although it is well known that religious houses never neglected an opportunity of strengthening their title to property bestowed on them, by confirmation from the successors or heirs of the original donor. Besides, the Coker charter was not followed by possession, there being no trace that the Abbey ever held an acre of land in Coker.[20]

Had it (as Collinson asserts) retained any down to the reign of Henry V, the fact would surely have appeared on some records, but no allusion to it or to any grant to the Priory of Montacute can be found. The Priory certainly did hold a small property in Coker, but that was the gift of "Edward the Staller," after the manor had come into the possession of the de Mandevilles.

The only other land in Coker that belonged to the Church was a small property held by the Abbey of Glastonbury, shortly before its dissolution, lying principally in West Coker, but partly in East Coker and Hardington. It is not mentioned in the Monasticon, and the only information respecting it is in Abbot Beer's survey, 9-10 Henry VIII,[21] which does not state how the Abbey acquired it.

---

[17] Dugd. Mon. ii, 957.   [18] Neustria Pia, p. 628.
[19] Dugd. Mon. i, 571.   [20] Hist. Somt., ii, 344.
[21] Harl. MS., 3,961.

The most probable solution of this extraordinary story is that if the
charter of William Rufus was ever made at all, it was repudiated by
one or other of the parties on some grounds of which we are now ignorant, and that the precious ornaments remained in the possession of
the Abbey until they were redeemed by Henry I; which is confirmed
by the fact that Burton, as well as Frampton and Bincombe, were
held by it until the dissolution of alien priories, whilst Coker continued in the hands of the Crown.

It will be observed that in the charter of Hen. I there is no
confirmation of the gifts of Crewkerne and Corsham, but none was
wanted, as it appears from the charter of Hen. II that Burton had
been given by Hen. I not only in exchange for the crown and
ornaments, but also for the churches and lands of Crewkerne and
Corsham. By this means Crewkerne was restored to the crown,
and was afterwards granted to the great house of de Redvers, and
remained in that family down to the reign of John or Henry III,
when it was given by William de Redvers, called de Vernon Earl de
L'isle, to Robert de Courtenay in free marriage with his daughter
Mary, and descended from them to the Courtenays Earls of Devon.[22]

There is every reason for believing that Coker was granted with
Crewkerne to de Redvers. By a charter, sans date, of Baldwin
ed Redvers, second Earl of Devon, who sometimes styled himself
Earl of Exeter, he released to the Priory of Montacute parts
of Sutton Bingham and Closworth from all customs and dues,[23]
and as both were tithings in the hundred of Coker, which
was appurtenant to the Manor of Coker,[24] it is to be inferred that
the Earl was at that time lord of both.‡ He or some of his

‡ This charter is alluded to also in Chapter III (p. 40). The text is as follows :
" Carta Baldewyni Comitis Exonie de donatione excluse molendini de Clouesworth.
  B. Comes Exonie, Omnibus Baronibus et amicis et hominibus suis tam pre-
sentibus quam futuris de omnia terra sua salutem et amorem Sciatis certissime me
donasse deo et sancto Petro et Monachis ecclesie Montisacute unam esclusaille
ad unum molendinum in Clowesworde pro salute mea et pro salute anime patris
inei et omnium parentum meorum liberam ab omnibus consuetudinibus
et debitis, videlicet inter terram Willielmi Calveth de suhtuna et pontem heille.
Hiis testibus Gaufrido clerico Huberto de Valli[bus] Gauffrido de furn[ell]
Jordano de lestre. Valete." N.B.—" Esclusaille " means a mill dam.
    Cartulary of the Priory of Montacute, Trin. Coll., Oxford, MS. no. 85.

[22] Fine Roll, 6 John, pt. i, m. 8 ; Ass. Roll, 8 Edw. I, 5-13-7. Esch. 2, Edw. I,
no. 27. Cleaveland's Hist. of House of Courtenay, p. 140.

[23] Mont. Cart.

[24] Fines Div. Cos. ii, Edw. I, no. 128.

family must have granted Coker as a sub-fee to de Mandeville, for had it been granted by the Crown it would have been held *in capite*, which it was not, for John de Mandeville, at his death, 4 Edw. I, held the manor of East Coker of the heirs of the Earl de L'isle—*i.e.*, the Courtenays.[25] Assuming the grant to have been made by de Redvers, as the de Mandevilles were " of Cocre " three generations before the time of King John, any grant made by the Crown of Crewkerne and Coker to de Redvers must have been still earlier, and possibly by Henry I to his favourite, Richard de Redvers, father of Baldwin, on whom he conferred many honours and estates.

The De Mandevilles of the West were of Norman origin, and of the same stock as Geoffry de Magnaville (I), the Conqueror's companion in arms. By Athelaisa, his first wife, he had, besides William his eldest son, who was created Earl of Essex, two other sons, Roger and Geoffry (II).[26] Roger succeeded to his father's estates in Normandy, and was, it is believed, the father of a second Roger and of Stephen de Mandeville, an illustrious warrior, and a close ally of the above Baldwin de Redvers, who was one of the chief supporters of the Empress Maud in her contest for the English crown.§[27] He assisted Baldwin, it may be presumed, in his gallant defence of the Castle of Exeter, and after its evacuation he certainly joined him in a military expedition to Normandy.[28] He was not, however, destined to fall by the sword, but died from natural causes on his way to Jerusalem with the Earl, either in the second crusade (A.D. 1147) or in a devotional pilgrimage to the Holy Sepulchre.|| He left two sons—Roger, the third of that name, and William. Roger, by charter undated, to which Nicholas, prior of Montacute, and Ralph, Patric and Roger, his uncles, were witnesses, confirmed to the Abbey of St. Sauveur the gifts of his father Stephen, and he gave to the Abbey of Montebourg, which was founded by Baldwin, the churches of

§ It is believed that further investigation would establish a connection either by blood or marriage between the families of de Redvers and de Mandeville.

|| " Comes Baldwinus et Stephanus de Mandeville viri potentes apud West Saxones pictatis causa peregre profecti sunt quo itinera Stephanus obiit. Balwinus ægre domum reversus est." Baldwin died A.D. 1155.[29]

[25] Esch. 2 Edw. I, no. 27, 4 Edw. I, no. 48.

[26] Madox's Formulare Anglicanum, no. 397. Stapleton's Rotuli Normaniæ ii, clxxxviii.

[27] Gesta Stephani Regis, p, 965.

[28] Ordericus Vitalis (Bohn) iv, 196.

[29] Leland's Collectanea i, 446.

PEDIGREE OF The De Mandeville Family.

ARMS—QUARTERLY, ARGENT AND OR. (*)

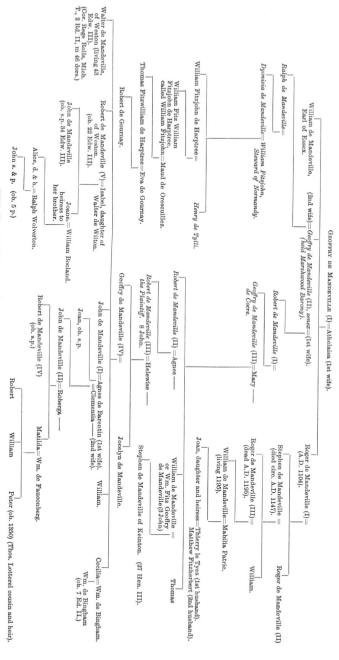

GEOFFRY DE MANDEVILLE (I)=Atholaisa, (1st wife).

William de Mandeville, Earl of Essex.

(2nd wife)=Geoffry de Mandeville (II), senez=(1st wife). (held Marshwood Barony).

Ralph de Mandeville=

Dyonisia de Mandeville= William Fitzjohn, Steward of Normandy.

William Fitzjohn de Harptree=

William Fitz William Fitzjohn de Harptree, called William Fitzjohn.=Maud de Oreseuillex.

Thomas Fitzwilliam de Harptree=Eva de Gournay.

Robert de Gournay.

Robert de Mandeville (V)=Isabel, daughter of (ob. 22 Edw. III). Walter de Wilton.

Walter de Mandeville, of Weston, (living 43 Edw. III.), (Cor. Rege Rolls, Mich. T., 2 Ed. II, m 46 dors.)

John de Mandeville (ob. s.p. 34 Edw. III).

Joane.=William Bocland. heiress to her brother.

Alice, d. & h.=Ralph Wolverton.

John s. & p. (ob. 5 p.)

Henry de Tylii.

Roger de Mandeville (I), (A.D. 1104).

Robert de Mandeville (I)=

Geoffry de Mandeville (III)=Mary —

Stephen de Mandeville (died circ. A.D. 1147).

Roger de Mandeville (II)

Roger de Mandeville (III) (dead A.D. 1195),

William.

William de Mandeville (III)=Mabilia Patric. (living 1195).

Joan, daughter and heiress=Thierry le Tyes (1st husband), Matthew Fitzherbert (2nd husband).

William de Mandeville = or Wm. Fliz Geoffry de Mandeville (3 John).

Thomas.

Robert de Mandeville (II)=Agnes —

Geoffry de Mandeville (IV)=

Robert de Mandeville (III)=Helewise the Plaintiff, 8 John. —

Jocelyn de Mandeville.

John de Mandeville (I)=Agnes de Barentin (1st wife), =Clementia —— (2nd wife).

Joan, ob. s.p.

John de Mandeville (II)=Roberga —

Robert de Mandeville (IV) (ob. s.p.)

Robert

William

Stephen de Mandeville of Keinton. (27 Hen. III).

William.

Matilda.=Wm. de Fauconberg.

Cecilia.=Wm. de Bingham. Wm. de Bingham (ob. 7 Ed. II.)

Peter (ob. 1350) (Thos. Lotterel cousin and heir).

NOTE.—The parts in italics are taken from the Pipe Roll, Som. and Dor. (10 John).

(*) The Arms—three lions passant—attributed to De Mandeville in Hutchins' History of Dorset are those of Fitzpain, who purchased the Manor and Barony of Marshwood.

Besneville in Normandy, and Stoche (*i.e.*, Earl Stoke) in the county of Wilts.[30] This Roger also gave to the Priory of Plympton the church of Arreton in the Isle of Wight, which gift was confirmed by Henry II.[31]

By another charter of Roger (III), undated, but to which his uncles Ralph and Roger were also witnesses, he gave to the Priory of Montacute, for the health of the soul of his father Stephen, who died on his journey to Jerusalem ("qui in prœcinctu vie Jerosolemitam obiit"), his mill of Stoches (Earl Stoke) with the land adjoining—the miller (hominem molendini) and his family and the service of his tenants at the mill; also the mill of "Gofford," with the land adjoining, in exchange for the land of "Dumett," and he also gave to it the churches of "Odecumb" and "Ciseburg" [Chiselborough].[32]

Coupling this with a charter of John de Mandeville in the Montacute cartulary, dated at "Cocre," 33 Edward I, by which he confirms the gift of "Stoches" mill made by his ancestor Roger de Mandeville for the health of the soul of his father Stephen, the line of descent from Stephen to John would apparently be established. But it may be doubtful whether it was a strict lineal descent, as according to the pedigree on the records John had no lineal ancestor named Roger; and according to the Pipe Roll, William, brother and heir of Roger, paid his relief on succeeding to the land of Stoches.[33]

Recurring to Geoffry (II), the other younger son of Geoffry (I), his relationship to Roger (I) appears by a charter, dated before A.D. 1104, whereby Roger granted the church of St. Martin Grouville to the monastery of St. Sauveur; Geoffry de Mandeville, one of the witnesses, being styled "the brother of Roger."[34] This Geoffry is supposed to have been the Geoffry de Mandeville who held the office of Constable of the Castle of Exeter under Henry I, coupled with the manor of Wonford in Heavitree[35]; and it can hardly be doubted that he was Geoffry (II) of the Coker family.

In another part of Sir Wm. Pole's valuable collections (p. 155) he says that the manor of Woodbury was given by Henry I to Roger de Mandeville, Castellan of his castle of Exeter, whose son Stephen granted it to William Carbonell, and that the grant was confirmed by Roger de Mandeville, the son of Stephen; but unless Roger and

---

[30] Stapleton *ubi supra.*
[31] Dug. Mon., ii 8.
[32] Mont Cart.
[33] Pipe Roll, 9 Ric. I, Wiltshire.
[34] Stapleton, *ub. sup.*
[35] Testa. de Nevill, p. 194; Pole's Devon, p. 233.

Geoffrey were constables in succession, it is questionable whether this is not another version of the Wonford story, both Woodbury and Wonford being Royal manors.

One of the earliest possessions of the De Mandevilles in the western counties was the Barony or Honour of Marshwood in Dorset, held of the King *in capite,* and of which Geoffry de Mandeville senex (II), is the earliest recorded owner. The *Caput Baroniæ* was at Whitchurch Canonicorum, the domain extending over the vale of Marshwood and the adjacent parishes. Neither Whitchurch nor Marshwood is nominally mentioned in the Domesday Survey, being probably included in the royal demesnes of forest and waste.¶ Besides the home domain the lords of Marshwood possessed many manors which from time to time (previous to the statute *Quia Emptores,* 18 Edward I) they had granted out by way of subinfeudation, all which became members of the Barony, and at the date of Testa de Neville as many as eleven knights' fees were held under it in Devonshire alone, and several more in Dorset, Somerset, and Wilts, so that in the height of its prosperity the family must have been one of the most influential in the West of England.

The church of Whitchurch at one time belonged to the de Mandevilles. It had been granted away by the Crown before the creation of the Barony, for the Domesday Survey records that the Conqueror had bestowed it on the Abbey of Fontanell in Normandy. Afterwards the Abbey granted it to the See of Salisbury, but A.D. 1215 Robert de Mandeville (III) presented to the church, and he (Robert) added considerably to the endowments of it by gifts of lands in Whitchurch and elsewhere. About the year 1239 his son Geoffry (IV) granted the advowson to Jocelyn, Bishop of Bath, " to dispose thereof as he pleased," and he appropriated it to the Dean and Chapter of Wells, subject to an endowed vicarage, the patronage of which was vested in the Bishop. In return for this liberal gift the Dean and Chapter gratefully promised that Geoffry should for ever have the benefit of their prayers.[36]

In the reign of Richard I the Barony of Marshwood was the subject of litigation between the senior and junior branches of the De Mandeville family, the origin of which was an arbitrary act of

---

¶ That there was a forest appears from a charter, without date, in the British Museum (Cott. Ch. xii, 38), whereby Geoffry de Mandeville, son of Robert de Mandeville, grants to Richard de Piritune, son and heir of Osmery de Piritune, land in the ville of Piritune in the manor of Merswood, and *Parsuage in the Forest of Merswode,* and also all the land juxta Cerne [*i.e.,* Charmouth.]

[36] Hutch. Hist. Dors., ii, 271. Liber Albus, Wells, f. 450.

Henry I in taking away the Barony from the eldest son and heir of the last Baron and giving it to the youngest.

Although at that early period in English history the Prerogative of the Crown carried everything before it with a high hand, the Sovereign will respected, with very rare exceptions, the right of succession to real property, which had then become inheritable even under the feudal law. One of such exceptions occurs in this case, but still there is something to be said for the King. In the creation and distribution of dignities—pure and simple—the Crown, as the fountain of honour, was undoubtedly supreme, and it may be that the King, in this case, was advised that, the Barony being a dignity, it was within the limits of his prerogative. A Barony, however, as originally constituted, was not a mere personal dignity conferred by the King on whom he delighted to honour, but a territorial domain bestowed by the Conqueror or his sons as a reward for military achievements, which carried with it the annexed dignity of a Baron, descendible with the land, according to the law of inheritance. But as feudal tenant, the grantee could not alien the Barony without the King's licence, neither could his heir take his place and rank until the King had approved of him as the successor and accepted his homage and service. The King's advisers might, therefore, with some reason have argued that as the land and the dignity were inseparable, the power the King had over the latter necessarily extended to the former also. But the mistake was that they treated the land as appertaining to the dignity over which the King had control, instead of the dignity appertaining to the land, over which legally he had none. By the decision in this case the pre-eminence of the law was established.

It appears by the records that Geoffry de Mandeville senex (II), who held the Barony, was married twice. By his first wife he had an only son, Robert (the first of that name), who, therefore, was entitled, at his father's death, to succeed to the Barony as his heir. By his second wife, Geoffry had another son, Ralph, and King Henry conferred the Barony on him, because, as it is said, " he was a better knight (melior miles), than his brother Robert." From Ralph the Barony wrongfully descended to his daughter Dyonisia, who became the wife of William Fitzjohn, the King's Seneschal of Normandy, and from her it came to their eldest son Henry (called " de Tylli," from his father's possession at Tylli in Normandy), and he held it in the year 1195.

Robert (I) was then dead, leaving Geoffry (III) his son and heir, who commenced an action against de Tylli for the recovery of the Barony, and paid 100 marks for having, as the record runs, the judgment of the King's Court respecting his inheritance in England and Normandy, of which Henry de Tylli had deforced him.[37] This was all that was done in Geoffry's lifetime, and what little we know of him may be noticed now. He was called Geoffry de Mandeville *de Cocre*, from which it may be inferred that he had settled there. He paid scutage for his possessions in both Somerset and Dorset several times, and 14 Hen. II he certified that he held Hardinton of the king in chief, an ancestral estate which belonged to the de Mandevilles from the time of the conquest.[38] It is probable that he was one of the rebellious Barons who joined King John (when Earl of Moretain) in conspiracy against his brother Richard I, during his absence from the kingdom, and was punished by seizure of his lands, as the Crown Receiver in 1195 accounted for 33s. 9d. for the farm of Hardinton for one quarter of a year, and for the rents of certain lands at Cocre for half a year.[39] Geoffry (III) must have died soon after, as he was dead 1st John, and after that event the family thread gets very tangled.

Geoffry had three sons, Robert (II), William, and Thomas. Robert, the eldest, died in his father's lifetime, leaving a son Robert (III), who became his grandfather's heir. In the face of this, William, the second son, on his father's death assumed to be his heir, and continued the action against De Tylli, by paying (1st John) 100 marks for the judgment of the court in the suit between his father and Henry de Tylli concerning the Honour of Marshwood.[40] Not only so, but he took possession of the paternal estate in Somersetshire, and the sheriff accounted for two marks received for scutage of " William Mandeville de Cocre."[41]

The question is—What claim had William to be his father's heir? The answer may be that Robert (III) was a posthumous son, and the following charter from the Montacute cartulary favours that presumption. By it Geoffry de Mandeville and Mary his wife, with the consent of their sons William and Thomas, confirmed the gift which Robert, their son and heir, when about to go the way of all flesh *(viam universe carnis ingressurum)* had made to the Priory for the redemption of his sins, of a virgate of land called "at Hach," in his manor of Hardintone, which manor he (Geoffry) and his wife

[37] Pipe Roll, 6 Rich. I, Dors. and Som.
[38] Lib. Nig., p. 95, Testa de Nevill, p. 163.
[39] Pipe Roll, 6 Ric. I.
[40] Rot. Obl. Fin. temp. John, p. 44, Rot. Car. Reg. ii, 245.
[41] Pipe Roll, 3rd John.

had given to Robert before his espousals with Agnes his wife. But the charter goes on to say that if by any means he (Geoffry) should be unable to warrant the said virgate, he and William, " his son and heir," bound themselves by oath, at the holy altar of the church of Montacute, that within one year after the burial of Robert in the chapel *(capellâ)* of Montacute, he would give to the Priory another virgate of equal value. The charter is undated, and the witnesses are Wm. de Milbourne, Wm. Fitzwilliam, Thos. de Merioth, Ansger de Nuderstoke, John de St. John, Gerold de Cocre, Geoffry his son, Wm. Fitzroger, Roger de Cocre, and Walter de Montacute.[42]

Upon the face of the charter it is apparent that it was made within a year after Robert's death, and that he died soon after his marriage, without issue born, by which event William, the second son, became his father's heir presumptive only, being subject to the contingency of a posthumous child of Robert turning up. Provisions for substituting an equivalent in case of any defect of title to the original gift were not uncommon in donative charters to religious houses, and the priory was well advised to insert one in this instance, as Robert, according to the pedigree, had a son, Robert (III), who could question his father's gift. Whether or not he did so does not appear.

It must have been on some substantial grounds, not now to be ascertained, that William refused to recognise his nephew as the heir of his grandfather. Possibly his legitimacy was in question, and there is some colour for the conjecture, as it is remarkable that in the charter of King John confirming the judgment of the court respecting the Barony, it is expressly stated with regard to this Robert that he was *ex legitima uxore*, whereas his father and grandfather are said to be *ex uxore disponsata*.

William endeavoured to pacify his nephew by settling on him for his life part of the manor of Keinton Mandeville, one of the paternal estates. This manor, it may be observed, after the death of both William and Robert, was claimed by William's son Stephen o Geoffry (IV) under a settlement his father had made ; but by a final concord made before the justices at Ilchester, Stephen released the land to Geoffry in consideration of one mark in silver.[43]

Robert was not to be disposed of so easily. He therefore proceeded by writ of "*assize of mort d'ancestor*" against his uncle, to

---

[42] Montacute Cartulary, fo. 53.

[43] Assize Rolls Q.B., Somt., 27 Hen. III, m-5-13—1.   Feet of Fines, Somt., 27 Hen. III, no. 89.

recover " one knight's fee in Cocre and West Cocre with the Hundred," and was charged 80 marks in silver, nine palfreys, and four
Norway hawks for obtaining the judgment of the Court.[44] The dispute, however, was amicably arranged in Robert's favour, with the
sanction of the Crown as supreme lord. This appears from an
ancient calendar of the muniments of Edmund Mortimer, Earl of
March, the owner of the Barony of Marshwood, temp. Edw. III,
one of which was a Royal charter, whereby King John confirmed the
release and surrender made by " William FitzGeffrei de Mandeville
to Robert de Mandeville of divers lands in Est Cocre and elsewhere,
and also of the Barony of Marshwood."[45] The date of this release
was probably about 6th John, as in that year Robert de Mandeville
paid six marks for having seisin of the Manor of Hardington, which
was held by his father Robert, saving the dower of his mother
therein.[46]

Robert (III), having settled with his uncle, proceeded with the suit
against de Tylli, and at the trial (6 John) by grand assize, a jury of
twenty knights gave a verdict in his favour,* after which by Letters
Patent, tested 14 Feb., 8 John, all knights holding of the Honour of
Geoffry de Mandeville, senior, Lord of Marshwood, were commanded
to acknowledge the right of Robert de Mandeville thereto, as the
heir of Geoffry.[47] This was followed by a confirmation charter of
the King, dated at Porchester, 24th May, 8 John, which runs as
follows :—

" Johes dei gr̄ Rex Angl. Salut̄. Sciatis Q̄d. Recognitum est in curia
nr̄a coram nobis et Baronibus nr̄is et plene declaratum p̄ sacramen-
tum legalium militum de Baronia de Mershwode Q̄d. Galfridus de
Mandevil senior tenuit predictam Baroniam de Mershwode sicut jus
suum et hereditatem et genuit ex uxore sibi desponsata Rob. de
Mandevil, idem vero Rob. genuit ex uxore sibi desponsata alium
Galfridum de Mandevil seu Galfridum de Cocre, qui ex legitima

---

* The jury was composed of twenty of the leading men of Dorset and Somerset.
Their names were Osbert Fitz Wi'liam, Robert Fitz Reginald, Robert Fitz
Richard de Hac, Henry de Stok, Alexander de Waddon, Ralph de Vallibus,
Walter de Wudiet, Ralph de Torum, William de Vallibus, Gerard de Brocton, Philip
de Horsy, Theodoric [Terricus] de Mudiford, Richard Fitz Robert, Hugh de
Givelton, Ralph de Cruket, William de Cinnoc, John Malherbe, William Fitz
Geoffry, Hugh de Greinton, and Simon Buzun.

44 Rot. Obl. and Fin., pp. 302-360.

45 Addl. MSS., Brit. Mus., no. 6,041.

46 Fin. Rot., 6 John, pt. 1, m. 8.

47 Pat. Roll, 6 John, part 1, m. 8.

uxore suo genuit Rob. de Mandevil patrem Rob. de Mandevil qui jus clamavit in predcam Baroniam. Predcus vero Galfridus senior, mortua prima uxore sua de qua genuit Rob. de Mandevil ut dcm est, aliam uxorem sibi desponsavit de qua genuit Radum de Mandevil qui post obitum patris sui tenuit predcam Baroniam de Mershwode per voluntatem Regis H eo quod melior miles erat quam Robtus primogenitus frater suus Robert quem predcus G. de prima uxore sua genuit ut dictum est. Idem antem Radus genuit filiam Dionisiam nomine qui nupta fuit Willo fil Johis tunc Senesch. Normann qui de ea genuit Hen. de Tylli. Nos ergo cnm ista constarent nobis et curie nre de jure prenominati Robto de Mandevil qui processit de primogenito filio, et recto herede prefati Galfridi de Mandevil semoris reddidimus ei et heredibus suis et presenti carta nra confirmavimus totam predictam Baroniam de Mershwode cum oibus ptn et libertat."†[47]

Being now fully installed in his rights, Robert was charged by the Crown a fine of no less than £483 16s. 8d., seven palfreys, and four Norway hawks, " for having his Barony."[48] But he was acquitted by special writ from the King, of one hawk, which (as the writ states) "the said Robert by our command delivered to John de Lacey, Constable of Chester, to whom we gave it."[49] John de Lacy was Earl of Lincoln, and the bird must have been a very choice one to be worthy of his acceptance ; it may have been a noble peregrine falcon, as an Earl was privileged to carry one on his wrist.

It is worthy of notice that through the issue of his second marriage Geoffry de Mandeville senex was ancestor of the celebrated family of de Gournay. William Fitzjohn, the husband of Geoffry's daughter, was lord of Harptree, and besides Henry de Tylli, his eldest son, he had another son also called William Fitzjohn, to whom his brother Henry conveyed the Honour of Harptree, and for that reason he was called William Fitzjohn of Harptree, to distinguish him from William Fitzjohn of Weston, to whom further allusion will be made.[50] William Fitzjohn the father was the son of John de Harptree, lord of that manor. In the year 1137 he joined William Gouel

† The record and verdict are set out on the Roll[51] almost verbatim, with the Patent, the chief variation being that the second Geoffry de Mandevil is called *senex* instead of *senior*, and that the third is said to be of *Croere* instead of *Cocre*.

[47] Wells MSS., Liber Albus.
[48] Pipe Roll, 10 John, Dor. and Som.
[49] Close Rolls, 8 Hen. III.
[50] Lib. Nig., pp. 84-85.
[51] Rot. 11, m. 2, Dors.

de Perceval, lord of Castle Cary (the supposed ancestor of the house of Lovel), and William de Mohun, lord of Dunster, in fortifying their castles for the Empress Maud against Stephen, and by their ravages they cut off the supplies for his army then engaged in the siege of Bristol.[52] Ascelin Gouel de Perceval, the Domesday tenant under the Bishop of Coutances of Harptree Ferentone (now Farington Gurney) and Babington, and brother of the above William de Perceval, is said[53] to have been the father of John de Harptree; and certain it is that all those manors were afterwards held by William Fitzjohn. Either William Fitzjohn of Harptree or his son married Matilda de Orescuillz, owner of the manor of Sandford Orescuillz (now softened to Orcas), as co-heiress of Humphry the Chamberlain, Domesday tenant of that manor. Their son, Thomas FitzWilliam of Harptree, married Eva de Gournay, a great heiress, whose son Robert assumed her name and transmitted it to his descendants.

Robert de Mandeville (III) was, we may presume, amongst the Barons who rebelled against King John, and thereby forfeited not only his allegiance but his lands and liberty also, for (17 John) Peter de Mauley, Sheriff of Dorset, was commanded to give possession to Ralph de Fay and his brother of a moiety of the land of Robert de Mandeville, " who is in the prison of our lord the King at Corf,"[54] and a like mandate was directed to Robert de Curtenay, sheriff of Devon, as regards the lands of de Mandeville in his county. But on the accession of Henry III he made his peace, and the Sheriffs of Dorset, Somerset, Devon, and Cornwall were ordered by the King's writ (1 Hen. III) to restore to Robert de Mandeville the lands he held " when he withdrew his allegiance from King John our father," and he must have been in high favour with King Henry, as by another writ Robert de Curtenay was ordered to deliver seisin of all lands of the King's enemies *(inimicos)* within his bailiwick to de Mandeville for his support during the king's pleasure.

Robert (III) may have been the Robert de Mandeville who was exempted from scutage, 6 Henry III, because he served with his own knights,[55] but he paid scutage in Somerset and Dorset, 8 Henry III.[56]

He appears to have conveyed a large portion, if not the whole, of his estates to his son Geoffry. The Mortimer calendar records a charter (sans date), made by Robert de Mandeville to Geoffry his son, of the manor of Marshwood, and also an indenture of covenant made between them concerning divers manors and fees. In the year

---

[52] Gesta Stephani. [53] Anderson's History of the House of Yvery.
[54] Close Rolls, 17 John, m. 19. [55] Miscell. Rolls Chan., 6 Henry III, no. 8.
[56] Dodsworth's Coll., xv, 70.

1239 he conveyed to his son his estates in Somersetshire and Wiltshire also, and by fine between Geoffry de Mandeville, querent, and
Robert de Mandeville, deft., the manors of Sutton (in Wilts), East
Coker, West Coker, Hardington, and Kington (Keinton), in Somerset,
were acknowledged to be the right of Geoffry, who in return agreed to
find Robert and Helewise, his wife, in all reasonable estovers, viz., for
Robert, one palfrey with harness, trappings and furniture, and for
Helewise the like, and also one groom, one chambermaid and one
laundress (" unum garcionem, unam camerariam, et unam lotricem"),
and one esquire in food and clothing.[57] Robert, who was probably
in his last illness at the time the fine was levied,[58] must have died
soon after, leaving his wife surviving, as, 27 Hen. III, " Helewise,
who was the wife of Robert de Mandeville," paid one mark for
license to agree with Geoffry de Mandeville.‡[59]

Assuming his death in 1243, he cannot have been the Robert de
Mandeville who paid an aid for 14½ knight's fees belonging to the
Honour of Marshwood, unless the tax was due in his lifetime, and
left in arrear for several years.[60]

Dugdale supposes[61] that Geoffrey was the brother of Robert, but
although it is quite possible that Robert had a brother Geoffrey, there
is cogent evidence to show that the Geoffrey who succeeded him was
his son. For instance, there is in the Montacute Cartulary a charter
whereby " Geoffrey, son of Robert de Mandeville," confirmed the gift
which Edward the Staller (Stabularius) had made to the Priory of
the land held by him in the ville of Cocre. There is no date to the
charter, but amongst the witnesses are Sir Nicholas de Meriet and
Sir William de Dommere, both of whom flourished in the reign of
Henry III. Again, by another charter, also undated (the original of
which is preserved amongst the Manor muniments at Coker Court),
Geoffry de Mandeville confirmed a grant made by Walter de Ete-
minstre, chaplain to Gilbert de la Burtune, of one virgate of land which
he held, by homage and service, " of Robert de Mandeville, father of

---

‡ A charter in the British Museum (Addl. MSS., 15437) suggests who Helewise
was. By it Gunnora de la Hulle gives to Helewise, her daughter, all her right
to the lands given her by Robert de Mandeville. Test., Ivo de Pilesdone, Ric.
Long, Will. Clavile and others. No date.

The locality of La Hulle appears by another charter (15436), whereby Geoffry
de Mandeville releases to Yerin de Bavent 30d., part of an annual rent of 3s.
for land " de la Hulle in the manor of Merswode." Test., Dom. Rad. de
Basinges, Mag. Will, persona de Cocre, Rob. de . . . steward of Geoffry,
and others. No date.

[57] Fin. Div. Cos., 23 Hen. III, no. 145.
[58] Plac. Abbrev., p. 112.   [59] Ass. Rolls, Q.B. Somt., 27 Hen. III, m—5—13—1·
[60] Pipe Roll Dors. & Som., 38 Hen. III.   [61] Baronage, i, 206.

him, Geoffry, in his Manor of Est Cocre at la Burtune "— [Burton, a hamlet in the parish of East Coker] —and " la Hesse." Witnesses, Girard de la Hesse, William de Cocre, Benedict de Hacche, William Burel, Roger de Suttone, William de Huwenbear. The seal to this charter is a heater-shaped shield of green wax, the charge being Quarterly arg. and or, but the legend is defaced. These were the proper arms of de Mandeville. Hutchins, in his notice of the family,[62] ascribes to it three lions passant in pale arg., debruised by a bendlet az., but this was the coat of Fitzpain, who purchased the Manor of Marshwood from John de Mandeville, in the reign of Edward I.

Geoffry (IV) must have been much embarrrassed with debts. In 1239 he acknowledged that he owed Giles de Bridport 300 marks, and agreed that, if not paid in three years, Giles might hold the Manor of East Coker, with the Hundred and Church, in perpetuity, according to the terms of an agreement between them, and of a charter deposited in the Abbey of Glastonbury. In the same year he gave to Richard le Dune, parson of the Church of Hardington, security for 40 marks on his Manor of Kington[63] in lieu of a mortgage made by Robert his father on the Manor and Advowson of Hardington[64] whereupon le Dune reconveyed that Manor to Geoffry, who, in return, discharged le Dune from suit and service for certain lands held by him in it.[65]

It should be noticed here that Geoffry (IV) was the over-lord of the manor of Weston (now called Buckhorn Weston), Dorset. This manor was a member of a Barony created by William the Conqueror[66] in favour perhaps of the Earl of Moretain, under whom " Haimo " held Weston at the time of the Domesday survey. His son, John FitzHamon, was the father of William Fitzjohn of Weston, who held it 14 Hen. II.[67] On his death, which happened before 13 John, he was succeeded by John FitzRichard, who, as his heir, paid 14 marks relief for seven fees of the Honour of Moretain.[68] John was followed by Henry FitzRichard, probably his brother, on whose death before 27 Hen. III,[69] his estates, of which Weston was part, descended to his four collateral heirs, one of whom was Thomas le Bretun. By purchase of another fourth in addition to his own, le Bretun had a moiety, which he sold to Geoffry de Mandeville (IV), who gave it to his younger son Robert before 15 Edw. I,[70] for there was a dispute

[62] Hist. Dorset ii, p. 261.
[63] Ass. Rolls, Q.B., Somt., 27 Henry III, m—3—13—1.   [64] Ib.
[65] Somt. Fines, 27 Henry III, no. 94.   [66] Testa de Nevill, p. 165.
[67] Lib. Nig. i, 85.   [68] Pipe Roll, Dors. and Somt., 13 John.
[69] Rot. Fin., i, 401.
[70] Hundr. Rolls, i, p. 100 ; Placita de Banco, Hil. T., 15 Edw. I, dors. Rot. 6.

that year between this Robert and the Priory of Stavordale, respecting the advowson of the church of Buckhorn Weston.

From Thomas le Bretun, Geoffry (IV) acquired also the over-lordship of Charlton Adam or Charlton FitzAdam, Somerset. This manor, of which the Earl of Moretain was Domesday tenant in chief (Reginald de Valletort being his under tenant), was afterwards held by John FitzHamon, already noticed, and he bestowed the church of Charlton on the Priory of Bruton, which gift was confirmed by a charter of his son William FitzJohn, addressed to Robert Bishop of Bath. But, 8th John, the over-lordship of Moretain had vested in Wm. FitzAdam, whose connection with FitzHamon, if any, does not appear. He released to the Priory all his right to the church, and his son Wm. Fitz-Wm. FitzAdam (called Wm. FitzAdam) by charter bestowed the manor also on the Priory in free and perpetual alms, " Sir Geoffry de Mandeville " being one of the witnesses. Lastly, there is a charter whereby Geoffry de Mandeville, for the salvation of his soul and the souls of Mabel, his wife, and his children, released to the Priory all his right to one knight's fee in the Manor of Charlton Adam, and notifies to Wm. FitzAdam that he had authorised the Priory to take possession of it, " which," he declares, " is my fee by the gift (ex dono) of Thomas le Bretun."§ Notwithstanding this, Charlton appears to have remained subject to the Lord of Coker. In a survey of the manor of East Coker, 14 Edw. II, made by a jury on oath, it is found " that the Prior of Bruton holds the manor of Charlton FitzAdam of the Lord by service of one knight's fee, and the Lord of Aysshehull sold that manor, but the homage say that the lords were accustomed to take scutage there, and Geoffry de Mandeville, then Lord of Coker, gave one knight's fee in Charlton FitzAdam to the Prior and his successors in free and perpetual alms for ever, reserving therefrom nothing save their prayers, and scutage when it shall happen to be due.[71] The tenure is again referred to in a Court roll of the Manor, 10 Hen. VI.

There was probably some relationship between de Mandeville and le Bretun which induced Geoffry to purchase Weston and Charlton. In 1257 Robert de Mandeville gave security to the Crown for 110 marks for having Scolastica, daughter and heir of William Briton, as his wife.[72] In an assize of lands in Suffolk, late of " William le Bretun,"

---

§ The foregoing Charters are taken from the Cartulary of the Priory of Bruton, in the possession of the Earl of Ilchester.

[71] Manor Muniments.

[72] Mem. Rolls, Trin. Term, 41 Hen. III.

in 1287, it appeared that he left three daughters his co-heirs, one of whom was married to Robert de Mandeville; but her name is said to be Nicholai.[73] Then, by deed dated 31st May, 1284, Geoffry de Mandeville grants to Thomas le Britthun his Manor of "Chedehoc" for his life, and moreover agrees to lend him 15 marks to pay off a mortgage on the manor of Studland, and the said Thomas [Geoffry] undertakes to indemnify Geoffry [Thomas] from any claim by Mabel his wife on the manor of Chiddihoc, and William de Cocre is appointed to deliver seisin to Thomas.[74]

The embarrassments of Geoffry (IV) induced him to lay claim to other estates which had been held by Henry de Tylli.

The Manor of Dogmersfield, Hants, was given by Henry I to Godfrey, Bishop of Bath,[75] but in the reign of Henry II was the subject of litigation between Bishop Robert and William Fitzjohn of Harptree, who claimed to hold it as a knight's fee, the Bishop insisting that it was part of his demesne.[76] The dispute continued between Reginald, the next Bishop, and Henry de Tylli, who had succeeded his father William Fitzjohn; but it ended in a compromise by which for the sum of 100 marks Henry de Tylli relinquished all claim to Dogmersfield, and also to the manor of Dinder, near Wells, which he had held under the Bishop, and both manors were granted by the King to the Bishop.[77] How Wm. Fitzjohn acquired Dogmersfield does not appear, but it may be presumed that it was part of the possessions of Geoffry de Mandeville (II), and that it was seized by Henry de Tylli, as his father's heir, on the same grounds as he claimed the Barony of Marshwood. Geoffry de Mandeville (IV) must have based his claim as heir of Geoffry (II), who, as he alleged, was seized of Dogmersfield in the time of Henry II; and the de Mandeville pedigree, as set out in the pleadings, tallies exactly with that in the verdict in the Marshwood case. Geoffry (IV) failed, however, in his action—apparently on technical grounds.[78]

Geoffry (IV) died before 53 Hen. III, as in that year John de Mandeville did homage and had seizin of all the lands of his father, "then lately dead."[79] The entries in the Pipe Rolls, 7 and 15 Edw. I,

---

[73] Plac de Banc, Hil. Term, 15 Edw. I, Suff.

[74] Hutch. Dors. ii, 255.

[75] Wells Liber Albus, 16—46 dors.

[76] Lib. Nig. i, 87.

[77] Lib. Alb., ub. sup., Archæologia, vol. 50, pt. ii, p. 354.

[78] Coram Rege. Rolls, no. 107, Hil. T., 43 Hen. III, m. 7.

[79] Fine Rolls, Printed Extracts ii, 495.

of £29 10s. due from Geoffry de Mandeville for scutage on 14 fees and a half and the fourth part of one fee of the Honour of Merswode, must refer to an assessment made 42 Hen. III, in his lifetime, but continued in charge for non-payment, except £2 paid by William de Bingham.

John de Mandeville (I) was married twice. His first wife was Agnes, daughter of Dru de Barentyn,|| who, it appears, had purchased of Geoffry the manor of Sutton, Wilts, in order to assist him in discharging his debts to the Jews, and on the marriage of his daughter with Geoffry's son he settled that manor on them. The only issue of this marriage was a daughter Joan,[80] and Sutton must have reverted to the De Mandevilles, as, 9 Ed. I, the King presented to the church there as guardian of John de Mandeville.[81] This was John (II), son of John (I) by his second wife Clementia, who survived him and became the wife of Simon de Montalt. Towards the end of his life John (I) became deranged, and (3 Ed. I) the King, as his guardian, took charge of his estates, making provision out of the rents for the lunatic, his wife and children.[82] But he died in the following year, and the inquisition taken after his death furnishes us with important particulars relating to Coker. It finds that John de Mandeville held the manor of the heirs of Earl de L'Isle by the service of one knight. It then proceeds to say that the court (*i.e.*, the mansion or residence), garden, dove-houses, vineyard, and curtilages were worth by the year 20 shillings ; 148½ acres of arable, in demesne, worth 6d. per acre; 226½ acres of arable worth 4d. per acre ; 11 acres of meadow worth 2s. per acre ; 16 acres of meadow worth 20d. per acre, and 9 acres of meadow worth 8d. per acre ; and in the Park outside the wood 105 acres of pasture worth 4d. per acre, and 110 acres more of pasture, of which 27½ acres of underwood could be sold yearly at 6d. per acre. There was also a windmill worth 26s. by the year ; rents of freeholders, £5 5s. 6d.; rents of villeins (*i.e.*, copyholders), £6 15s. 6d., together with pleas and perquisites of court, 60s.; also 16s. 8d. rents in the borough of Murifield. There was also a Church, the advowson of which belonged to the Lord of the Manor, worth 24 marks by the year, £13 6s. 8d. That William de Bingham

---

|| A writer in *Notes and Queries* (4th series, iii, 485) confuses the Mandevilles of Marshwood with the family of Fitzpiers, Earls of Essex, and assigns this Agnes as wife of John Fitz Geoffry Fitzpiers.

[80] Esch. 4 Ed. I, no. 40 ; Cal. Gen., p. 240 ; Test. de Nev., p. 142.

[81] 50 Rep. D.K., Pub. Rec. App., 220.

[82] Close Rolls, 3 Edward I, m. 33. Originalia 3 Edward I, Ro. 7.

held the Manor of Hardinton of the said John, which he held of the king in chief by the service of one knight; and William de Mandeville held the Manor of Kington (Keinton) of the said John by the service of one knight, which he held of the heirs of the Earl of Moretain. That the said John held the Manors of Merswode and Cydiok, which Geoffry his father conveyed to John Gervays and his heirs under the rent of £20 a year,§ and that he held the said manors of the King in chief by Barony, and the service of two knights in the army with their lord. Then the inquisition enumerates many fees held by the said John in Somerset, Dorset (one of which was the ville of Gissic, an escheat of the Crown, granted by King John to William de Mandeville),[84] Oxfordshire, Wilts, and Devon—that of Wonford in the last named county being one—and it concludes with finding that his son John, aged 16, was his heir.[85] Amongst the fees were two knights' fees held of him by William de Morteshorne in Morteshorne (*i.e.*, Mosterton), belonging to his Manor of Marshwood, and this, coupled with the fact that Richard de Redvers was the Domesday tenant of Mosterton, renders a connection of the families of de Redvers and de Mandeville more probable.

The tenure of Coker, with some variation, appears also in " Kirby's Quest," taken about 12 Edw. I, where, under the head " Hundred of Coker," it is said " John de Mandeville holds Est Coker and West Coker for one knight's fee of the heir of the Earl of Vernon, of the honour of Christchurch of Twineham, and the heir of the King in chief." The Earl of Vernon was William de Vernon, Earl de L'isle, and the Honour had descended to the Courtenays as his heirs.

The record goes on to say, " The same John holds Hardington, which belongs to his ' Barony of Merswode,' held of the king in chief by the service of one knight," from which it may be presumed that after the recovery of that Barony, Robert de Mandeville, or one of his successors, had attached Hardington to it, unless the Barony was at the time of the Conquest coupled with the grant of Hardington. This, however, is rather inconsistent with the entry in " Testa de Nevill " (p. 163), that Robert de Mande-

---

§ In Inq. p. m. of John Gervase it is said that he held the manor of Chideok only of John de Mandeville, at a rent of £20.[83]

[83] Esch. of Edw. I, no. 18.

[84] Testa de Nevill, p. 166.

[85] Esch. 4, Edward I, no. 48.

ville holds Hardington, in the hundred of Coker, of our Lord the King by the service of one knight from the [time of the] conquest of England.

Between 14 Hen. II (when Geoffry de Mandeville certified that he held Hardington in chief) and the reign of King John, the de Glamorgans of the Isle of Wight laid claim to the whole or part of it, for, 1st John, there was an action pending between Ralph de Glamorgan and Robert de Mandeville, respecting five hides of land in Hardington;[86] and, 2nd John, de Glamorgan paid one mark for recognizance of *mort d'ancestor* for half a knight's fee in Hardington.[87] An assize of *mort d'ancestor* would only lie where the plaintiff's claim was founded on the seizin of his deceased father or mother, or some near collatoral relation ; and as Hardington was one knight's fee, this proceeding looks as if the estate had descended in moieties to two co-heirs, represented by de Mandeville and de Glamorgan. How the action ended does not appear, but de Mandeville certainly held the entirety.

John (II) being a minor at his father's death, the King continued in possession of his estates as guardian, and the Sheriff accounts, 4 Edw. I, for 51s. 6d. received for corn sold from the demesne of East Coker, which was cropped at the time John (the father) died.[88] The Manor of East Coker and the third presentation to the Church and one fee in Kington were assigned to Clementia, his widow, for her dower.[89]

On the 23rd April, 25 Edw. I, the King, by letters patent, dated at Bruton, presented Robert de St. Nicholas to the church of East Coker, " in the King's gift by reason of the custody of the land and heirs of John de Mandeville ; "[90] but if, as the Inquisition states, the heir was 16 in 4 Edw. I, he must have been of age 11 Edw. I, and in that year we find a fine levied between John de Mandeville (son and heir of John de Mandeville) and Simon de Montalt and Clementia his wife, whereby, after stating that John complained that they held more than their share of the estate for her dower, they released to John, inter alia, the manor of East Coker and the advowson and hundred, in exchange for the manor of Sutton Mandeville, Wilts,

---

[86] Rot. Cur. Reg. I, 245.

[87] Rot. de Obl. and Fin., p. 59.

[88] Pipe Roll, 4 Edw. I, Dors. and Somt.

[89] Close Rolls, 28 October and 15 March, 4 Ed. I.

[90] 47 D.K. Rep. App., p. 195.

and a rent of 103s. 4d. out of the manor of Marshwood for the life of Clementia, who retained her right to the manor to Shotwell, Berks.[91]

10 Edw. I, John (II) proferred his services against the Welsh for two knight's fees held by him in Dorset.[92]

22 Edw. I, he was summoned to attend the king at Portsmouth with horse and arms in his expedition to Gascony,[93] and 28 Edw. I he was again summoned to perform military service against the Scots as holding lands in Somerset and Dorset of the yearly value of £40.

33 Edw. I.—In this year he parted with his ancestral estate in Dorsetshire, and by charter, dated 8th May, 33 Edw. I, license from the Crown having been obtained (which license states that besides Marshwood he held the manor of Coker, worth £31 a year, with the Hundred of Coker thereto appurtenant, and also the manor of Sutton Mandeville, Wilts),[94] he conveyed the manor of Marshwood, with the Hundred of Whitchurch held of the king in chief by Barony, to Robert Fitzpain and Isabella his wife and the heirs of Robert. From them it devolved upon their adopted son Robert, surnamed Fitzpain, who with Ela his wife settled it in 1327 upon themselves and their issue, and in default of such issue on John Maltravers, to whom they had sold the reversion. Upon the attainder of Maltravers it escheated to the Crown, and was afterwards granted to the Mortimers, Earl of March.¶[95]

In the same year John (II) confirmed to the Priory of Montacute several of the donations made by his ancestors. By charter, dated at Coker, Sunday after the Feast of St. Mary, A.D. 1305 (33 Edw. I), wherein he is styled "Sir (Dominus) John de Mandeville, son of John de Mandeville," after reciting the gift of land in Coker to the priory by Edward the Staller, and another gift of a rent of 3s. issuing out of lands at Ford, in the manor of Coker, by Geoffrey, son of Gerald de Coker, which gifts his ancestors, Robert de Mandeville and Geoffrey his son, had confirmed; and reciting also the gift of the mill of

---

¶ Some charters relating to this transaction are transcribed in the cartulary of the Abbey of Ford (now in the possession of Mrs. Fenwick, daughter of Sir Thomas Phillipps), part of the Abbey estates being within the hundred of Marshwood.

[91] Feet of Fines, Div. Con. 11 Edw. I, no. 54.

[92] Parly. Writs, vol. i, Alph. Digest.

[93] Rot. Vascon, 22 Edw. I, m. 9 Dors.

[94] Inq. ad. q. d., 33 Edw. I, no. 182.

[95] Mortimer Register; Coker's Hist. Dors., p. 14.

Erlestoke (Wilts) by his ancestor, Roger de Mandeville, for the soul of his (Roger's) father, Stephen, and a release to the Priory of suit and service for the Manor of Closeworth, made by Geoffry de Mandeville, his grandfather; he confirmed all the said gifts for the good of his own soul and the soul of Anastasia, daughter of Lord John de Mautravers, late wife of Herbert de St. Quintin, " whose body is buried in the newly-erected Chapel of the Blessed Mary in Montacute," and for the good of the souls of his father and mother and all his ancestors, and of Stephen, then Prior of the Convent. Amongst the witnesses to this charter are Lord John de Beauchamp, Philip de Maubanc, and John de Dummere.[96]

It is impossible now to say what induced John de Mandeville to interest himself for the soul of this Lady Anastasia. She does not figure in the exhaustive pedigee of the Maltravers family compiled by Mr. Steinman,[97] but was probably a third daughter of Sir John de Maltravers, who died in 1296. Herbert de St. Quintin, her husband, was of a very ancient family holding large possessions in Dorset, Somerset, and Wilts. He was son of Herbert by Margery, daughter of Walter de Fauconbridge, and died in his father's lifetime, leaving issue Herbert de St. Quintin, who died 31 Edw. I, seized of the manor of Frome St. Quinton, Dorset.[98]

The charter would naturally be received as ample evidence of the burial of the lady at Montacute, but, strange to say, on the testimony of the industrious cavalier, Richard Symonds, she was buried at Hinton St. George. In his diary for 1644 is the following entry relating to the church of Hinton : " In the north chapel lyes a blew flat stone with five shields all gone, as also the brass letters which were in old caracters round about. YCI : GIST : ANESTEISE : DE : SAINT : QUENTIN : FILLE : SIRE : JOHAN : MATRAVERS : PRIES : LI : KE : DU : [Dieu] DE : [S] ALME : EUT : MERCY : + " Underneath is a sketch of a flat tombstone with a small blank escutcheon at each corner, and another in the centre.

It is very evident that Symonds made no mistake, for the stone is there still—only instead of being *in* the church it is outside and converted into a doorstep. The de Quintin family held property in Coker, as lessees of de Mandeville, but no trace has been found of any connection of either St. Quintin or Maltravers with Hinton St.

---

[96] Mont. Cart.

[97] Coll. Top. and Gen., vol. vi, p. 335.

[98] Hutch. Dors. ii, 643. Pedigree of St. Quintin, Vincent's coll., Coll. Arm., no. 2, f. 297, cited in Gough's Sepulch. Mon., vol. i, p. 200.

George. It is just possible that on the destruction of the Conventual Buildings at Montacute, temp. Hen. VIII (?), some of the materials were purchased for paving the church of Hinton, and amongst them this memorial slab.

Upon his marriage, John (II) settled the Manor of East Coker upon his wife, Roberga, and his issue by her, and died before 1 Edward II, leaving a son, Robert (IV), and his wife surviving. In that year Roberga recovered from Michael de Morville one-third part of the hundred of Coker and of divers messuages and lands in East Coker and North Coker which she claimed in dower, but a claim she made against John de St. Quintin (lessee of the premises) was dismissed.[99]

We now come to the end of the connection of the De Mandevilles with Coker (*i.e.*, both East and West Coker), which was occasioned by some serious offence committed by Robert de Mandeville IV) in 34 Edward I, when he could hardly have been of age. What the offence was we do not know, but it was found by Inquisition, 3 Edward II, that Robert, son of John de Mandeville, was outlawed *for felony*, 34 Edw. I, and that he held the manors of East Coke and West Coker of Lord Hugh de Courtenay (1st Earl of Devon), who was bound to account to the King for the rents for a year and a day.[100]

In consequence of this forfeiture the feudal tenancy of the De Mandevilles in Coker became merged in the over-lordship vested in Hugh de Courtenay as the heir of De L'isle, and in the Nomina Villarum, 9 Edw. II, Hugh de Courtenay is returned as the Lord of East Coker and West Coker.

Robert appears to have been advised that the forfeiture did not extend to a part of Coker, the legal estate in which was outstanding, and 4 Edw. II he brought an action against Hugh de Courtenay, John de Veer, Philip le Do, parson of West Coker, and others, for disseising him of a tenement in East Coker and West Coker pertaining to the Manor of East Coker and Hundred of Coker. Hugh de Courtenay, who was the real defendant, alleged that the manor was in the seisin of one Michael de Morville, but he having alienated it in mortmain to the house of Bockland,[101] Hugh took possession of it as a forfeiture. This Robert denied, asserting that Michael had

---

[99] De Banco Rolls, 1 Edw. II., m. 9.

[100] Inq. ad. q. d., 2 Edw. II, no. 11.

[101] See Hugo's History of this Religious House, Somt. Archl. Socy. Proceedings, vol. x.

enfeoffed him of the Manor, but failing to appear at the trial at Chard his claim was dismissed. Poverty and durance vile compelled him to make the best terms he could with de Courtenay, and having done so[102] by charter, dated at London, 8 Edwd. II, wherein he is styled "Robert de Mandeville, of the county of Somerset," he granted to Hugh de Courtenay and John de Stonhouse the reversion of all his lands in East Coker and North Coker which Clementia de Montalt (his mother) held for her life, and which John de St. Quintin held for his life by the demise of John de Mandeville, whose heir he (Robert) was.[103] The reason of this charter being made in London was puzzling, until explained by a contemporary entry in the register of John Drokensford, Bishop of Bath and Wells, which tells us that the Bishop, Dec. 6, 1314 (8 Edw. II) presented a petition to the King setting forth that Robert de Mandeville, clerk, was a prisoner in Newgate for debt, and praying that he might be liberated, it being contrary to the statute that clerks should be imprisoned for debt as laymen.[104] We learn also from this entry that Robert was a clerk in holy orders.

About the same time Clementia his mother, then widow of Simon de Montalt, recovered from Hugh de Courtenay her dower right of presentation to the Church of East Coker, then vacant by the death of Robert St. Nicholas,[105] but shortly after she sold to him all her rights in dower, and they were conveyed 13 Edw. II.[106]

As felony caused a forfeiture only of the real estate of which the offender was seized ; it is probable that it did not touch Hardington, which was outstanding on a lease for life granted by John de Mandeville, his grandfather, to William de Bingham, son of William de Bingham, of Sutton Bingham, and Cecilia his wife, daughter of Geoffry de Mandeville (III). On the death of William de Bingham, the son, it was found by inquisition[107] that he held for his life certain lands in Hardington, by lease of John de Mandeville, and that Robert de Mandeville, surviving son of the same (ipsius) John, was his next heir, and aged 26 years. In the same year, Robert did homage for all the lands held by William de Bingham in

---

[102] Ass. Rolls., Div. Cos., 4 Edw. II, n—2—15—2.

[103] Close Rolls, 8 Ed. II.

[104] Drok. Regr., 1st Vol. Somt. Record Soc.

[105] De Banco Rolls, 2 Edw. II, Trin. 1—9—2—39.

[106] Close Rolls, 13 Edw. II.

[107] Esch. 7 Edw. II, no. 15.

Hardington by lease of the said John, who held the same of Henry, late King, the King's grandfather, by the service of half a knight's fee.[108] But Robert soon lost Hardington also. 11 Edw. II license was granted to him as " Robert, son of John de Mandeville," to enfeoff Alexander Loterel and his heirs of the manor of Hardington Mandeville, reserving a life interest to Robert, " and nothing remains to Robert beyond the said manor."[109] Loterel was perhaps only a trustee, for, 17 Edw. II, he conveyed the manor to John de Pointyngton and Alianor his wife, and Lawrence their son.[110] Robert died in the prime of life, before A.D. 1332, and leaving no children, his sister Matilda, widow of Sir William Fauconberg, was his heiress. In that character she tried to impeach the claim of Sir Hugh de Courtenay to Coker, but was unsuccessful, and 9 Edw. III she executed a full release of it to Sir Hugh by charter, dated at Stoke-under-Hamdon, to which Matthew la Warre, John de Clyvedon, Richard Pike, and Henry de Urtiaco, knights, were witnesses.[111]

But this compromise did not affect her claims to Hardington, which she asserted against the Pointyngtons and 8 Edw. III there was an assize to try whether she had disseised Alianor, widow of John de Pointyngton, and Lawrence her son, of that manor.

In support of her claim Matilda pleaded that she and her husband recovered the manor in an action 6 Edw. III, on proof of a grant made by Michael de Morville to one Roberga and her issue by John de Mandeville, that from them it descended to Robert de Mandeville, their son and heir, upon whose death without issue it came to her (Matilda) as his sister and heiress. On the other hand, Alianor said that Michael de Morville never made the alleged grant to Roberga, but that one Andrew Luterel was seized of the whole manor in fee, and thereof enfeoffed John de Pointyngton her husband, and herself and Lawrence, their son.

The jury found that the manor had been granted to John de Mandeville and Roberga, and their heirs in fee simple, subject to a lease to William de Byngham for his life ; that Robert de Mandeville was their son, and that after the death of William de Byngham he

---

[108] Excerpt e Rot. Fin., 7 Edw. II, m. 14.

[109] Inq. ad. q.d., 11 Edw. II, no. 26.

[110] Inq. ad. q.d., 17 Edw. II, no. 4.

[111] Coll. His. Som., ii, 341, Harbin MSS.

granted the Manor to Andrew Luterel and his heirs, who conveyed it to the Pointyngtons. There was, therefore, a verdict in their favour.

Alianor survived her husband, and was married to Walter de Otterhampton, otherwise Walter de Romesey.[112] Her son Lawrence must have died previous to 44 Edw. III, for in that year his son (or brother probably), Thomas de Pointynton, sold the reversion of Hardington, after the deaths of Walter de Otterhampton and Alianor his wife, to John de Cary.[113] From Cary it came to John Wadham, who, 13 Hen. IV, died seized of this manor and the manor of Muryfield (in Ilton) and of one moiety of the manor of Chilton Cantelo, leaving William his son and heir, aged 21.[114] From the heirs of Wadham, Hardington was carried by three co-heiresses to the families of Strangways, Wyndham, and Martin, but is now the sole property of Viscount Portman.

Matilda, the sister and heir of Robert de Mandeville, appears to have had, by her husband Wm. de Fauconbridge, three sons—Robert, William, and Peter—of whom Peter was the survivor; and none of them could have left any issue, as on the death of Peter, in 1350, Thomas Lotterel, his cousin, was found to be his heir.[115] By this means the main line became extinct, but the Buckhorn Weston branch survived for a considerable period. Robert de Mandeville had license from the Crown to give 6s. 8d. rent in Buckhorn Weston to the Priory of Stavordale,[116] and at his death, shortly after, he held the manor jointly with Isabel his wife, of the Earl of Devon, as of his manor of Coker, by render of one sparrowhawk, value 2s.[117] Their son and heir was John de Mandeville, who died 34 Edw. III, without issue, and Joan, his sister and heiress,[118] was the wife of William Bokeland,[119] from whom Weston came to the family of Stourton.

Hugh de Courtenay, first Earl of Devon, to whom the De Mandeville estates escheated, became consequently lord and owner of the manors of East and West Coker, the advowsons of the churches

---

[112] Ass. Rolls, Div. Cos., 44 Edw. III, n—2—21—6.

[113] Harl. MS., 4,120, p. 192.

[114] Ib., . 281.

[115] Ass. Rolls, 2 Edw. III, no. 16, n_{18}^2 } 3. 8 Edw. III, no. 19, n_{19}^2 } 7. Esch. 23 Edw. III, no. 56. Coll. Som. III, 67.

[116] Inq. ad. q. d. 19 Edw. III, no. 39.

[117] Esch. 22, Edw. III pt. 1, no. 13.

[118] Esch., 34 Edw. III, pt. 1, no. 41.

[119] Cor. Rege. Rolls, 2 Ric. II, no. 46 dors.

of Hardington and West Coker, and the hundred of Coker. He
was the first Courtenay Earl of Devon, that title devolving on him
as heir of Isabel de Fortibus, Countess of Devon. He died in 1340,
and was succeeded by his son Hugh, the second Earl, a warrior of
great renown, who accompanied King Edw. III in several expedi-
tions into France. The year after his father's death, having obtained
the King's license for that purpose, he settled by fine (inter alia) the
manor of East Coker and the advowson of Hardington on his son
Hugh and Elizabeth his wife (daughter of Sir Guy de Bryan) and
their issue, with remainder to Hugh the Earl in fee.[120] As there was
only one child of this marriage, who died s.p. in his grandfather's
lifetime, the settled estates reverted to the settlor absolutely,
and he afterwards entailed them on his sixth son, Sir Peter de
Courtenay, in tail male, with remainder to his other sons and their
issue.[121] He died in 1377, but his wife, the Lady Margaret de Bohun,
lived until 1391, and held for her life the manor of East and West
Coker, the advowson of West Coker, the hundred of Coker, and
four acres at Burel's Mill, under the settlement made by the first
Earl on her marriage.[122] Sir Peter de Courtenay dying s.p. in
1405,[123] the property came to his brother, Sir Philip de Courtenay
(to whom his mother also gave Powderham by her will), and on the
death of Sir Philip in 1406 it devolved on his son, Richard de
Courtenay (afterwards Bishop of Norwich)[124]. The Bishop died in
1415, s.p., and his nephew Philip, son of John his brother, then a
minor, succeeded him.[125]

Philip (son of John) married Elizabeth, daughter of Walter Lord
Hungerford, and died in 1463,[126] leaving Sir William Courtenay of
Powderham his son and heir, who died 1485, and from him the
manor descended in direct succession to Sir William Courtenay of
Powderham, who died 1630. He was the last of his family who
held East Coker, and in 1591 he sold it and the advowson of Hardington to Robert Dillon, Esq., of Chimwell, Devon. Coker is
described in the conveyance as "the manor or lordship of East
Coker, and the capital messuage, barton, and demesnes of East

---

[120] Esch. 49, Edw. III, pt. 1, no. 27.

[121] Esch 49, Edw. III, pt. 1, no. 27.   Esch. 15 Ric. II, no. 16.

[122] Esch. 15 Ric. II, no. 16.

[123] Esch. 6 Hen. IV, no. 38.

[124] Esch. 7 Henry IV, no. 51.

[125] Esch. 3 Hen. V, no. 49.

[126] Esch. 3 Edw. IV.

Coker, and the lands, pastures, and woods called East Coker Parke or the Parke of East Coker," and a lease thereof granted to Walter Grove and Mary his wife for their lives is excepted.

In 1598, the Dillons sold both the manor and advowson to Edw. Phelipps of "Mountagu" (afterwards Master of the Rolls), and in 1616 they were sold (with the exception of the farm of Nash) by his son, Sir Robert Phelipps, Kt., to the Very Rev. William Helyar, canon of the Cathedral Church of Exeter and archdeacon of Barnstaple, whose lineal descendant, Horace Augustus Helyar, Esq., is the present owner.

The manor and advowson of West Coker and the hundred of Coker had been settled by fine, 9 Edw. II, made between Hugh de Courtenay (afterwards 1st Earl of Devon), plt., and Alianor, late wife of Hugh de Courtenay, his father, deft. (2nd Earl), on the 1st Earl for life, with remainder to his son Hugh (2nd Earl), in tail, remainder to Robert, another son, in tail, remainder to Thomas, another son, in fee.[127] At the death of Hugh (2nd Earl) in 1377, whose issue, as we have seen, failed in his lifetime, his brother Robert was dead without issue, consequently the limitation to Thomas in fee took effect, and he being also dead, the estate descended to his nephew and heir, Edward, 3rd Earl (son of Edward, brother of Thomas), and from him to Thomas (6th Earl). He died s.p. in 1462, and his sisters—Joan, wife first of Sir Roger Clifford, Kt., and secondly of Sir William Knyvett; and Elizabeth, wife of Sir Hugh Conway, Kt.—became his ultimate co-heirs; but West Coker and his other estates had been forfeited to the Crown by his attainder. They were granted by Henry VII to Edward Courtenay on his creation as Earl of Devon,[128] but he afterwards released West Coker to the King, and it was granted to Sir William Knyvett and Joan his wife, and the heirs of her body, with remainder over to the Courtenays.[129] This grant must have been afterwards surrendered, for by a special Act of Parliament[130] West Coker (subject to a yearly rent-charge of £6 13s. 4d. to Sir William Knyvett for his life) was entailed on the issue of Lord William Courtenay, late Earl of Devon, and the Princess Katherine of York, his wife, failing whom it was to revert to "the King and his heirs for ever." The Crown had not, however, to wait for the failure of issue, for

---

[127] Somt. Fines, 9 Edw. II, no. 48.

[128] Pat. 1, Hen. VII, pt. 2.

[129] Pat. 6, March 5, Hen. VII. Esch. 16 Hen. VII, no. 11.

[130] 4 Hen. VIII, c. 12.

it was forfeited 31 Hen. VIII by the attainder of Henry Courtenay,
Marquis of Exeter (son of William and the Princess Katherine), and
was afterwards granted to Edward, Duke of Somerset, the Protector.
He was the owner of West Coker in 1550, and gave it to Barlow,
Bishop of Bath and Wells, in part exchange for the manor of Wells
and other episcopal manors,[181] but on their forfeiture to the Crown
on the Duke's attainder in 1552 the King restored them to the
Bishop in exchange for West Coker, which, by this means, reverted
again to the Crown. It so remained until the reign of Queen
Elizabeth, when by letters patent[182] the manor of West Coker
and the hundred of West Coker and the advowson of the rectory of West Coker, late parcel of the possessions of Edward
(sic) Earl of Devon, were granted to Edward Busshe and Henry
Parker and their heirs, to be held in chief by the service of
one-twentieth part of a knight's fee. Not long after, the
manor and hundred became the property of the Portman family,
and the arms of Sir John Portman, created baronet A.D. 1612,
impaling those of his wife Ann, daughter of Sir Henry Gifford, of
Kings Somborne, Hants, Kt., are over the entrance to the old manor
house, which still remains standing, although much altered by an
amateur restorer. The Portmans by degrees parted with the
manorial lands, but the hundred of Coker (whatever that may now
mean) remains the property of Viscount Portman. The advowson
was severed from the manor by the grantees or their successors in
the reign of Queen Elizabeth, as Francis Whitton presented to the
church in 1583. It is quite possible that Whitton may have been
an intermediate owner of the manor and hundred between the
grantees and the Portmans.

We must not omit to notice a family closely identified with East
Coker as well by their names as their property—the de Cokers,
who, according to Hutchins,[183] were the ancestors of the Cokers
of Mappowder. There is no doubt that those Cokers were
descended from the de Cokers of Worle, in this county, but no
documentary evidence has been found showing any relationship
between the de Cokers of Worle and the East Coker family. It
would be a very important genealogical fact if the connection could
be established, and it is hoped that the evidences now collected may
assist in solving the problem. The de Cokers were possibly of the

[181] Wells Index, p. 237.
[182] Pat. Roll, 2 Eliz., pt. 8.
[183] Hist. Dors., iii, 722.

MANOR HOUSE, WEST COKER.

To face p. 138

de Mandeville stock, and in some way descended from the Geoffry de Mandeville who, in the reign of Hen. II, was distinguished as "Geoffrey de Cocre." Passing by him and discarding the Robert Coker who Hutchins says lived in the time of Henry I (which is a clerical error for Edw. I), the earliest occurrence of the name we have met with is in a charter (sans date) of Robert Bishop of Bath (1136 to 1165) respecting the church of Charlton Adam, to which " Master Arnold de Coker " was witness.[184]   Then in 20 Hen. III a fine was levied between Robert de Coker, plt., and John de Chinnock and Matilda his wife, defts., whereby one virgate of land in West Coker, and half a virgate in Merswode, Dorset, were conveyed to John and Matilda and her heirs, subject to the yearly rent of 3s.,[185] and the fact that this Robert was owner of land both in Marshwood and Coker strengthens the probability that he was related to the Mandeville family.

There was a William de Cocre, who, by charter (sans date, but probably, from the style of writing, of the reign of John or Hen. III), granted to Roger, son of Adam de Cocre and his heirs, for his homage and service, the moiety of a messuage or curtilage in Gyvel (Yeovil), to hold of the said William and his heirs under the yearly rent of 6d., and to the Church of Gyvel one penny, as Adam his father had been accustomed to pay for the whole of the said tenement.   To this charter is appended a seal on which is a fleur de lys with the legend " S. Wilelmi de Coker," and amongst the witnesses are Dominus William de Cocre and Ralph de Cocre.[186] This, no doubt, was the William de Koker who was presented for withdrawing the suit and service for a tenement in Yeovil from the Hundred of Stone [187]   William, son of Roger de Coker, was a witness with Gerald and Geoffry de Coker to the grant of land in Hardington by Geoffry de Mandeville already noticed, but he could hardly have been the William of this deed.   Ralph de Coker was probably the person referred to in an Assize mort d'ancestor of Edward I, brought by John, son of Ralph de Coker, against Beatrix, late wife of Ralph, and Alice his daughter, for the recovery of certain messuages in Yeovil.[188]

Gerald de Coker was a witness with Geoffry de Mandeville (IV) and others to a charter, whereby William Calvel released to Guy, the

---

[184] Bruton Cart.
[185] Som. Fines, 20 Hen. III, no. 187.
[186] Transcript of Yeovil Almshouse Deeds, penes J.B.
[187] Hundred Rolls, vol. ii.
[188] Pat. Roll, vide 50, D.K. Rep., p. 265.

Prior of Montacute, all his right to a mill-dam between Sutton Bingham and Closworth. The deed is not dated, but Guy was prior from 1269 to 1284.[189]

The De Cokers, as well as the De Mandevilles, looked for spiritual help to the priory of Montacute. Geoffry, son of Gerald de Cocra, for the salvation of his own soul and that of Matilda his wife, granted, by charter, to the Priory of Montacute, a perpetual rent of 3s., out of his land, "De la Ford," in West Coker, for the use of the monks dwelling in the infirmary. To this grant, Matilda his wife, Geoffry Chaplain of Coker, Robert Parson of Coker, Geoffry de Hardinton his uncle, William de Cocre, Richard his son, Geoffry son of Richard his nephew, and Hamond de Cocre were witnesses, and it was confirmed by Robert de Mandeville (III), and afterwards by his son Geoffry (IV), and also by Gerald, son of Geoffry de Coker, the donor.[140]

By another charter, dated at West Coker A.D. 1280, Isabel, daughter and heir of Gerald de Coker, in her widowhood, for the health of her soul and the souls of John de Chalke, her late husband, and those of her father and mother, Gerald and Alice, gave to the priory a perpetual rent of 2s., issuing out of a messuage adjoining the land of La Forde, from which the priory had the foregoing rent of 3s. Thomas de Coker and Helyas de Coker were witnesses to this charter, and as Isabel is said to be her father's heir, we may conclude that the male line of Gerald de Coker (the first of that name) had failed.[141] In 28 Edw. I, Thomas de Coker had license to give a rent of 10s. out of his lands at East Chinnock to the Priory of Montacute, the jury finding that he would still have 100s. worth of land yearly in East Coker and East Chinnock.[142]

35 Ed. I, by agreement made at East Coker, Thomas de Coker agreed to give to John, son of William de Coker, an acre of land in Allethemede, in exchange for an acre of land in Redelonde, both in the manor of East Coker. To this agreement William le Ju, Roger de la Buretone, Joh. Elys, Joh. de Angulo, and Matt. Bubbe are witnesses.[143] By another deed, dated at East Coker, 10 Edw. II, he released to John de Coker, his son, all his right in a messuage, lands, and rents in the manor of East Coker, and also in a croft

---

[189] Mont. Cart.

[140] Mont. Cart.

[141] Mont. Cart.

[142] Inq. ad. q. d., 28 Edw. I, no. 137.

[143] Harl. Charters, Br. Mus., 48, f. 52.

called East Croft. The witnesses are John de Bingham, John Musket, Wm. Burel, Joh. Pen, Joh. de Angulo, Wm. Pylard, John de Clyftone ; John Musket and John de Clyftone affixing their seals also.[144]

In the year following, 11 Edw. II, a fine was levied between Thos. de Coker and John de Coker and Margaret his wife, plts., and John Musket, deft., whereby 12 messuages, 82 acres of arable, 14½ of meadow, six acres of alder, and 1d. rent in East Coker were settled on Thomas for life, remainder to John and Margaret and the their issue, remainder to the right heirs of John.[145] According to the manor survey, 14 Edw. II, John de Coker held one carucate by knight service, subject to a rent of 20s. 7d. and suit at the Hundred Court, two pounds of wax yearly, and a heriot ; and in 16 Edw. III there was a grant of lands in East Coker by John de Coker to Joanna, daughter of Walter de Hewston, and Thomas, son and heir of John, probably a settlement on the marriage of said Thomas and Joanna.[146] 24 Edw. III (1450), Robert Coker is a witness, with John de Salisbury and John Elys, to a lease of lands in the manor of East Coker by Adam, son of Richard Attemere, of West Coker, to John le Doo, of West Coker, and Joan, his wife, for their lives.[147]

10 Rich. II, a fine was levied between John Manyngford, John Fitelton, and John Tracy, plts., and Robert Coker and Johanna his wife, defts., of 8 messuages, 1 ferling, 160 acres of arable, 8½ acres of meadow, and 15 acres of pasture in West Coker and Hardington Mandevyle, which were limited to the said Robert Coker and Johanna his wife for their lives, with remainder to " John, son of Robert Coker and Katherine his wife," and his heirs.[148]

In 1346 license was granted to Richard de Coker to give 19a. arable, and 6½ meadow in Charlton Adam and Charlton Mackrell to the Priory of Bruton, there remains to Richard, 100 acres of land and rent at " la Brigge," held of Ralph de Albini by homage and fealty.[149] This is no doubt the benefaction alluded to by Hutchins in his account of the Coker family.[150] There was also Robert de Coker, 1st Edw. III, who was Canon and Cellarer of Bruton Priory, and afterwards promoted to the office of Prior, which he held until his death, 35 Ed. III, or shortly after.[151]

---

[144] Ib., f. 53. [145] Somt. Fines, 11 Edw. II, no. 100.
[146] Harl. Ch., 48, f. 54. [147] Addl. MSS., Br. Mus., 25, 886.
[148] Som. Fines, 10 Rich. II, no. 73.
[149] Inq. ad. q. d., 19 Edw. III, pt. 2, p. 66.
[150] Hist. Dors. vol. iii, p. 722.
[151] Bruton Cart.

It appears that in or before the reign of Hen. IV the de Cokers dropped the prefix " de," for at a court held for the manor of East Coker, 16 Richard II, Robert Coker was presented as a freeholder, owing homage and suit of court for lands in North Coker ; John Coker, of Stouford, for Cokersham ; and Nicholas Coker, for lands in East Coker. At the Michaelmas Court in the following year the death of Robert Coker was presented, and John Coker, his son, admitted in his stead. Nicholas Coker and Alice his wife were at that time the owners of the manor of Chilthorne Domer, but 8 Hen. V they sold it to Simon Sydenham. After that there is no further mention of the family in the annals of East Coker.

The advowsons of the churches of East Coker, West Coker, and Hardington were appendant to those manors until 33 Edw. I, when John de Mandeville (II) sold them for £100 to Robert de Tothale, Prior of the priory of Minchin Buckland, Somerset.[152] Probably Tothale was only a trustee, as 4 Edw. II he conveyed the advowsons of both Cokers to Hugh de Courtenay, 2nd Earl of Devon.[153] The church of Hardington was not included, but 12 Edw. II it was, with the King's license,[154] also conveyed by de Tothale to the Earl, and it has been held by the owners of East Coker down to a very recent period.

The earlier title to the advowson of Hardington is involved in much obscurity. In the reign of Henry I Bernard de Newmarch bestowed it on a Priory he had founded at Brecknock, in Wales.[155] But not long after Geoffry de Mandeville, by charter,[156] gave it to the Abbey of Quarr, in the Isle of Wight, founded by Baldwin, Earl of Devon, A.D. 1132. As might be expected, a dispute as to the ownership soon arose between the two claimants, but a compromise was effected by which the advowson was ceded to the Abbey. This arrangement was confirmed by Robert, Bishop of Bath,[157] who occupied that see from A.D. 1135 to 1165. But then it appears [158] that Simon, son of Hugh de Mandeville, had given the church of Hardington to the Abbey of Quarr; and Richard, Earl of Exeter, son of Earl Baldwin, who died A.D. 1162, confirmed the gift by his charter. Hugh and Simon are new names in the de Mandeville

---

[152] Somt. Fines, 33 Edw. I, no. 142, Som. Arch. Soc. Proc., vol. x.

[153] Helyar MSS. and Lord Devon's Muniments, 9th Hist. Com. Rep., p. 405.

[154] Inq. ad. q. d., 12 Edw. II, no. 112.

[155] Dugd. Mon. I, 305.

[156] Madox Form. Angl., no. 434.

[157] Madox Form. Angl., no. 72.

[158] Dugd. Mon. ub. sup.

pedigree, and the connection between them and the donor Geoffry has not been ascertained; but this charter increases the probability that the family of de Redvers were the Over-lords of the whole hundred of Coker, of which Hardington formed a part.

The patronage of the rectory of East Coker was retained by the Courtenays until late in the reign of Edward III, and from the extent of the glebe it must have been a valuable piece of preferment. In the Nona Roll, 14 Edward III,[159] it is rated as follows :—" William Rogh, John de Salesbury, John Williams, John de Nevyle, William in la Hurne, and John Wygod, parishioners of East Coker, say on oath that the ninth of the corn, wool, and lamb is worth only 106 8d., and so is not payable, because the rector is endowed with 80 acres of land in demesne worth 60s. a year, and also with rents, mortuaries, tithes of hay, oblations, obventions, and small tithes worth £7 13s. 4d. a year."

Hugh, 2nd Earl of Devon, not long before his death* (which occurred A.D. 1377), contemplating probably the burial of himself and the Lady Margaret his wife in the Cathedral Church of Exeter, procured the appropriation of this rectory, with that of Honiton, to the Dean and Chapter as an endowment of a chantry for the good of the souls of himself and his family. For this purpose he conveyed both churches to his son Sir Philip Courtenay and others, upon trust to carry out his intentions, and they, after the Earl's death, with license from the Crown, 1st Rich. II,[160] granted these rectories to the dean and chapter. The chantry was known as the Courtenay chantry, and the divine services were performed at the founder's tomb, which stood originally in the nave of the cathedral, the effigies of himself and his wife lying on it. Although the foundation took place before the statute of 15 Richd. II, which required that on an appropriation a proper provision should be made by the Bishop for the endowment of a vicar who had the cure of souls in the parish, the Bishop of Bath and Wells took care that it was done in this case, and what was technically termed " the ordination of the vicarage of East Coker " was made by the Bishop under his episcopal seal, 24th June, 1385 (8 Ric. II).

It first sets out the foundation of the Courtenay chantry for four priests, who were to offer, at the tomb of the founder, daily masses

* The Earl must have been a very devout man, according to the light vouch-safed to him, as, two years after, he founded another chantry, richly endowed with lands, at Colcombe, near Colyton, Devon, where he resided.

[159] Excheq. Lay Subsidies, 169—14.
[160] Pat. Roll, 1st Rich. II, part 3, M 35.

for his soul and for the good state of Margaret his relict (who
proposed to be there buried), and for the souls of their parents, and
of William, Archbishop of Canterbury, and of Philip and Peter de
Courtenay, and that for the support of the chantry the churches of
East Coker and Honiton were appropriated to the Dean and Chapter,
subject to the payment of £6 a year to each of the four priests, and
subject also to an adequate provision to the perpetual vicar of East
Coker.

The Bishop then directed that the vicar should have for his residence the hall of the rector, the chambers adjoining, the kitchen, the
brewery, and all other buildings within the hall, together with the
gardens and dovehouse; the profit arising from the herbage and
trees in the churchyard, two acres of the better kind of meadow, and
the alderbed of the rector's demesnes, panage for hogs in the lord's
wood, sufficient firewood and a trunk of a tree at Christmas from the
wood, as the rectors had been accustomed to have. He was also
to have all the small tithes and oblations, and an annual pension of
60s. from the Dean and Chapter at Easter. In return for this
endowment the vicar was subjected to the very unusual burthen of
maintaining the chancel in repair, and if need be of new building it,
and he was to pay all tenths and subsidies to the Pope and King,
procurations, paschal rent, and Martin's gift, and 2s. to the Chantry
of the Blessed Mary in the said church; to find wax lights for
processions, and pay a pension of 40d. to the Bishop of Bath and
Wells, and another of 13s. 4d. to the Dean and Chapter of Wells,
and to discharge all other burthens which would appertain to
the rector if the church were not appropriated; with this additional
one, that whenever the Canons of Exeter should come on business
to East Coker, they should be lodged at the vicar's house, and be
provided by the vicar during their stay with fuel from the alderbed,
but nothing else.[161]

On the dissolution of Chantries, 1 Edward VI, this chantry came
to the Crown, but by letters patent, 5th June, 27th Elizabeth, the
rectory appropriate of East Coker and the advowson of the vicarage
were granted to the Dean and Chapter of Exeter, and they still hold
the rectorial tithe rent-charge, but they sold the glebe some years
ago to the late George Bullock, Esq. It is this impropriate rectory,
with the lands belonging to it, which Collinson erroneously calls the
Manor of North Coker, belonging to the Bishop of Exeter;[162] but
there never was a manor of North Coker, it being part and parcel

---

161 Liber Albus of Dean and Chapter of Wells i, fo. 287; iii, fo. 137.

162 Coll. Somt. ii, p. 345.

Old Vicarage, East Coker.

of the manor of East Coker. The rectory was leased out by the Dean and Chapter apparently to the de Courtenays, and a quasi court was held for it, called "East Coker Personatus," with a tythingman and a bailiff or proctor, who collected the tithes, rents, and mortuaries, and paid the pension to the vicar and other out-goings. Afterwards, in or before the reign of James I, it was called the manor of Roddon, or Rotton Row, and was known by that name in modern times.

In 1624 (21 James I) we have a second description of the vicar's residence. The Dean and Chapter and William Ford, the vicar, fell out respecting a piece of land adjoining the vicarage, which the former claimed as part of the rectory, and in a law suit that followed a plan of the vicarage was produced and verified by a witness who deposed that the house consisted of " a hall with a little porch on the north side, a parlour, a kitchen, two chambers over the kitchen and parlour, three under rooms at the west end of the hall, with two chambers over, one other little room adjoining on the south side, which was a pigeon house, one stable, &c." This description agrees substantially with that in the ordination; and, in fact, the venerable vicarage stood untouched until it was taken down about 40 or 50 years ago, to make room for the present house, the exterior of which is in striking contrast to its predecessor. The old house was singularly picturesque, within and without. The writer knew it well, and can vouch for the fact that the description of 1624 was a correct one in 1824, so that we had here a most remarkable example of a mediæval parsonage, occupied without structural alteration from the reign of Edward III until that of William IV—a period of nearly 500 years.

The house was entered from a porch, and on the right, separated from the passage by a stout oak partition, was a spacious hall in which were two lofty pointed windows with trefoiled heads, closely resembling those in the old mansion we shall notice at North Coker. It was a lofty room, of one story only, showing no doubt originally the timbered roof, but desecrated by a ceiling in modern times,—the result, it may be, of evil example at the hall of the 'Squire. Beyond the hall and approached by a separate staircase were two chambers, one of which had the appearance of an oratory ; on the other side the passage was the living room, with a massive mullioned bay window towards the east (apparently an addition), and a square-headed Edwardian window on each side of the fireplace, which stood in the east wall. The heads of these windows contained fragments of painted glass, one of which was a crowned monogram of the Virgin in a rich golden colour. At the back of this room was a turret stone staircase leading to the bed-chambers, the principal one being over the sitting-room, with side windows of the same style as those below. Altogether it was a gem, the loss of which is much to be deplored.

There were at least two chantries in the church of East Coker. The earliest was that of the Virgin Mary. The date of its foundation has not been discovered, but the founder was probably Geoffry de Mandeville (IV). In an ancient minute of grants by the Mandevilles amongst the Helyar MSS. there is an entry, under the date 4 Edw. I, "Galfridus de Mandeville concessit, &c., Willo Tankard et successoribus suis Deo et Be Marie ecclesie de Est Coker . . . . &c., domum quandam Walteri Godwin, &c., cum diversis pcell terr, &c.," but the date cannot refer to the foundation, as Geoffry died 49 Hen. III.

In the Manor Survey, 14 Edw. II, the advowson of the church, with the glebe, worth 6d. per annum, is said to belong to the lord, as well as the advowson of the " Chantry of the Blessed Mary, from which the lord received no profit, but furnished bread and wine or 12d., also wax for torches at the altar, and a waggon-load of wood for the chaplain at Christmas ; and an acre called Shortenacre belonged to the chantry, as appeared by its charter." There is a discrepancy between the survey and the minute, as according to the former the chantry was endowed with a house and several parcels of land, and not one acre merely. The patronage of this chantry continued in the lord of the manor. 17 Edw. III, William le Couper, priest, was admitted chaplain by the Bishop, on the presentation of Hugh de Courtenay, Earl of Devon, and there are several subsequent presentations in the Bishop's registers, the last being the admission of John Wytte in 1453 (31 Henry VI), on the presentation of William Courtenay, after which we hear no more of it. Probably it had been suppressed long before the Statute of Edw. VI, or may have been blended with the chantry of the Holy Cross. But there is an important entry on the Court roll, 16 Ric. II, requiring John Strange (who was no doubt the chaplain) to show by what title he claimed one messuage and half a virgate of land, the endowment of the chantry of the Blessed Mary of East Coker, which Geoffry de Mandeville had granted to William Tancard, chaplain, and his successors, together with the rent of assize of 15s., payable by Walter and Richard le Yarde and their heirs, out of which Geoffry reserved 12d. and suit at the court of Marshwode, besides wards, reliefs, homage, and escheats. At another court, held 19 Hen. VI, presentment was made that William, chaplain of the chantry of the B.M., did not reside on it nor perform the divine offices incumbent on him, and, therefore, it was ordered that all the issues and profits should be taken into the lord's hands. This was no doubt a seizure for forfeiture, under the statute 13 Edw. I—" De Religiosis."

The other chantry was that of the Holy Cross, founded within the Church of St. Michael the Archangel at East Coker by Hugh de Courtenay, Earl of Devon, by license of the Crown,[163] and endowed with four messuages, 60 acres of land, and eight acres of meadow in East Coker, North Coker, and West Coker, for providing a chaplain to offer daily prayers for the souls of himself and Margaret his wife and their heirs, also of Emma Penny, Robert Penny of West Coker, and Joan his wife; also the father and mother of William de Middleton, late rector of East Coker, deceased, and Sewald his father, and Christiana his mother, and John de Hardington, John de Berewik, William de Middleton, late sacristan of Wymbourne Mynster, John Penny, and all faithful people deceased.*

---

* The particulars of the lands are given in one charter. They are described as a messuage with curtilage in North Coker between a tenement of Philip de Tytenhull and a tenement of Walter de Otterhampton. Thirteen acres and half of arable in the manor of Coker, whereof two acres lie in Langeland, between the land of the parson of East Coker and the Colecrofte, one acre and half at Grymesgore between the lands of John de Coker and John Hillard, five pieces lie at Radesborgh between the lands of William de Pechalle and John Clode, one acre lies in the furlong which streches (extendit se) into Foxmanslade next the land of Edithe Glide, and one acre in the same furlong between the lands of the said Edithe and of Christina Ebs, one acre lies at "la Holedich" between the lands of John de Salisburie and John de Nevyle, one acre lies in Wibbergh between the lands of Walter Rous and William Panyer, one acre lies in Brodesharde between the lands of William Pechalle and William Hoggs, one acre lies in Langburgh between the lands of John de Salisburie and William Bigum, two acres lie on the same furlong between the lands of William Gillet and the parson's, one acre lies at Stodeleghe, one acre of meadow lies at Kempthorne between Ingeston and the meadow of John de Salisburie, half-an-acre lies in Brofurlonge [Brode?] between the meadows of John Attware and Richard Buril, one acre lies in the same furlong, between the meadows of William Wayne and Editha Glide. And also all rents and services due from William Wayne and Johanna his wife, and from William Rogh for lands held by them for their lives, together with the reversion after their deaths, as appeared by a certain charter made to the said Earl by Robert Penny. And also three acres of meadow, which Sir William de Middleton, parson of the church of East Coker, had acquired by grant of William in the Hurne, Walter Row and Margaret his wife, and Sir Philip de Poyntyngton, parson of the church of Honyton, whereof one acre lies in Coker Mere, in the culture, which is called Boghholm Furlong, between the meadows of Walter de Montalt, and Wm. Wayne; another acre lies adjoining the meadow called Hamcroft, between the meadows of William in the Hurne and Richard

163 Inq. ad. q. d. 18 Edw. III, pt. 2, no. 38.

The charters and documents by which the foundation was legally effected are set out in the confirmation of them by Ralph de Salopia, Bishop of Bath and Wells, which is recorded in his Register, p. 310, but the exact date is omitted.

By the final charter the Earl grants the lands to Thos. de Malling (the chaplain) and his successors, reserving to himself and his heirs the right of presentation. It is dated " at our Manor of East Coker," Monday after the feast St. Margaret the Virgin, 18 Edw. III, and is tested by Thos. de Courtenai, Wm. de Chiverston (?), John de Chiverston (?), Henry de Welyngton, and John Lutene, Kts., Richard de Brankescombe, Robert de Rodeston, and others.

We hear of this chantry again at the manor court, 16 Ric. II, when the homage presented that before the statute " de religiosis " the lord of the manor had given land to the value of 42s. a year to the chantry of the Holy Cross for the performance of divine offices, and that John Cadby, the chaplain, had received the profits for a long time past, but for two years had neglected to perform such offices, and they prayed that the lord would take possession of the lands until the chaplain did his duty.

As far as can be ascertained now, the two chantries were blended together before the reign of Henry VIII, the Valor Ecc. made in 1535 mentioning one only, of which William Tanner (rector of Sutton Bingham) was the chaplain. Tanner died in 1541, and was succeeded by Wm. Slade,[164] who was the last chaplain.

At the dissolution of chantries, 1 Edw. VI, the lands belonging to it consisted, according to the survey of chantries, 2 Edw. VI, of several messuages and more than 108 acres of land, and 3 Edw. VI the capital manse of the chantry and about 36 acres of land were granted to Giles Kelway and William Leonard ;[165] and 1 Philip and Mary about 67 acres more were sold to, or rather exchanged with, Edward Nevill, Esq.,[166] leaving about five acres unaccounted for.

Besides the chantries in the church there was at Burton, in North Coker, a chapel called " The Chapel of our Lady of Burton," of the foundation of which nothing is known, and which appears to have possessed only the piece of ground whereon it stood. It was

---

Buril, and the third acre lies between the meadows of Wm. le Jew on the west and the meadows of Walter de Montalt on the east. And also one messuage, with the curtilage adjoining, at " la Aissh," between the land of John Williams on the east and the land of Wm. Wayne on the west.

[164] Bishops Certif., 33 Henry VIII, Rec. Office.
[165] Particulars of Grant, 3 Edw. VI, sec. 3.
[166] Pat. Rolls i, P. and M., pt. 8, m. 12.

covered with lead and furnished with a bell weighing 40lbs., but as no plate or ornaments were found, Divine services had probably been discontinued, especially as there was no mention of a chaplain.[167] Both the chapel and land belonging to it were included in the grant to Nevill.

In 1624 Archdeacon Helyar, who had lately purchased the manor, called upon Mr. Ford, the vicar, to perform Divine service in the chapel. He refused to do so, and the Archdeacon appealed to the Bishop, and amongst the State papers now in the Public Record Office is the report made by him (William Piers) to the Archbishop of Canterbury of an inquiry he held at Wells, 16th December, 1634, in the presence of Dr. Goodwyn and Dr. Wood, Canons of Wells. It sets out that a controversy had arisen between Mr. Archdeacon Helyar, farmer or lessee of the Impropriation of East Coker, and Mr. Ford, vicar of the Church, about the Chapel of St. Mary the Virgin, in that parish, the question being whether the Vicar was bound to celebrate divine service in the chapel. The proctor, for the Archdeacon—who, being old and infirm, did not personally appear— alleged two reasons against the Vicar—(1) that an arbitrament was in 1419 made by four divines, arbitrators between the Dean and Chapter of Exeter and the Vicar of East Coker, and confirmed by the Bishop of Bath and Wells, the Dean and Chapter of Wells, and the Prior and Convent of Bath, under their respective seals, wherein are these words : " Vicarius de East Coker at successores sui divina servitia celebrant in capella beate Marie Virginis in parochia predicta ; and (2) that three vicars before Ford,—viz., Buckland, Tucker, and Gold (and before Gold no man living could remember)—read prayers in the chapel on Saturday in every week, and upon no other day.

Ford admitted the alleged agreement, but appealed to a composition made in 1385, between the Dean and Chapter of Exeter and the vicar of East Coker, in which there is no mention of the vicar's reading prayers in the chapel, which composition is recited verbatim in the agreement. 2. He answered that the agreement bound only the then vicar upon forfeiture of 100 marks if he stood not to the award, and that some of the arbitrators were Canons of Exeter, and so parties. 3. He proved by ancient deeds that it was a free chapel, and had a peculiar chaplain, 8 Edw. III, and was endowed with land, 20 and 23 Edw. II, and 13 R. II. 4. He alleged that the chapel came to the Crown with the land thereto belonging, by the statute of Chantries, 1 Ed. VI, and was sold by the Crown, 1 Phil. and Mary, to one Neville, but the conveyance was questioned, 10 James, and

---

[167] Charity Certif., Som., no. 42, 1 Ed. VI.

then one Pitt and Floyd bought the chapel with the land belonging to it, inter alia, as concealed lands, and sold it again to Walter Grove, deceased, who left it to his son Robert Grove, then living, who had told Ford that he would turn it into a school or a hospital. Lastly, he answered that he had been vicar 16 years, and was never called on to read prayer in the chapel till Helyar came to East Coker, which was seven or eight years since. The report further states that the chapel is distant from the Church a quarter mile, and that Helyar's house is not near the chapel but close to the church ; that the Dean and Chapter of Exeter did not meddle in the business, but only Helyar, as an inhabitant of East Coker, and not as Canon of Exeter; that the chapel had been profaned divers ways, as by wedding dinners, and dancing at those weddings, and by lighting of hemp and other commodities there, and had of late been defiled by vagrants and by cattle, but was repaired about seven years since by the profit made by a church rate, and £40 had been bestowed in making seats and beautifying the chapel. The Bishop leaves the determination to the Archbishop.† What the legal decision was (if any) we have not ascertained, but the vicar seems to have taken the law and the chapel into his own hands, and having acquired the chapel from Grove, by his will he bequeathed it as " The Chapel at North Coker and the rod of ground whereon it stands to the use of the poor in the parish of East Coker, to be disposed of by the vicar who shall be in those days and by consent of the churchwardens." The vicar died in 1663, and the building from that time was used as a parish poor-house, and was standing in 1784, when having become ruinous it was, by order of the Vestry, taken down, and the materials used in the erection of a workhouse. But the parishioners were disturbed by rumours that they had irreverently and illegally meddled with holy ground, and therefore in 1788 they prayed the Bishop to sanction what had been done, and he granted a faculty, the only effect of which was to quiet their consciences, as if there had been any desecration the faculty could not condone it.

The Church of East Coker stands close to the manor house, on the northern slope of the hill which overshadows the village below, and, as might be expected from its elevated position, is dedicated to St. Michael.

Whenever a church is found, as this is, contiguous to the manor house, it may be taken for granted that the lord of the manor was the founder ; and—if in a rural district, remote from the mother

---

† This report is taken from the MSS. of the Rt. Honble. Henry Hobhouse, sometime keeper of Her Majesty's State Papers.

church,—the probability is that originally it was only an oratory or domestic chapel, built by the lord for the use of himself and his immediate dependants. In process of time, when the tenants and inhabitants of the manor increased, it would become a parochial church; endowed with rights of baptism and burial, which relieved those who resorted to it from their dependance on their mother church, and gave "the cure of souls" to the chaplain or priest appointed by the lord with the sanction of the bishop. It is not unreasonable to suppose that this, or something like it, was the case at Coker.

The church presents no features of peculiar architectural interest, and consists of a nave, chancel, north and south aisles, and transepts in the Perpendicular style. Remains of an earlier building are to be seen in the southern arcade, the piers of which are circular columns of the Decorated period, if not before, and the western corbelled respond terminates in a pendant of the same character. A fragment of Decorated work appears also in the exterior of the east wall of the chancel, the plinth moulding being enriched with the four-leaved flower. Probably this at one time formed the sill of the window, with similar ornaments in the jambs.

The aisles open, through arches panelled with Perpendicular tracery, into what are called transepts, as they project beyond the aisle walls, but it is questionable whether they did so originally, and if not, the church could hardly have been cruciform in the proper acceptation of that term, although Collinson speaks of it as "a high handsome structure in the form of a cross, with a tower in the centre." The tower was supported by four arches, and the two western piers are said to remain in situ, cased over with the new work which now forms the square pilasters of the modern semi-circular arches of the transepts.

About the year 1791 the old tower was taken down, and the present one built. It was designed by a Yeovil marble mason, and is a respectable example of the so-called Gothic of that period. The present chancel arch and the doorway leading into the tower are still more modern.

With regard to the transepts, it is questionable whether they were originally anything more than chapels at the east end of the aisles. It is certain from the church books that the north transept was re-built in 1793 without any projection beyond the aisle wall, that being quite a modern enlargement; and as regards the south side, it is very possible that at some early period of the Helyar ownership the head of the house added just enough to the chapel to allow a doorway to

be made direct from his grounds into it, and shifted the window out
to its present position. Over the door is a small window, now blocked
up, which cannot have been original work, and it is hardly credible
that an architect would not have continued the parapet round the
transept uniform with that of the aisle.

There are no ancient monuments in the church, with one exception.
Collinson says, "In the chancel by the side of the north wall is the
mutilated effigy in stone of a female of the Courtenay family, many
of them having been interred within this church." It was removed
when the chancel was newly paved, and it now rests on a slab at the
western end of the nave. The figure is evidently that of a lady of
quality, but little beyond its general form can be distinguished. The
drapery is long and flowing, the waist girdled by a narrow band
fastened with a buckle in front—a similar one confining another band
attached to the right shoulder. The head-dress fits close, ornamented with a small beading at the edge and bound round by a whimple.
The right arm hangs down close to the side, but the left is laid
across the breast, and holds something up in the bend of the elbow. The
feet are gone, but on the left side of the base is what may perhaps be
the noduled end of a staff. From the general character of the figure
and dress it may be conjectured that it is 14th century work, but any
attempt to identify it is futile. Collinson's statement that it represents
a Courtenay can rest on no better foundation than village tradition,
on which no reliance can be placed without something to back it up.
Of course it *may* be a Courtenay, but there is in fact no evidence
that any of that family were ever buried at Coker; indeed the
evidence is quite the other way. We know that after they succeeded
to Coker the Courtenays resided at their castle, either of Cowick or
Powderham, and that their remains, if not resting at either of these
places, were entombed at the Cathedral of Exeter or at Ford Abbey,
which they founded.

A confident expert some time ago laid it down with authority that
the effigy was that of Elizabeth Courtenay (the widow of Hugh
Courtenay, jun.), who died 49 Edward III, on the ground that she
held Coker in dower, but as her husband was buried at Ford
Abbey,[168] it is to be presumed that she was buried there also,
especially as there was no issue of the marriage to continue the connection with Coker.

Besides this effigy, there was in Collinson's time "a very ancient tomb
in a niche of the wall of the northaisle, but without any memorial,
and on the east wall of the same aisle a benetoire" [benitiere].

[168] Beltz History of Order of Garter, p. 53.

This tomb could hardly have been in the wall of the north aisle properly so called, for in that case it would be there now, as no alteration is believed to have been made in that part of the church ; it probably therefore stood in the north wall of the north transept, and was carelessly destroyed when the transept was rebuilt. The so-called benitiere was no doubt a piscina, belonging, we may conclude, to the altar of the Chantry of the Virgin—the east end of an aisle being a very usual position for a chantry altar. Perhaps the tomb was intended for the founder, de Mandeville, and as no effigy is mentioned, the monument may have been only a simple tomb, which would correspond with the supposed de Mandeville tomb in the church of Whitchurch Canonicorum.

In the vestry there is another mutilated effigy, which was found in the churchyard when it was levelled a few years ago. It is hazardous to say whether it is intended for a female figure or an ecclesiastic. There was also found buried in the churchyard a massive coffin cover or slab of Ham Hill stone, exhibiting a full-length incised figure, loosely draped and with the hands uplifted, but here again there is nothing to assist in identification.

The burden of maintaining the chancel being by the endowment laid on the poor vicar, it is not to be wondered at that nothing was done beyond what was absolutely necessary. From the evidence of Wm. Daniell, of East Coker, one of the witnesses in an Exchequer suit in the reign of James I, we learn that about 30 years before, Mr. Gould, the vicar, had blocked up with stones and mortar a window on the south side of the chancel, $9\frac{1}{2}$ft. high and $4\frac{1}{2}$ft. wide, and part of another in the same manner ; that the pavement was then much out of repair, in some parts gone, leaving only the bare earth, and that the chancel door was quite in decay. Nearly a century after something was done, for there is a tablet in the south wall, dated in 1711, recording that the north and south walls had been re-built and the roof renewed, at the expense of the vicar, Mr. Richard Short. As he died in 1703, we presume that his estate was saddled with the cost as dilapidations. It remained pretty much in the same state down to a recent period, excepting that the east window was blocked up with a plaster altar-piece in the Italian fashion of the day, but it was removed about the year 1857, and a new east window, with Perpendicular tracery, introduced.

The display of heraldry in East Coker must at one time have been considerable. The earliest notice of it occurs in Br. Mus. Harl. MS. 1559, which is a composite copy by R. Mundy (who was connected with the College of Arms in the reign of Chas. I) of the

Somersetshire visitations of 1573 and 1591, page 235 of which is headed, " Notes Taken in the Visitation of Somerset, 1591, in East Coker."

Then follow tricks of four shields.

1.—Party per pale, quarterly within a bordure (but no bearings) impaling quarterly (1) a bend and in chief two mullets, (2) a fesse between six birds with a mullet for a difference ; (3 and 4) blank.

2.—" John Arundell and Catherine, his wyf," six swallows (Arundel) imp. an inescutcheon with an orle of martlets (Chydiok).

3 and 4.—" James, Earle of Ormond, and Amye, his wife, in Est Coker Church, knelling." Two shields—(a) Az. a chief indented, or, (b) or a chevron gu. within a bordure engr. sab.

Only Nos. 3 and 4 are said to be in the church, and it may be inferred that they were kneeling effigies in stone, surmounted by the two shields of arms. Probably Nos. 1 and 2 were in the church also, as all four undoubtedly relate more or less to the same family. None of them are mentioned by Collinson, so that they were destroyed between 1591 and 1791, perhaps in the civil wars.

Taking Nos. 3 and 4 first—they are the arms of James, Earl of Wilts and Ormond, and Avice, his first wife. He was Sir James Butler, Kt., son of Thomas, Earl of Ormond, and was born in 1420. In 1449 he was created Earl of Wiltshire, and succeeded his father as 5th Earl of Ormond in 1452. In the wars of the Roses he sided with Henry VI, and had the misfortune to be taken prisoner at the battle of Towton, March 29th, 1461. What his fate was is uncertain. According to one account he was beheaded on the spot ; to another he was captured by Richard Salkeld and executed at Newcastle; and a third says that Thomas de Courtenay,Earl of Devon, was beheaded with him, but a fourth mentions Courtenay's execution at York or at Pontefract immediately after the battle, but says nothing of the Earl of Wilts. In Gregory's Historical Collections[169] it is said :—" And the Erle of Wylteschyre was take and brought unto New Castell to the Kynge. And there his hedde was smete of and send unto London to be sette upon London Brygge. And Doctor Morton the Prynces Chanceler, was take with him and put in the Toure, but he schapyd a way longe tyme aftyr, and ys by yond the see with the Quene." Looking at these conflicting versions, it may be, as a recent writer has suggested,[170] that the Earl escaped from his captors and fled to a hiding place in the south, but why he should select Coker is a mystery.

---

[169] Cam. Soc. N.S., no. 18, p. 21.

[170] Genealogist N.S., vol. 1, p. 74.

His first wife, to whom he was married about 1438,[171] was a great heiress—Avice Stafford, daughter of Sir Richard Stafford, of Hooke, and Maude, his wife (née Lovel). Avice died in 1456, and the Earl married secondly Alianor, daughter of Edmund Beaufort, Duke of Somerset, and Alianor his wife, daughter of Richard Beauchamp, Earl of Warwick. By neither of these ladies had he any issue.

The arms of the Duke—France and England quarterly within a bordure company—were, no doubt, intended to be tricked in No. 1, but the 2nd quarter of the impaled arms is the coat of Beauchamp of Bletsoe, and the 1st quarter looks very much like the arms of the St. John family. Margaret, a daughter and heiress of the Bletshoe house, was married first to Sir Oliver St. John, and secondly to John Beaufort, 3rd Earl and 1st Duke of Somerset, father of Edmund. They were both buried in Wimborne Minster, and in some of the windows of that church the arms of Beaufort and Beauchamp of Bletshoe appear.[172]

The only connection that has been traced between the Earl of Wilts and this part of the county was with Clifton Maubank—about four miles from East Coker, then the seat of the Horsey family. There is no recorded relationship between the two families, but for some reason, now unknown, Henry Horsey, the owner of Clifton, in the reign of Henry VI, was induced, in certain events, to settle it on the Earl. By a deed, dated 18 February, 33 Hen. VI,[173] after reciting that he (Henry Horsey) had enfeoffed certain feoffees of the Manors of Horsey and Charleton Makerell, Somerset, and the manor of Clyfton Maubank, with the advowson of the church or free chapel, upon trust to perform his will, he declared his will to be that his feoffees should convey all his said manors to James, Earl of Wilts, and one other person to be nominated by the said Earl, in fee simple (except an estate in the Manor of Horsey reserved to himself and the heirs of his body), but subject to forfeiture on alienation, in which event all the said manors were to devolve " to the use of the said Earl and his heirs for evermore." Henry Horsey died, s.p., 1st Edw. IV, which regnal year began March, 1460-1. The battle of Towton was fought 29 March, 1461.

Now Leland says, " Ormond Earl of Wiltshire, about King Edwarde the 4 tyme, invaded Clifton and possessyd it by violence withe a pretencyd title and began a greate foundation there for

---

[171] Top. and Gen. ii., 333.

[172] Hutch. Dors. iii., 212.

[173] Close Rolls, 33 Hen. VI, m. 10.

stables and howsys of office, and entendyd to have buyldyd a castle there ; but shortly after Clifton was restoryd to Horsey." [174] The foundation of his claim no doubt was, that Henry Horsey had made some alienation causing a forfeiture of the settled estates and the " invasion " (presuming the Earl was executed after the battle of Towton) must have occurred some time between 33 Hen. VI (1454) and 1 Edw. IV (29th March 1461) ; it may have been after his wife's death, 35 Hen. VI, by which event he lost all her large estates. But looking at the date of Henry Horsey's death and supposing, as is not unreasonable, that the Earl did not press his claim until after that event, the probability for believing that he escaped after the battle is materially increased.

No. 2. Arundel impaling Chydiok refers to Sir John Arundel, Kt., of Lanherne, who married Katherine, daughter and co-heiress of Sir John Chydiok, Kt., and widow of Wm. Stafford, of Hooke, by whom she had Humphry Stafford, who was in 1469, after the attainder of Wm. Courtenay, Earl of Exeter, created Earl of Devon, and beheaded at Bridgwater the same year. A sister of this Humphry was married to Sir Walter Courtenay, second son of Sir Hugh of Boconnoc, but he does not appear to have had any interest in Coker. Wm. Stafford was a brother of Richard Stafford, the father of the Countess of Wilts.

In Collinson's time there were several coats of arms in the east window of the chancel, which he describes as (1) Arg. on a bezant a cross Tau or ; (2) Arg. a cross gu. ; (3) Arg. a saltier or ; (4) Arg. three escallops or—but to what families they belonged it is impossible now to say. No. 4 may be Malet. He mentions also two ancient coats in the north transept—(1) A chevron between three garbs or, and (2) or three torteaux in pile, surmounted by a label of three points az., each charged with as many bezants [annulets]. (Courtenay differenced.) Not a vestige of these coats remains, and may be that those in the east window were all removed—probably purloined when it was plastered up in order to receive the Italian altar-piece— and that those in the transept were lost or destroyed when it was taken down and rebuilt.

In the traceried head of the south transept window six coats are preserved. Collinson describes them, but so inaccurately that it throws considerable doubt on the correctness of his blazon of the arms in the other windows.

---

[174] Lel. Itin. vi., fo. 21.

They have been also described in another publication[175] as follows :—

I. Quarterly 1 and 4. Or Three Torteaux 2 and 1 (Courtenay).
2 and 3 or, a lion rampant az. (Redvers).

II. Az. a cross flory arg. between four mullets pierced or (Helyar).
impaling arg. on a bend sab., three roses of the first (Cary).

III. Gules a sword and key in saltire arg. and or (intended for See of Exeter).
N.B.—Peter Courtenay, Bishop of Exeter, and afterwards of Winchester, ob. 1492. The arms of the See of Exeter are gules a sword in pale two keys in saltire or. Those of the See of Winchester are a sword and two keys, but differently disposed.

IV. Repetition of No. II.

V. Quarterly 1 and 4 sab., six sea swallows 3 2 and 1 (Arundel).
2 and 3 az. a bend or (Carminow).

VI. Quarterly 1 and 4 arg. three greyhounds statant sab.
2 and 3 a saltire gu. within a bordure bezantee (De la Pole).

Nos. II and IV are enamelled glass, and Jacobean in style. They must have been introduced by Archdeacon Helyar or his son after his purchase of Coker in 1616. Both the father and son married a Cary.

The first and fourth quarters of No. VI are also enamelled, and of a later period than the other shields, and were apparently put in at the same time as Nos. II and IV. They may have been intended for the arms of Maleverer, but the Maleverer hounds were courant, not statant. Halnath Maleverer was sheriff of Devon,[176] and bore sab. three hounds courant in pale arg. His wife was Joan, daughter and a co-heir of Thomas Carminow, and widow of Thomas Carew ; and her sister, Margaret, was the wife of Hugh Courtenay, of Boconnoc.

The second and third quarters are earlier, and parts of the original window, but on close examination no bordure can be seen.

No. V (Arundel and Carminow quarterly) refers either to the son or grandson of Sir John de Arundel, of Lanherne, and Elizabeth his wife, daughter and co-heiress of Sir Oliver Carminow. The grandson, Sir John Arundel, was found to be heir of his grandmother, 19 Ric. II. It was his grandson and heir, Sir John Arundel (third of that name), who married Catherine, daughter and co-heiress of Sir John Chidyok, and widow of William Stafford, whose arms are in shield No. 2 in the Harl. MS. already noticed.

175 Herald and Genealogist ii, 341.

176 2 Ric. III.

None of the arms in these windows are mentioned in the MS. notes of the visitation of 1591 ; but they must have been there at that time, with the exception of the Jacobean coats, and it is therefore strange they were not copied by the herald who examined the church. Coupling this with the difficulty of accounting for the introduction of any memorial of the Earl of Wilts and his wives in East Coker Church, it is questionable whether by some misarrangement of the herald's notes, or some error of R. Mundy in copying them, East Coker was not written in mistake for some other place.

From the Church we proceed to the Manor House, in modern times styled " Coker Court." It is a quadrangular pile, surrounding an inner court, on the south and west sides of which are the offices, with a base court beyond. No part of it can be ascribed to the de Mandevilles, whose lordship ended early in the reign of Edward I, except possibly some massive masonry and pointed arches standing near the kitchen. With that exception, the house has at different times been so altered and remodelled that no remains of the original building can be recognized, and the main part of the old fabric as it appears now was the work of the Courtenays about the reign of Henry VI. The principal entrance is on the north side, through a porch leading into the usual passage separating the hall from the butteries, the arched openings to which are still discernible on the face of the wall. Passing through an arcaded screen on the east side of this passage we enter the hall, which in its original state must have been a noble apartment. It is lighted on the north side by three lofty two-light Perpendicular windows, with trefoiled heads and transoms, and flanked in the exterior with buttresses of the same style. Similar windows, it may be observed, are to be seen in the Courtenay Manor House at West Coker and in the Hymerford mansion at North Coker. The oriel, if ever there was one, must have stood at the north end of the dais, but both oriel and dais had to give way for modern improvements. In the south wall traces of a Perpendicular window were discovered a few years ago, the loss of which is to be regretted, as the sunbeams through it must have added much to the cheerfulness and comfort of the interior. Before the last century the hall was open to the roof, which, from recent examination, appears to have been of simple design without hammer beams or other artistic enrichments usually found in mediæval roofs. The minstrels' gallery and the arcade which supports it, as well as the fire-place, are Jacobean. Whether they were the work of the Archdeacon we cannot say, but we may fairly look on him as the moralist

COKER COURT.

who adorned the gallery front with three shields (now unfortunately gone) bearing the arms of (1) Courtenay; (2) Helyar; (3) Phelips; and underneath these mottoes—Olim-Nunc-Nuper. Perhaps the Archdeacon had been reading Camden's "Remains," who quotes " an old verse which a right worshipful friend of mine not long ago writ upon his new house :—Nunc mea—Mox hujus—Sed Postea Nescio cujus."

About the year 1760, the eastern wing, which had a gabled front, was taken down, and the present handsome suite of rooms erected on its site, in the classical style, from designs of the celebrated architect, Sir William Chambers. The plan involved the necessity of destroying the dais of the hall, but the new building being on a higher level, the architect very skilfully compensated for the loss by constructing a spacious corridor, open to the hall, and reached by an ascent of three steps, with a column of noble proportions on either side. The north end of the corridor opens into a small room lighted by a Perpendicular window, but it is doubtful whether it is part of the Courtenay house. The architect evidently considered the style incongruous with the new wing, and therefore he unfortunately modernised it by introducing a flat ceiling, with a modillon cornice, which cuts off the open roof, and conceals the pointed heads of the windows, thereby destroying the mediæval character of the hall.

South of the house the ground rises rather abruptly to nearly 400 feet above the sea level. It is a breezy down-like slope, about 150 acres in extent, and called, according to modern fashion, The Park ; but in our youth it was content with the old English name of the Sheep's Sleight. Not that Coker was without a park, for one is mentioned in the Manor Survey of 14th Edw. II, but it was nearer Coker Wood, and no doubt an ancient park then. It was probably of much larger extent than the present enclosure, and included that part of the lord's demesne now called Darvhole, which is evidently a corruption of Deerfold, a term indicating a place where deer were harboured for sport or captured by " toils."

Below the house, by the entrance gates, stands a picturesque range of almshouses for 12 poor women, founded and well endowed by the Archdeacon not long after he purchased the Manor.

Before we leave Coker Court something more should be said respecting the Archdeacon himself. He was the son of William Helyar, a substantial landowner, residing on his estate called Lower Ernesettle, in the parish of St. Budeaux, near Plymouth, and was born there January 8, 1559. Nothing is known of his ancestors, and therefore it is a mere conjecture that he was of the same family as Richard Helyar, who in 1441 was Canon of Exeter, in the following year Archdeacon of Barnstaple, and in 1444 Archdeacon of Cornwall. He died in November 1446, and is buried under an inscribed ledger stone in the north choir aisle of Exeter Cathedral. It is to be presumed that our Archdeacon believed that he was related to his predecessor in office, as he laid the remains of his wife in a grave contiguous to that of Richard Helyar, with a memorial inscription on the stone over it.

William Helyar received his University education at Exeter College, Oxford, graduated as M.A. in 1587, and in the following year married Mary, daughter and heiress of William Cary, of Ladford, Shebbear, North Devon. In 1581 he became rector of Dunchideock, Devon, and in 1587, being chaplain to Wm. Blount Lord Mountjoy, he had license to hold with it the rectory of Cheriton, Devon. Subsequently he held other livings in the diocese of Exeter.

In 1602 he was appointed Canon of Exeter Cathedral, on the recommendation of Sir Walter Raleigh, whose letter to Sir Robert Cecil on his behalf is preserved amongst the Cecil papers at Hatfield House. It is as follows :—

To Sir Robert Cecil.

Sir,—I have written to Doctor Cæsar [afterwards Sir Julius Cæsar, Master of the Rolls] in the behalf of Mr. William Hilliard, a Master of Arts, and very learned, to move her Majestic for her letters to the Deane and Chapter of Exeter for his admittance to the next place that shall be void of a Prebend and Cannon therein.

I beseech your Honour to further him in his suite for the obteyning thereof. He will in dutifull service acknowledg your honorable favour, and I shal be bound for his sake to remember it to my power. And so I humbly take my leave. From Plymouth, the 26th of May, 1596.

Your Honors to do yow service,

W. RALEGH.

[Postscript.] Sir,—I beseiche yow for my sake because it standeth miche on my creditt to favor the sute, and I shall evermore acknowledge it in the highest digre. W.R.

In 1605 the Canon was preferred by the Bishop (Dr. Cotton) to the Archdeaconry of Barnstaple. In 1608 he was again favoured with Royal patronage. James the First, in his love for polemical divinity, devised a scheme for founding a college of learned divines under the title of King James's College in Chelsea, who were to devote their whole time and abilities to the study and teaching of controversial divinity, especially those points in dispute between the Churches of England and Rome. The College was to consist of a

Provost and Fellows, and it speaks well of the attainments and standing of the Archdeacon that the first Provost, Dr. Sutcliffe, Dean of Exeter, selected him as one of the Fellows, and his selection was confirmed by the King. The scheme, however, failed, principally for want of funds, and the College buildings, after remaining for many years in an unfinished state, were converted by Charles II into a Royal Hospital for disabled soldiers, now Chelsea Hospital.

In 1616 the Archdeacon purchased Coker of Sir Edward Phelips, but he had an earlier connection with it, as he was lessee of the impropriate rectory, under the Dean and Chapter of Exeter, who had a grant from the Crown, as already mentioned.

He was getting a very old man when the civil war broke out, but, notwithstanding his age, he showed himself a determined Royalist, and suffered much for his attachment to the King. In 1643, under colour of certain ordinances of the Parliament for demolishing superstitious ornaments in cathedrals and churches, a band of fanatical Independents mutilated the fabric of the cathedral, pillaged its contents, and inflicted large fines on the dignitaries who resisted them. Amongst the most strenuous of their opponents was the venerable Archdeacon, then in his ninetieth year. If the accounts which have come down to us are to be relied on, he was most cruelly treated, being dragged out of his bed at midnight, beaten, pelted with mud, and hustled away to a ship stationed in the port, and only regained his liberty by payment of a fine of £800.[177] He did not long survive this attack, and died at Coker, November 26th, 1645. From contemporary writings and facts we gather that he was a High Churchman of the Laudean school, a great stickler for the rights of the Church, and a strenuous reformer of abuses and irregularities in the chapter of which he was a member. At Coker, as has been already noticed, he instituted proceedings for compelling the vicar to revive the performance of Divine service in the chapel of Burton.

His son, Henry Helyar, died in his father's lifetime, leaving by his wife Christian, daughter of William Cary, of Clovelly, a son William, who succeeded his grandfather as owner of Coker. He also was an ardent Royalist. He raised a troop of horse for the King in 1643, and was engaged with Colonel Wyndham in the defence of Bridgwater in 1645. He was afterwards raised to the rank of colonel in the King's army, and in 1655 compounded for his delinquency by the payment of the large sum of £1,522.

---

177 Mercurius Rusticus.

On the restoration of the monarchy his civil services were soon
enlisted by the King, who appointed him sheriff for the county in
1661-2. In the same year, having occasion to petition for the
King's interference in a claim he had on the Dean and Chapter of
Exeter, his Majesty was graciously pleased to accede to it, from
"the sense," to quote the King's own words, " wee have of the
loyall services performed by him to our Royall Father of glorious
memory, which occasioned him many sufferings, even to exile."

Colonel Helyar lived to see the peace of this part of the country
again disturbed by the " Monmouth Rebellion," and joined the
King's forces in suppressing it. He died in 1697, leaving, by his
wife Rachel, daughter and heiress of Sir Hugh Wyndham of Pils-
don, Bart., William Helyar, his eldest son, and several other children.

The Lordship of the Manor and Hundred of Coker, with its regal
rights of Sac, Soc, and Theam, must, in its full vigour, have been a
franchise of great local power, exercising in its courts extensive
jurisdiction, both civil and criminal. An examination of the
constitution and procedure of these courts would extend beyond the
prescribed limits of this work, and we can only therefore notice some of
the facts recorded in the rolls which bear on the history of the manor.

The Court Rolls do not, unfortunately, go back to a very early
date—the earliest being a solitary one for the year 1398 (16 Ric. II).
This is followed by an irregular series, continuing down to the time
of Charles II. But, notwithstanding these deficiencies, many
interesting and curious details are to be found in the collection at
Coker Court, and we are happy to hold out a prospect that Mr.
Helyar will, at some future day, publish them, with such explana-
tory comments as may be expected from the pen of so competent
an editor.‡

Our knowledge of the manorial rights anterior to the Court Rolls
is derived from two isolated documents of the reign of Edw. II,
one being the manor survey already referred to, and the other a
bailiff's annual account. The former, which is the more important,
is a presentment made at a court held in 1321 (14 Edw. II), by a
jury of 12 tenants on their oath, of " The customary of the manor,"
that is, a detailed survey of the lands, the tenants, and the rents
and services rendered by them to the lord. The immediate
occasion of this survey was probably the recent change in the
ownership of the manor from de Mandeville to Courtenay, and the
necessity for the new lord to be officially advised of his rights.

---

‡ This prospect is, alas, suddenly swept away, by the melancholy death of my
kind friend Mr. Helyar, whilst these pages are passing through the press.

It was essential to the existence of a manor that some of the tenants should be freeholders (liberi homines vel tenentes), and the lord of Coker had a goodly array of them. They held their estates by military service, and were bound to do homage and fealty at the lord's courts. A second class of tenants were the copyholders, holding by grants for lives, under certain rents, heriots, and suit of court. Then there were the tenants in villeinage, holding simply at the will of the lord according to the custom of the manor. These, besides paying rent, heriots, &c., were bound to labour on the lord's farm at stated times in the year, and at fixed prices, being paid partly in money, and partly in food and liquor. This is what is generally called a base tenure, and the nature of it will be illustrated by the following example, taken from the survey.

William Capon held half a virgate of land at 10s. rent, subject to these services—To help the lord, if he had oxen, in ploughing so many days at 2d. per day and one meal—to harrow at seed time, both autumn and spring, if he had plough beasts, doing as much harrowing as there was ploughing, receiving 1d. for a whole day and ½d. for half-a-day—To work "ad precarias" (*i.e.*, at the lord's request) at spring sowing, receiving 1½d. for food and 3d. for the work—To be bailiff, if chosen, having an allowance out of his rent with his meals for eight weeks in autumn and four bushels of wheat. To be carter, if chosen, being allowed out of his rent 6s. 8d. and raw meat (caro) every other Saturday—If he carried the hay with the lord's waggon and his corn in the autumn, he was to have two average sheaves for a whole day ; if half-a-day only one sheaf—To be shepherd, if chosen, with an allowance out of his rent—To weed for half-a-day for nothing, the work being valued at ½d.—To help haymaking for one day—that is, turning it over before dinner and carrying it in the afternoon—the work being valued at ½d., having liquor at the lord's expense—To provide a man to assist in making the hay rick and the corn mow in the lord's barton, the lord providing him two meals a day until the work was finished—the hay rick work being valued at ½d. and the corn mow work at 1d.—Although he was carter, to pay a heriot of his best beast, and if he had none then his best half-acre of corn—To pay for pasturing cattle in Hethefield 1d. per head for each beast three years old and ½d. if younger.

In addition to these tenants in the manor, four foreign manors are entered in the survey, which were held as dependencies on the Lordship of Coker by military and other services.

The Lord of Kyngton (now called Keinton Mandeville), held that manor by the service of half a knight's fee, and subject also to scutage, wardship and marriage, and the render of three arrows at Michaelmas.

The lord of Weston Mandeville (now Buckhorn Weston) held that manor by the service of one knight's fee, and the render of a sparrow-hawk.

The Prior of Bruton held the manor of Charleton FitzAdam by the service of one knight's fee and scutage.

Nicholas Cheyney held the manor of Pyneford by knight's service, the homage being ignorant of the precise tenure, " but they say that John de Maundevyle distrained there for scutage and took it [*i.e.*, the things distrained] to Coker, and it is held of Coker." As we have seen, John de Mandeville held, at his death, 4 Edw. I, two parts of a knight's fee in Pyneford.

The lord of the adjoining manor of Barwick held a meadow at Cay (Key), rendering to the lord a pair of gloves at Easter.

As Coker was not a Barony, it is difficult to understand how these manors could be so engrafted on it as to pass to the Courtenays, whose right by forfeiture could only extend to the over-lordship of the original manor, granted by the Crown to their ancestor, De Redvers. Charlton was purchased by Geoffrey de Mandeville ; Weston came to him from Fitzjohn of Weston, and neither Keinton nor Pyneford, as far as we know, was held by the de Mandevilles as Lords of Coker. Still, as the lords of these manors submitted quietly to the yoke, we must suppose there was some valid ground for imposing it.

The bailiff's account is from Michaelmas, 1309, to Michaelmas, 1310 (2 and 3 Edward II). It is headed " West Coker," but it concerns East Coker as well, and relates to the management of the Lord's demesne, the purchase and sale of live and dead stock—the perquisites of the courts, &c.

The entries are interesting as regards prices, &c. For instance, four oxen were bought at 66s. 4d., or 16s. 6d. apiece. Hemp and flax were both cultivated.

The Lord found his house—no doubt from de Mandeville's poor circumstances—in much need of repair, and a considerable sum was laid out on it, including the erection of a new room and solar.

There is an entry of 13s. 4d. paid by the direction of Sir (Dominus) William de Burton to Peter de Draycote, the King's coroner, and to the clerks of the sheriff, for transacting business touching the manor of Coker. This was, perhaps, delivering possession of the manor to the Earl, owing to the absence in prison of Robert de Mandeville.

Then there is an item for carrying letters to Bromore (?) and Limington for summoning a court; another letter to William de Burton, informing him of the death of the rector of East Coker; and also letters from Lord Robert Fitzpain to the lord (*i.e.*, the Earl of Devon) at Okehampton.

The account closes with an item of the payment of £6 on account to Sir William de Clopton, the lord's receiver.

The first Court Roll is in 16 Ric. II. To this was summoned William de Courtenay, Archbishop of Canterbury, to do homage for 1 carucate of land called *Byrelsmyll*; also Sir Walter de Clopton and Sir Matthew Gournay for lands held by them, and John Wadham, for the Manor of Hardington, which, although sold, still rendered homage and fealty to Coker.

The Prior of Montacute was also summoned to do homage for lands held by his priory, which appear, from an entry in a roll (34 Henry VI), to have been in West Coker. The prior, claiming exemption, disregarded the summons for many years, but at length, being required to prove his claim, he established it by producing, at a court held in 1432 (10 Henry VI), a charter, without date, whereby " Geoffry, son of Robert Maundevyl " confirmed to the church of the blessed St. Peter and St. Paul, of Montacute, and the monks serving God there, the land which Edward the Staller used to hold in " *Croca*," and which by permission of the said Geoffry he gave to the said church. And moreover the said Geoffry granted that the said land should be for ever quit and free of all services and exactions, and should have community—[that is, share, in all the manorial rights and privileges]—in the ville of *Croca*, as favourably as, or better than, it enjoyed in the time of his father.

But at the next court the Prior tried to escape from doing suit for his manor of Closworth, and produced another charter, also without date, of Geoffry Maundevyl, releasing the priory and their freemen and bondmen (servi) in the manor of Closworth from all suit to the Hundred of Coker, except on the king's writ or on forfeiture for felony before the Justices itinerant. The Prior was unsuccessful, as the charter only related to Hundred service to which the lord made no claim, and the bailiff was ordered again to summon the Prior to do his suit [at the Manor Court].

There is a schedule of expenses annexed to the bailiff's account for 1473 (2 Edw. IV) which deserves notice. The Lord of Coker at that time was Sir William Courtney of Powderham. By his wife Margaret, daughter of William Lord Bonville, he had two sons, William and Edward, for whom these frugal expenses were incurred, and who we presume were being educated at the Abbey of Muchelney. The exact entry is :—" When my maister William and maister Edward cam fro Mychelney. In primis for brede 1d. ob., itm for ale iijd., itm for candel, ob., itm for ij busshallys of wots vid. Another tyme when ye rede [they rode] to my Lorde of Clarens ayenst Cristys masse. In primis for brede 1d., itm in ale 1d. ob., itm on a henne ijd., itm in candel ob., itm for Underwode is borde [*i.e.*, Underwood's board] for ij wekes whyle ye were in Devenshire evy weke ixd. the sume is ijs. iijd. Itm for halfe a quarter of wots for your ij horses for the same iij wekes xd."

" My Lorde of Clarence " was George, Duke of Clarence, the king's brother, who was drowned in a butt of malmsey in the Tower, 1477. He had a grant of the Manor of Sampford Courtenay, Devon, and in 1473, the date of the account, he was at Exeter, and " honourably received and entertained at the cities public charge."[178] Probably he was also a guest of Sir William Courtenay, and the young gentlemen came home to be introduced to so distinguished a visitor.

A small area of land lying at the southern extremity of the parish, in and near the Marsh, formed a distinct ville, although belonging to the same lord. It was called the Borough of Murifield—on the Court Rolls " Burgus de Murifield "—a word which means, probably, the boundary field of the manor, and the name still survives in that of an adjoining meadow, known as Merryfield. This borough had its own court, distinct from that of Coker, with a separate homage or jury, a bailiff or provost, and its own Court Rolls. It was, in fact, a free borough, and the tenants were the burgesses. Their burgages were held by burgage or socage tenure, that is, at a fixed rent, free from those military and personal services which were introduced by the Normans, with privilege of alienation and devise; but they were subject to a small rent—to suit and service at the lord's court, and to a fine payable on a change of ownership. In 1309 there were, according to the survey, 18 burgesses, with burgages varying from half-an-acre to an acre, the whole being 19 acres and a-half, but there are grounds for supposing that in earlier times both the burgages and the burgesses were more numerous.

The number of small inclosures which, until recently, existed in this part of the parish always attracted the attention of observers, and many theories have been offered to account for it. One made

---

[178] Isacke's Memorials of Exeter.

by Captain Dampier has already been alluded to; but we may perhaps attribute the existence of these little plots to the wants and energies of the burgesses of the Free Borough of Murifield.

It would be futile to attempt to explain how this exceptional state of things arose, but it must have originated at a very early stage in English history. Burgage tenure is of itself a mark of præ-Norman origin, and we may have here the vestiges of a Saxon independent community, modified after the Conquest by the protection of a feudal lord and the imposition of a small tax in return. But as the whole of Coker was equally subject to the general Saxon land laws, there must be some special reason why this small part of the territory should have been carved out and separated from the rest.

Allusion has already been made to the number of freehold estates in the manor which were held by the owners as feudal tenants, subject to manorial services, and we will close this imperfect sketch of the history of Coker with such gleanings respecting them as we have been able to collect.

A considerable part of North Coker was at a very early period severed from the rest of the Manor. In the reign of Richard I, Richard de Argentine claimed of Geoffry de Mandeville "the land of North Cocre which had been given to his ancestors for one hundred solidates of land," *i.e.*, of the annual value of one hundred shillings. His claim, however, was contested in the King's Court · by Geoffry and his son Robert (III), Lords of Coker, but ultimately it was agreed that the land should be divided, and that one moiety should belong to Robert and his heirs in demesne, together with the over-lordship of the whole, and the other moiety to Richard and his heirs, subject to the services appertaining thereto, and the sheriff was directed to summon a jury to make partition accordingly, and to return their verdict by a certain day, so that a fine might be made between the parties.[179]

No such fine is to be found, but it may be concluded that the partition was duly effected, and that the de Mandeville allotment descended with the manor, but as to the other allotment we are left entirely to conjecture. A family of Argentine, of great distinction, flourished at that time in the eastern counties, which traced its descent from Sir Giles de Argentine, who accompanied William the Conqueror in his invasion of England, and it is possible that the Coker landowner was Richard de Argentine, steward of the house-

---

[179] Pipe Roll, 1 Ric. I, Som. and Dors.; Close Rolls, 8 John, m. 3.

hold of Henry III, who died in 1246.|| We cannot ascertain now the
origin of the dispute, but the parties may have had a common
ancestor, from whom the land descended through co-heiresses.
The name of Argentine does not appear again in any record
relating to Coker, and we can only surmise that the Argentine
allotment was sold and divided into several manorial tenements,
including some of those we are about to notice.

One part may have been the estate for some time in the possession of the de Montacute family. In 1320 William, 1st Baron of
Montacute, and Elizabeth his wife, held Coker Mill, four bovates of
land, one messuage, 91 acres of arable, and 10 acres of meadow
and pasture of John de St. Quentin, who was lessee of the
Manor for life, under the yearly rent of 16s. 8d.[180]   Coker Mill
was in fact the mill now known as " Pavyot's Mill," as in the
survey of 1321 it is called " The tenement of Pavyot's Mill,"
held by Wm. de Montacute by the service of the fourth part of
one knight's fee, besides suit at the Hundred Court and a customary
heriot.   It continued in the Montacute family as late as 1415, when
Elizabeth, widow of the second Earl of Salisbury, held one-third
of it in dower.[181]

Pavyot's Mill stands on the boundary line between the parishes of
East Coker and Yeovil. It was so called from a former owner named
Pavyot, and in 1280 John Maltravers, Lord of the Manor of Hendford, in Yeovil, brought an action against John Pavyot, for
disturbing him in his right of way along the side of the
mill pond, alleging that the pond was in Yeovil; but the jury
found that it was in Coker, and so Maltravers was defeated.[182]
It is singular that Pavyot's Mill continued to be debateable ground
between the two parishes down to modern times, the question
cropping up again in a settlement case under the old Poor Law.

From de Montacute Pavyot's Mill came to the family of
Micheldever. In 1388 (11 Ric. II) Richard Micheldever obtained
license to endow a chantry at Ryme, Dorset, with a messuage, mill, and carucate of land in the manor of East Coker;
but the intention must have been abandoned, as he continued to hold the property down to his death in 1401.[183]

|| After inspecting the Pipe Roll, 1 Ric. I, Som. and Dor., it seems tolerably
certain that he was the Richard de Argentine who was implicated in the treason-
able attempt of " Earl John " to supersede his brother as king; especially as in
the same Roll he fined for having a writ of right against Geoffry de Mandeville.
If he did not die until 1246, he must have lived to an age unusual in those
perilous times.

[180] Esch. 13 Edw. II, no. 31.   [181] Esch. 2 Hen. V, no. 39.
[182] Assize Rolls, Div. Cos. 8, Edw. I, 5—13—38.   [183] See Court Rolls.

HYMERFORD HOUSE, NORTH COKER.

He also died seized of two messuages and 40 acres of land formerly " San Cleres " (St. Clere's), which were held by the service of finding one man, armed, to ride with the lord for 40 days anywhere in the Kingdom of England, at his own expense.[184] This particular service enables us to identify these lands as the tenement described in the survey as " a certain place called Le fyshce weir held by Matilda de Senclere " at the yearly rent of 6d., also one croft called " Le Down haye " and two virgates of land, which were held by the same military service.

Matilda de St. Clere was, not improbably, a daughter by a former husband of Isabella, wife of James de Fyfhide, and the foregoing lands held by her were part of the messuage and one carucate of land and 27s. 6d. rent in West Coker, North Coker, East Coker, Attenashe, and Hardyngton Marsh, which, in 1202, by fine between James de Fyfhide and Isabella his wife, plts., and Robert de St. Clere and Matilda his wife, defts., were settled on James and Isabella for their lives, with remainder to Robert and Matilda, and her heirs.[185]

Richard Micheldever was succeeded by John Micheldever, and ultimately both Pavyot's Mill and the St. Clere lands descended by the distaff side to Henry Helmbridge, or Hambridge, of East Coker, and after his death in 1505 to his son and heir William.[186]

The old farmhouse in North Coker—now called Bridge Farm—but more correctly Bridge's Farm, was the seat of the Hymerfords. It was never part of the Courtenay estate, and therefore may have been another portion of the de Argentine allotment.

The house is a good example of a country gentleman's " modest mansion," and is called in the Court Rolls, 11 Edw. IV, the Mansion of John Hymerford. It has an entrance porch—passage dividing the hall from the offices—with another porch on the opposite side. To the left of this passage is the hall, which is probably earlier than the porch. Originally it was open to the roof, as the hall at Coker Court, but now it has a chamber over, the original Perpendicular windows still remaining. The hood mould of the arch over the entrance in the west porch terminates in corbelled shields, one of them bearing the arms of Hymerford—a chevron between three ducks ; the other shield is blank, or at any rate defaced. The proper blazon of the Hymerford coat, which could not be well shown

---

[184] ib.

[185] Som. Fines, 20 Edw. I, no. 141.

[186] Court Rolls.

on the stone, is arg., a chevron sab. between three ducks of the same, collared gu.[187] There are fragments of old traceried work in a cottage adjoining, and the deeply cut mouldings of the buttresses of the barn mark them as coeval with the house.

The Hymerfords were seated at East Coker as early as the reign of Richd. II, if not earlier. At the Manor Court in 1393 Henry Hymerford appeared as a freehold tenant doing homage and fealty for his lands, and his name, and the names of his successors, Robert and John Hymerford, are to be found on the rolls down to the reign of Richd. III. In 1484, John Hymerford held a tenement called "Le Waynes" and other lands, and at a court held 13th November, 1500, John Hymerford, senior, "armiger," is presented for making default in suit and service. This homage was no doubt due for a messuage and upwards of 110 acres of land in Burton, formerly held by Richard Wayne, which belonged in 1440 to William Bogell, chaplain, whose sister or daughter Alice was married to John Hymerford before 1451, when the same lands were entailed by Bogell on them and their issue.[188] Joan Hymerford, widow, made similar default at a court held in 1505, and in the bailiff's account for 1509 he craves allowance for repayment of 18d. to this Joan out of the chief rent for Waynes' land, and 4d. for half-a-pound of wax for rent of the same.

There is little doubt that this John Hymerford was the "John Hymerford of East Coker" whose will, dated 12th November, 1500, was proved at Canterbury 14th February following. By it he desires to be buried in East Coker parish church, and after bequeathing to the Cathedral Church of Wells 3s. 4d., to the church of East Coker 6s. 8d., and to the chapel of the B.M. there 3s. 4d., he gives all the residue of his goods to his wife Joan.[189] Although he does not mention his children, it may be assumed that his son and heir was William Hymerford, who succeeded to Waynesland, subject, apparently, to his mother's jointure. With him the male line of the Hymerfords of Coker became extinct, and his estate was divided between his two daughters, Margaret and Joan, and on the marriage of Joan with John Hambridge, son of William Hambridge above mentioned, he settled all his lands in East Coker, North Coker, and Waynys, by deed dated January 16th, 1529, on her and the issue of the marriage.

---

[187] Harl. MS., 1559, p. 108.

[188] Somt. Fines, 18 Hen. VI, nos. 12 and 43; 29 Hen. VI, nos. 92 and 93 ; and Esch. 4 Hen. VIII, nos. 4 and 5.

[189] Register Prior and Conv. of Christ Church, Canterbury, fo. 36B.

A branch of the Hymerford family owned the manor of Folke, Dorset, and the manor house there is still a very respectable building which has evidently seen better days. In the reign of Henry VIII it was the seat of Henry Hymerford, who served the important office of escheator for the counties of Dorset and Somerset. He left an only son, Robert, who died in 1548, s.p., by which event the male line of this branch ceased, and his two sisters, one of whom was married to Molyns, of Westhall, succeeded as heirs. It may also be mentioned that Edith, a daughter of John Hymerford, was the third wife of Thomas Trenchard, of Wolveton, near Dorchester, and on one of the shields in the windows of the hall were the arms of Trenchard impaling Hymerford, with the legend, " Scutum Thome Trenchard arm et Dne Edith uxor ejus."

William Hambridge, the husband of Joan Hymerford, died in 1540, and it was found by Inquisition, taken at Axbridge, 10th October in that year, that he died seized of Pavyot's Mill and the St. Clere lands, consisting of two messuages, one garden, one orchard, 47 acres of land, six acres meadow, and 48 acres pasture in East Coker; and two messuages, one dovehouse, two gardens, 16 acres land, six acres meadow, and 10 pasture in West Coker; and seven acres pasture in Hardington, which he had settled on his wife Joan (who survived him) for her life; and of one messuage, one water mill, one orchard, 10 acres meadow, and 17 pasture in East Coker, of which he died seized in fee; that the first mentioned premises in East Coker were held of William Courtenay, Esq., in socage, by fealty and 6s. 6d. rent, and the said mill and other premises in East Coker were held of the same by fealty and 6s. 7½d. rent, and the premises in West Coker of the king by reason of the attainder of the Marchioness of Exeter; that he died 2nd September last, and that John Hambridge was his son and heir, and aged 23.[190] John Hambridge died in 1569, when all his estates descended to his son and heir Richard Hambridge,[191] who died in 1578, and at the next Court presentment was made that he held of the Lord " the capital mansion of Hambridge, late Hymerford's," by military service, and that his son John, then aged 16, was his heir.[192] John the son afterwards sold Pavyot's Mill to Sir John Portman, Bart., in whose family it continued down to a recent date, when it was purchased by the late George Bullock, Esq.

---

[190] Esch. Inq. Som. and Dor., 30 and 31 Hen. VIII, no. 10.

[191] Inq. Som. and Dor., 11 Elizabeth.

[192] Court Rolls.

John Hambridge (son of John, grandson of Richard) married, in 1630, Mary, daughter of Archdeacon Helyar, and on the same day Grace, sister of John, was married to William Helyar, junior, a younger son of the Archdeacon. Towards the end of the 17th century the male line of Hambridge failed, and the Coker estate, which they had inherited from the Hymerfords (except Pavyot's Mill), passed to Nathaniel Bridges, a descendant of Jonathan Bridges, and Phyllis his wife (daughter of William and Grace Helyar), who sold it to William Helyar, Esq.

The arms of Hambridge were sab. a chevron between three acorns pp[2] and a crescent for a difference, with a right to quarter the arms of Hymerford, and also those of Micheldever, which were Checky arg. and sab. on a bend gu. three mullets.[193]

A farm in North Coker, still called Chelworth or Morton's Farm, was formerly in the possession of the de Cokers. At the time of the survey, 14 Edw. II, John de Coker held it as one carucate of land in East Coker, by knight service and the render of 2lbs. of wax, and by sale or descent it passed to the Chelworths, as in the survey 14 Edw. II, the words " now Chelworth " are written over the name of de Coker in a later hand.

The family of Chelworth seem to have migrated to Coker from Wells, but were apparently connected with the de Bynghams. William de Challeworth, of Wells, died prior to 1362, possessed of property there, which Adam de Chelleworth formerly held. In 1362 Wm. de Chelleworth, son and heir of Wm. de Chelleworth of Wells, by charter made at Sutton Byngham, granted all his tenements in Wells to John de Chidiock, William Aumale, Kt., Robert de Panes, and William de Byngham, and the heirs of the said Wm. de Byngham. The witnesses are John De Meriet, Walter de Romeseye, Kts., John Atteforde, Thomas de Panes, William de Welde, John Fauconer, John Leddred, junior, John Leugh, Thomas de Mertoke de Wellys, Thomas Draycote, Robert Forde de Yevele, John le Doo, Robert de Coker, and William le Doo.[194]

The Coker estate continued in this family until the death of Robert Chelworth, a person of unsound mind, in the reign of Edw. IV, when it passed to his heir, Robert Morton,[195] who in a pedigree of Morton[196] is said to be son of Wm. Morton, of Cerne, and Agnes his

---

[193] Harl. MS., 1559, p. 208, 235.

[194] Index Wells Cathedral MSS., p. 167.

[195] Esch. 18 Edw. IV, no. 20.

[196] Hutchins' His. Dor. ii, 394.

wife, daughter and heiress of Robert Chelworth, of East Coker. After passing through various hands it was purchased in 1763 by John Bullock, Esq.

A considerable area of land belonging to Mr. Chafyn-Grove, lying to the west of his house, was anciently known as " Le Hurne." The derivation of that name is not very clear. Some think it means a hermitage, and one learned writer defines Hern or Herm to be " a cell or Hermitage, as Potherne, Whitherne, &c., so that it signifies no more than a cloister built and set apart for a number of religious to dwell in."[197] Probably its primary meaning was derived from the Anglo-Saxon word oern, a secret place, house or cottage, without necessarily implying it to be a recluse for religious devotees. This was probably the opinion of another author, who, writing in the year 1618 respecting a place in Gloucestershire called Hurne, says " It is so called from the little thicket or grove of thorns, small shrubs, or the like, called an Hurne, adjoining."[198]

In the survey, 14 Edw. II, " Henry in the Hurne " appears as a tenant holding 30 acres by military service ; and by charter in the year 1397, to which Robert Cokere, Thomas Bingham, Henry Hymerford, William Chelleworthe, and Thomas Boubb are witnesses, " John in the Herne, Clerk, " settled lands in East Coker on his daughter Joan, the wife of John Wygot.[199] The name occurs again in 1589 (31 Elizabeth) when Francis Whitton, *alias* Whittington, of West Coker, and Henry, his son and heir apparent, conveyed to William Daniell, of East Coker, two tenements in " le Hurne in North Coker," the one called " Bellepool Place," and the other " Morres Place," together about 50 acres. William Daniell was the ancestor of the opulent family of Daniell, of Yeovil, and the Coker property was held by them down to the year 1815, when it was sold by George Daniell, M.D., to Mr. Samuel Hutchings.

A wanderer, engaged in the hopeless task of threading the labyrinth of lanes which interlace the sandy tract above North Coker, may, perchance, find himself in front of a venerable pile of building which will not fail to attract his attention. An intelligent native (if by good luck he sees one) will tell him it is Nash. With this information he had better be content, for should he pursue his enquiries and

---

[197] Drake's Eboracum, p. 562.

[198] Smyth's History of the Hundred of Berkeley, p. 106.

[199] Coker Court Muniments.

endeavour to learn anything of its history, he will be involved in another puzzle as intricate as the maze in which he is immured. Wisely rejecting the many tales and traditions which will be volunteered to him, and preferring to judge for himself, he will, with a little knowledge of architecture, come to the conclusion that the building before him is the shell of an old mansion of the Tudor period which has undergone such alterations and embellishments that it is difficult to distinguish the original work from the restorations.

At present it is a long parallelogram of three compartments, united as one dwelling house, but so late as 1853, when the Somersetshire Archæological Society visited Nash, the centre section was a mere outbuilding, only one storey high, with a pointed archway in the eastern wall on the ground floor leading into the western compartment, but it has recently been made part of the house, with chambers over. The eastern part of the building is the most important. The northern entrance from the road, now blocked up, gives it the appearance of a gatehouse. It is a pointed arch, nearly 10 feet wide, with bold mouldings and enriched corbels, now defaced. The ancient oak door remains *in situ*, the head being panelled in quatrefoils and trefoils and four small escutcheons, but unfortunately all blank. The massive upper hinge, extending almost across the door, is so simple and clumsy that its antiquity may be reasonably doubted. It seems to defy any decay beyond rust, but both "the door and its hinges" owe their preservation to an inside wall, which protected it from trial and rough usage. Directly over this arch is a small two-light oriel window, the roof of which was flat in 1853, but now altered and adorned with crocketed pinnacles. It stands on a base, the upper part of which is enriched with quatrefoil panels. The lower part is fashioned into an elegant double corbel of fan-shaped tracery, the ribs terminating in a floriated ornament which dies into the mouldings of the arch below, showing that both gateway and window were built at the same time. Opposite this entrance, in the south wall, another gateway, six feet in width, with a lofty panelled arch over it, was discovered during the alterations. There is no hall or appearance of one on the ground floor. The eastern gable, which is flanked by buttresses of two stages—simple in design—exhibits a good example of a late Perpendicular two-light window (now walled up), with traceried head and transoms. There is a smaller window near on the south side, and the hood moulds of both are supported by elegant corbelled heads, the Tudor style being apparent in the head-dress of one corbel representing a lady of quality. Probably these windows mark the

OLD MANSION, NASH.

position of the principal room of the house. The gable is surmounted by an elegant octagon chimney, with panelling filled in with quatrefoils.

The western compartment is apparently of earlier date. Its chief feature is the lofty angular buttresses which support the western end, and a very rich square-headed window on the ground floor of the south front.

The whole of the building was at one time converted into cottages, and consequently the leading features, especially in the interior, had been swept away. A weak tradition exists that there was once a central tower, but we are not credulous enough to believe it. It is more probable that originally there was no centre building, and that the two compartments were at one time separate houses, with an open space between them.

The prime attractions to the spot for a gentleman's residence were no doubt the dry soil, and the brilliant spring of water which rises in the hollow close by ; and considering that at the close of the reign of Henry VII Nash belonged to James Courtenay, second son of Sir William Courtenay, Lord of Coker, probably we are indebted to him for the rich example of Tudor domestic architecture which has come down to us.

The earliest mention of Nash is in the Manor Survey of 14 Edw. II, when the heirs of Richard Fromond, of Ivelchester,* held of the Lord half a virgate of land, which Wm. Atte Nasshe occupied, paying yearly one pound of cummin. By aid of the spice rent we recognise the tenement again in the reign of Henry VI, when it was held by Wm. Bogell, and at a Court in 1462 the homage presented his death, and that he held a messuage and 20 acres of land (which is half a virgate) by fealty, and the yearly render of one pound of cummin, and further that he had enfeoffed John Peny and others thereof.

Bogell also held a larger estate called Burel's Mill, which seems to have been treated as part of Nash, and we learn from a fine levied in 1291, between John Burel and Emma his wife, plaintiffs, and William Burel, defendant, that it consisted of a messuage and mill, one caracute of land, ten acres of meadow and 50s. rent in East Coker, West Coker, Hardington, and Penne, which were thereby limited to William for his life, with remainder to John and Emma

---

* Richard Fromond was a considerable landowner in Somersetshire. He was a feudal tenant of the de Montacute family. He held the Ville of Haggeshole, in Broomfield, of Simon de Montacute, and he was also lord of the Ville of Penne— *i.e.*, Penselwood—which Nicholas Cleymund held under him.—(Kirby's Quest.)

and the heirs of John.[200] It is probably the mill now called Hewhill or Holywell, which stands on the confines of East Coker but in the parish of West Coker. The sandy cliffs below it are still known as " Burel Rocks."

By another fine in 1315 between Walter de Montalt and Alice his wife, plts., and William Burel, deft., Burel's Mill tenement, by the same description, was settled on Walter and Alice in special tail, with remainder to William Burel in fee.[201] In the reign of Edw. III it had passed to Henry Hak and Margery his wife, who by fine, levied in 1363, conveyed it to William de Bingham in fee for 100 marks in silver.[202] From de Bingham it must have come into the possession of Hugh de Courtenay, 2nd Earl of Devon, whose widow, the Lady Margaret Bohun, held at her death in 1392 ten acres of land at Burel's Mill in dower. Then her son William, Archbishop of Canterbury, held it, for at the Court for 1393 he was summoned to do his fealty for one carucate, *i.e.*, 100 acres of land, " in Byrelsmyll." The Archbishop died in 1396, and in 1403 his brother, Sir Philip Courtenay, appears as the tenant of Sir Peter Courtenay the lord. Afterwards it was in the possession of Sir Humphrey Courtenay, only brother of Sir Philip Courtenay, the second of that name, and then we hear no more of it until 1460, when by a deed, dated Nov. 22nd, 1460, Sir Philip Courtenay, Kt., and William Courtenay, Esq., his son and heir apparent, after reciting that Wm. Bogell and Alice his wife, and John Shelford, clerk, Richard Cater, clerk, Richard Clavellshay, and John Peny, stood seized of divers lands and tenements in Burel's Mill, West Coker, East Coker, Hardington, and Pendomer, lately held by Humphrey Courtenay, Kt., and of a plot of land 40 feet in length and 20 in width, upon which parcel of land the capital messuage of the said Wm. Bogell stood, confirmed all their estate and interest therein, except the services due for the said plot of land. Warranty against the Abbot of Glastonbury and all others. The witnesses to this deed are John Sydenham, sen., John Sydenham, jun., John Porter and others.[203]

The allusion to the Abbot of Glastonbury raises a suspicion that he had some claim on this land as lord paramount, and it is singular that the Abbey were then the owners of an estate lying in the three

---

[200] Somt. Fines, 19 Edward I, no. 136.

[201] Somt. Fines, 8 Edw. II, no. 36.

[202] Somt. Fines, 37 Edw. III, no. 66.

[203] Close Rolls, 1 Edw. IV, m. 15.

parishes of West Coker, East Coker, and Hardington, which, in Abbot Beare's survey,[204] is called Peny's tenement.*

They were no doubt feoffees to the uses of Bogell's will, and on his behalf they appear to have settled some outstanding claim to the estate, as by a fine levied in 1460 between John Peny and Richard Clavelleshay, plts., and John Miller and Willama his wife, defts., Burel's Mill tenement, by the description of a messuage with 200 acres of land, 16 acres meadow, 130 acres pasture, 15 acres wood, and 15 acres elder, in Burel's Mill, in the parishes of West Coker, East Coker, Hardington Marsh, and Pendomer, was conveyed to the plaintiffs and the heirs of John Peny, in consideration of £100 sterling.[205]

The Fromond tenement continued in the possession of Bogell's widow and his son, Wm. Bogell, chaplain, until the end of the reign of Henry VII, when James Courtenay, of Upcot, Devon, second son of Sir William Courtenay, the then lord, became the tenant of it (no doubt by purchase), and in 1572 he accounted at the Manor Court for the pound of cummin rent accordingly. Under the will of his father, who died in 1573, James Courtenay obtained the fee simple of this tenement, which in the will is said to be "a tenement named Naishe, lying in North Coker, in the parish of East Coker, worth yearly three pounds," and there can be but little doubt that he purchased Burel's Mill tenement of Bogell's representatives, and by that means became absolute owner of both. His descendants sold off the estate, probably in parcels, before 1598, as in the Manor Survey of that year a part known as "The farm of Nash" was the property of Thomas Knight, and in the conveyance of the manor of East Coker by Sir Wm. Courtenay to Edw. Phelipps and his son, special exception is made of "the messuages, lands, and tenements called by the name of Nayshe, or the manor of Nayshe, in the parishes of East Coker, West Coker, Hardington

---

* The field names of these lands are worth preserving, many of them being still in use. The names in *West Coker* are Frontells Wode Lands at Chestly, Penys Pitt, Grey Abbey, Harper's Dyche, La Gurte, in Redewyll under Cleyhill, under Borghwyll, in Cockborgh, in Bigdon, on Cottsclyff, at Lansher Furlong, in Brodemede, in Deny under Thre Thornys, in Foxcrofte, at Okylond, at Dowkyn's Stede, in Chestelle, at Brodeshor, at Lez Bassells, at Penys Thorne, in Lang Bronley, in Cleyhill Slade, in Ryall, in Northfield, in Shortekytehyll furlong, at Hermits House, in Middlecrofte. *East Coker*—In East Coker field at Brodeshord, at Dokyn'stede, and in the north part of Nayssh. *Hardington*—In Apsmede, in Hardington field, in Ruydon, and in Elmore.

[204] Harl. MS. 3961.

[205] Somt. Fines, 1 Ed. IV, no. 1.

Mandeville, and Pendomer, which were the inheritance of James Courtenay the elder, esquire, deceased." The language of this exception will embrace both Nash and Burel's Mill tenements.

In 1607, 5 James I, Robert Knight, of Wayford (who was probably son of Thomas), died seized of the capital messuage of Naishe and land in East Coker and Pendomer, held of Henry Knight, as of his manor of Pendomer, leaving Robert Knight his kinsman and heir, aged 22.[206]

Between 1607 and 1614 Knight must have sold to Sir Robert Phelips, as in a Manor Survey, 1614, Sir Robert is said to be the freehold tenant of the farm of Nash, subject to military service and the render of a pound of cummin yearly. After his death it belonged to his second son Robert, who sold it to Lionel Harrison, and by a deed of feoffment dated 23rd March, 1639, the farm of Nash and 40 acres at Lyets were conveyed by Robert Phelips, the son, with the concurrence of Edward Phelips, his father's heir-at-law, to Lionel Harrison the younger, son of Lionel Harrison the elder, of Nayshe, yeoman. At the end of the 17th century, a descendant, Lionel Harrison, the then owner, mortgaged the estate to one Daw, who foreclosed the equity of redemption, and sold to Thomas Penny, of Keyford, Receiver General of Taxes for Somersetshire. In 1718 he sold it to Henry Moore, of West Coker, in whose family it continued until very recently,† when it was bought by Mr. Robert Harrison, the present owner and descendant of the original purchaser, and he now resides at Nash.

We will close these notices of the freehold tenements held of the manor by alluding to one which, in 1598, consisted of "a mansion house with seventy acres of land, held by John Peny, Esq."[207] The early descent of this estate is very uncertain, and we can only hazard an opinion that the mansion house is that now called Bubspool. Although modernised and altered, there are, in the interior, remains of pointed arches and traceried windows, showing

---

† A curious circumstance is mentioned in connection with Mr. Moore's purchase. Many years after, in 1771, his grandson was involved in litigation with the Dean and Chapter of Exeter, who claimed a field in East Coker as leasehold held by Mr. Moore under them ; whereas Mr. Moore asserted it was part of his freehold estate of Nash, and an old servant of Mr. Moore deposed that he remembered ploughing the field for his master 60 years before the lease was granted. He could not tell the year, " but it was when there was an eclipse of the sun, which obliged him, from the total darkness, to stop ploughing."

[206] Esch. Wards and Liveries, 5 Jas. I, no. 46.

[207] Manor Survey.

it to have been an ancient dwelling of consequence, and we know that it was held by the family of Bubbe, to whom reference is made in the Court Rolls for Richard II, but not afterwards. How it got into the hands of Peny we cannot say.

The family of Peny, Penny, or Penne, as it was variously spelt, were considerable landowners in Coker, and had resided there from an early period. As far back as 1393 (16 Ric. II) John Peny did homage at the Manor Court for the land held by him, and the name occurs frequently on the Court Rolls down to the time of James I. In the reign of Henry VIII Giles Peny, of East Coker, was standing attorney of the Abbeys of Athelney and Muchelney. In a return of the fees and pensions owing by the latter abbey shortly before its dissolution in 1540 there is an entry, " Itm Egidio Peny nostro attornato xxs."

It was no doubt the first wife of this Giles Peny who was buried at Yeovil in 1519. On the floor of the nave in Yeovil Church is a small brass (removed from the chancel floor in 1859), on which are incised figures of a lady and gentleman, surmounted by two heraldic shields bearing their arms—over the gentleman, on a chevron between three hunting horns, as many Maltese crosses, fitchy, being the arms of the family of Crewkerne of Childhay in Broadwinsor ; and over the lady, a chevron between three ermine spots impaling a chevron between three eagles' (or griffins') heads, erased. Neither of these coats have been identified ; the dexter coat may be Gerard of Trent. Underneath the figure, in old English characters, is this inscription :—" Of yor charitie pray for the soules of Gyles Penne, gentelman, and Isabell his wyf, which Gyles decessed the —— day of ———, in the yere of our Lord God MV., and the said Isabel deceased the xv. day of December, in the yere of our Lord God MVXIX., on whose soules JHU have mercy. Amen."

Mr. Peny was evidently a man of " frugal mind" to make this economical provision for his own monument, but it did not avail him, as he was buried at Coker. None of the arms on the shields are those borne by Penne or Penny, of Corscombe, descendants of Giles, which were six fleurs de lis. The coat of Crokhorne is in honour of his mother, who, according to an old pedigree,[208] was daughter and co-heiress of that family, and married to his father, Thomas Penny, of Coker. Giles Penny's second wife was Anne, daughter of Newton, of Harptree,[209] by whom he had a

---

[208] Harl. MS., 1067.

[209] ? Harl. MS. 1067.

son, Giles Peny, jun., who was 23 at his father's death, in 1560.

Giles Peny, sen., must have been an important landowner in Somerset and Dorset. By the inquisitions taken after his death, 2 Eliz. (1560),[210] the jury find that he died seized of a capital messuage and divers lands in Est Coker, which were held of the heirs of Sir Wm. Courtenay, Kt., in free socage as of his manor of Est Coker, and of divers messuages, lands, and tenements in West Coker, Nether Adber, Old Soke, Ashington, Modford Terry, Mersh, Kingeston, Yevyll, Est Chinnock, Est Charleton, and West Charleton, in the county of Somerset; and of divers lands in Burcombe, Alton Pancras, Brodewinsor, Burstoke, South Perrot, Chedington, Corscombe, Weke, and Halystock, in the county of Dorset.

By his will, dated January 9th, 1558, he gives his lands in Halstock, Wester Corscombe, and Chedington (which lands in Chedington he did buy of Thomas Bampfylde, Esq., and of his son and heir), and also his lands and rents in Nether Adber, to his son and heir and his wife Dorothy for their lives, and to his heirs for ever. He wills that his (testator's) wife and son should have and occupy the farm of Up Sydlynge in the county of Dorset, with the Tithing (*i.e.*, the lay Rectory) of the same farm, which he did buy of the Abbot of Mylton, and devises it to his son in tail male. He gives the sheep on his farm of Wraxal and Chilfrome to his wife for her life, and after her death to be divided between his daughters. Gives his lands in Borcombe in Alton Pancras to his wife and son equally. Gives to the churches of Yeovil, East Coker, and South Perrot xxs apiece. Gives residue to Anne his wife and Giles his son and heir, and appoints them executors, and Sir Hugh Poulett, Kt., supervisor of his will, proved P.C., 10th October, 1560.[211] He was an intimate friend of Sir John Fitzjames, the chief justice, who died in 1542, and gave "to Gyles Penye the cup that was used to drink claret wyne in."[212]

Giles, the son (who styled himself Penny), married Dorothy, daughter of Richard Strode, of Parnham, and their eldest son John succeeded to his father's Dorset estates, whilst William, his younger brother, took Coker. In 1622, he was involved in a Chancery suit with Archdeacon Helyar, as Lord of the Manor, which deserves to be noticed, as showing how strictly the courts upheld the customs of

---

[210] Wards and Liveries, vol. viii, p. 74.

[211] Mellershe, 48.

[212] Som. Arch. Proc., vol. xxiv.

a manor. William Penny held a tenement of the lord, but did not reside on it, and the Archdeacon contended that he had forfeited it, the custom of the manor being that every customary tenant must reside on his tenement on pain of forfeiture. Penny and his son Giles, a student of the Middle Temple, filed a bill in Chancery to be relieved from the custom as an unreasonable one, but the court upheld it, and at a manor court, held 15th April, 1624, William appeared and tendered his submission to the custom, whereupon license for non-residence was granted to him on payment of a fine.[213]

The Penny family quitted Coker for Corscombe, and their Coker property passed (probably by purchase) to the Orchard family, who were the owners of it towards the end of the 17th century. The ancient family of Orchard came originally from Devonshire, and bore for their arms a chevron between three pears. An heiress of the main line was married to Portman, who quarter this coat. The Orchards had long been residents and copyholders in Coker. In 1611 John, son of John Orchard, took of the lord the reversion of a tenement then held by Joan his mother, for the lives of himself and his brother William. In 1545 Lawrence Orchard was Rector of the free chapel or rectory of Pitney, *alias* Kingston juxta Yevell, which he held until his death in 1563, and in 1560 he was rector of Charmouth.[214] His descendant, Thomas Orchard, of East Coker, died in 1665, leaving a son, Lawrence Orchard, also of East Coker, who was a solicitor. He settled this Coker property on his marriage with Elizabeth, daughter of Edmund Brickenden, rector of Corton Denham, Somerset, and at his death left issue four daughters, co-heiresses, one of whom became the wife of Edward Burton, a maternal ancestor of the writer.

---

[213] Chancery B. and A., Jas. 1, pt. 26.

[214] Hutch. II., 217.

CHAPTER VIII.

LIMINGTON.*

THE great Norman baron, Roger de Curcelle, according to Domesday book, was the tenant in chief of the extensive manor of Limington, which his father had acquired by exchange with the Abbey of Glastonbury ; but there was another manor in the parish, called Dreicot— now Draycot—of which Robert, Earl of Cornwall and Count of Mortain, was the chief lord, William de Curcelle being his tenant,[1] and, according to Mr. Eyton,[2] he was the father of Roger.

There is in the *Liber Albus* of the Dean and Chapter of Wells a mandatory letter of William the Conqueror, addressed to this William de Curcelle, requiring him, by proclamation at Montacute and Bristol, to expedite the collection of the Peter Pence tax. All defaulters were to answer for their non-payment before Giso the Bishop, and himself ; and as the bishop at that day sat with the sheriff in the County Court, we may conjecture that William de Curcelle was the Sheriff, and probably the first after the Norman Conquest.† At Montacute, it should be noticed, was the castle of

---

* Reprinted from Som. Arch. Soc. Proc., vol. xiii, N.S.

† This very ancient document was first printed in Hickes's *Institutiones Grammaticæ, etc.,* p. 164 ; but very recently it has been published in a more accessible form, in the volume of the Historical Commission, called *Index to the Wells Cathedral, MSS.,* but which, in fact, is a full calendar and abstract of the archives of the Dean and Chapter. It is a most valuable addition to the materials for elucidating the early history of the diocese and the county, and great credit is due to the compiler for the very accurate manner in which he executed the laborious task confided to him.

[1] See Exon Domesday, p. 247.

[2] Somerset Domesday, vol i, p. 60.

the Earl, Willliam de Curcelle's feudal lord. We do not again meet with Draycot as a separate manor during the period of which we are treating, and no doubt, on the death of William de Curcelle, it descended to Roger, his son, and became part of Limington.

The superior lordship of the manor of Limington, and the advowson of the church, remained part of the De Curcelle barony, and descended, with many other manors belonging to that barony, to the families of —(1) Malet, (2) Vivonia or De Fortibus, by the marriage of Hugh de Vivonia with Mabel, daughter and co-heir of William Malet (whose forfeiture was condoned), (3) to the co-heiresses of William de Fortibus, and (4) to Beauchamp of Hatch, by the marriage of John de Beauchamp with Cecilia, one of such co-heiresses. But the land constituting the territorial manor was divided into three parts, and we will trace their descent separately.

One-third was at a very early period held by the family of Fitz Bernard, and was, we assume, the knight's fee held by Robert Fitz Bernard, of William Malet, 12th Henry II.[3] He held also half a knight's fee in Devonshire, of the King's son,[4] and was sheriff of that county 15th Henry II. He was probably the father of Ralph Fitz Bernard, who by charter without date gave to the church of St. Andrew, Wells, and to Reginald the bishop (who occupied the see from 1174 to 1191), the church of Holcombe, Devon—now called Holecombe Burnell (a corruption of Bernard), a manor which had descended to him from the Domesday tenant, Tetbald Fitz Bernard. With this endowment the prebend of Holcombe was founded, and it survives (in name, at least) to the present time.[5] We gather from a charter of Letitia, widow of this Ralph,[6] that he died soon after his gift of Holcombe, and Limington descended to his son Richard, who, in the year 1206, by the name of Richard Fitz Ralph Fitz Bernard, pledged to the Chapter of Wells "his Lands and Revenues at Limington," as an indemnity against certain claims of his brother William in respect of the manor of West Hatch, which the irfather, Ralph, held of the Chapter for his life.[7] Notwithstanding this, we find, that 19th Hen. III, Ralph Fitz Bernard and Hugh de Vivonia had licence to agree on an assize respecting the last presentation to the church of Limington, John de Balun and Auda his wife (sister and

---

[3] Liber Nig., p. 93.

[4] Ib., p. 120.

[5] Wells Index, p. 11.

[6] Ib.

[7] Wells Index, p. 11.

heir of William Paynel, Lord of Huntspill), and Gundreda de Tudenham, or Tudeham being amerced because they withdrew *(retraxerunt se)*.[8] This last Ralph could not have been the father of Richard and William, but he may have been their brother, and it yet remains to be cleared up by what title he claimed the advowson instead of Richard.

It is worthy of observation that there was a Ralph Fitz Bernard, who, according to *Testa de Nevill*,[9] married, in the reign of King John, Alianor, daughter and heiress of Wandregesil de Curcelle, a ward in the King's gift, inheriting from her father one-third part of a knight's fee at Frome Selwood. Some connection between this Wandregesil and the Limington Lords may be presumed, as, 2nd John, there was litigation between him, or at any rate one of the same name, and Geoffry de St. Martin (the owner, as we shall see, of one-third of Limington), respecting the manor of Fisherton Delamere, Wilts, of which Roger de Curcelle was the Domesday tenant.[10] If Collinson[11] is correct in saying, contrary to Mr. Eyton, that the father of Roger, the Domesday tenant of Limington, was Wandril or Wandregesil de Leon, the father of this Alianor may have been his descendant, but her husband could not have been son of the Limington Ralph, if, according to Collinson, the Frome Ralph left issue by his wife Alianor only one daughter, Joan (afterwards wife of William Braunche), to whom, as his heir, Frome descended. It is possible that Joan was heir of her mother, and that Richard, William, and Ralph were his sons by a second wife, Letitia, already mentioned.

Richard Fitz Bernard died seized of this part of Limington early in the reign of Edwd. I, when it descended to John, his son (?), and by Indentures of Fine, 9th Edward I, between William de Wylington, plaintiff, and Joan Fitz Bernard, defendant, one messuage, one carucate of land, and 100s. rent in Limington, were conveyed to the said William, in fee, subject as to one-third to the estate in dower of Joan, widow of Richard Fitz Bernard.[12] The Wylingtons were important landowners, not only in Somersetshire, but in Cornwall and Gloucestershire. The above William is assessed (about 12th Edw. I), in Kirby's *Quest*, for one-third part of the ville of Limington ; but he died in the same reign, as, 31st Edwd. I, Gregory de Wylington is recorded to hold " the manor of Limington " of Cecilia

---

[8] Rot. Fin. Extr., vol. i, p. 283. Dugd. Bar. i, 453.
[9] Pages 161, 167.
[10] Hutchins's History of Dorset, 3rd edition, vol. iv, p. 470.
[11] History of Somerset, vol. ii, p. 187.
[11] Somerset Fines, 9th Edw. I, no. 62.

de Beauchamp, by the service of half a knight's fee. Gregory died without issue, before 6th Edw. II, leaving his wife Joan surviving, and Gunnora, wife of Sir Richard de Gyverney, Kt., his niece, who inherited her uncle's part of this manor.[13] There seems to have been some litigation respecting the large estates of Gregory de Wylington, the nature of which is not very apparent, but the result was that his heiress, Gunnora, made two settlements of them, to the following effect. By indentures of fine, 6th Edw. II, between Richard Gyverney and Gunnora his wife, plts., and John Gyverney, deft., one portion, consisting of one messuage, 40s. rent, and the third part of one carucate of land in Limington, Yevelchestre, Wells, Pyure [Pury], Benhangre [Binegar], Eversey, Eston, and Bridgewater, was settled on the said Richard and Gunnora for their lives; remainder to Thomas, son of Godfrey de Sowey, in tail; remainder to the right heirs of the said Gunnora; and by another fine of even date between the same parties, one messuage, two carucates of land, twenty-seven acres of pasture, and £6 rent, in the same places, were settled on the said Richard and Gunnora, and the heirs of their bodies; remainder to William son of John Warre, in tail; remainder to the right heirs of the said Gunnora. To both these fines, John (son of John la Warre) and Henry de Woolavington put in their claims.[14]

Little is known of the De Gyverneys. They sprang originally, no doubt, from some place of that name in Normandy—probably Gyverny, near Vernon, the church of which was endowed in 1052 with " La Couture du Prè de Giverny";[15] but we have only fragmentary notices of them in England, as possessing lands in the marsh district of Somersetshire.

Amongst the Wells Cathedral charters are two relating to this family. One is a charter dated the third year after the translation of St. Thomas,—that is, A.D. 1175,—whereby Gilbert Gule and Christina his wife gave to the Church of Wells all the land which her father, Thomas de Bolonia, held in North Curry;[16] and the other is a grant without date (No. 73), whereby Thomas de Gyverney, son and heir of Roger de Gyverney the second, grants to Edward the Dean and Chapter of Wells land in the manor of North Curry, which belonged to Christina, daughter of Thomas de Bolonia, his great grandfather. The pointed oval seal appended to this grant bears an

[13] Ass. Rolls Div. Cos. 6th Edw. II, n. $\frac{2}{15}$, 5 a.

[14] Somerset Fines, 6th Edw. II, nos. 127, 128; see also Fines Div. Cos., 6th Edw. II, nos. 80, 81.

[15] Dawson Turner's Tour in Normandy, vol. ii.

[16] Liber Albus, vol. i, p. 12.

eight-leaved rosetta between two trefoils, with the legend " s. THOME DE GIVERNI." The Dean was Edward de la Knoll, who held that dignity from 1256 to 1284. No. 74 is a duplicate of No. 73, and No. 75 the like, but with different witnesses—one being Sir Philip de Cantelo, Kt.[17] We cannot trace the exact connection between the parties to these deeds and Sir Richard de Gyverney. He was the son of Gilbert Gyverney and Mabel his wife, and was three times married, which we learn from the record, in the Bishop's Register at Wells, of his foundation, in the year 1329 (2nd Edw. III), of a chantry in the church of Limington. The chaplain was enjoined to pray for the souls of him the said Richard, and Maud his wife, and of Gilbert Gyverney and Mabel Gyverney, father and mother of the said Richard; and of Lord Philip de Columbers and Eleanor, his wife; and of Gunnora, formerly wife of the said Richard; and of Margaret, also formerly his wife; and of Henry Power and Maud his wife.[18]

The chantry chapel forming the north transept, with its unique, high-pitched stone roof, is a very interesting feature in the church. In it are the Gyverney monuments, but the only historical information we have respecting them is Leland's account, in the reign of Henry VIII. He says in his *Itinerary*,[19] "From Ivelcestre to Limington Village about one mile; one Iuuerney was owner of this Towne and Lordship, he lyith richely buried yn a fair Chapelle on the North side of the Paroche Church of Limington. Ther lyith at the feete of Iuuerney a woman vaylid in a low Tumbe with an Image of Stone. Ther lyith also in the South Arch of the same Chapelle a Gintleman and his Wife, I think also of the Iuuverneys. There is a Cantuarie Prest of the Chapelle. Iuuverney dwellid as sum think in the farme at the North Est side of the Chirch. Iuuverney's Landes cam by Heires Generale to the Bonevilles of Devonshire. There was but one of the Bonevilles that was a Baron, and that was Syr Wyllyam Boneville, whose sonne married the Heire General of the Lord Harington; and Cecil, his Heire General, was married to Thomas the Lord Marquise of Dorset." Leland does not notice the arms on the shield of Sir Richard Gyverney's effigy. They are a bend between six escallops—which were borne also by the Foljambes of the north.

The effigy of a " woman vaylid," near to that of Sir Richard, is a distinct tomb, and was, we presume, erected by him in his lifetime to his wife Gunnora, by whom he acquired the Limington estate.

---

[17] See Index, pp. 6, 156, 297.

[18] Collinson's Somerset, vol. iii, p. 218.

[19] Vol. ii, p. 91.

The other two paired effigies are supposed by Collinson to be those of Gilbert and Mabel Gyverney, Sir Richard's father and mother; but we doubt this, as his family had no connection with Limington until his marriage with his second wife. It is more probable that they represent Henry Power and Matilda his wife—especially if, as it is said, she was a sister of Sir Richard. Henry Power may have resided at Limington, as he represented the county of Somerset in Parliament, 6th Edw. III.

1st Edw. III, the Gyverney one - third of the manor had de-volved (by some title independent of the fines) on John le Warre, who sold it, subject to the life interest of Sir Richard, for £200, to the above-named Henry Power, and it was conveyed as " the manor of Lymington," to the said Henry and Matilda his wife, and the heirs of the said Henry.[20] In a subsequent fine[21] it is called a moiety only of the manor ; and, 20th Edw. III, Henry Power is assessed for half a fee in Lymington, which Gregory de Wylington formerly held there.[22] On the marriage of his daughter, Joan, with William Shareshull, jun. (son, probably, of the justice itinerant of that name), Henry Power settled this part on her—reserving only a life interest—and died 35th Edw. III, leaving the said Joan his daughter and heiress, aged 28[23] ; Shareshull sold it to Sir William Bonville, of Shute, Devon, a great landowner in these parts.

Another third was sometimes described as the manor of Liming-ton Tudenham, from its former owners, and belonged, in the reign of Henry III, to John de Tudenham (of Todenham in the county of Suffolk), who, in Kirby's Quest, is assessed for it. He was also lord of the manor of Churchstanton, Devon. It continued in his family until the reign of Edward III, when Sir Robert de Tudenham sold it to Sir William D'Aumarle, Lord of Woodbury, Devon, and West Chinnock in this county.[24] 36th Edw. III, upon the death of Sir William D'Aumarle—his only son dying the same year, without issue—it descended to his daughters (as heirs of their brother), Margaret, wife of Sir William Bonville, and Elizabeth, wife of John Maltravers, by whom it was entailed on the issue of Margaret, and so came through the Bonvilles to the Marquis of Dorset, as stated by Collinson.[25]

---

[20] Somerset Fines, 1st Edw. III, no. 2.

[21] *Ib.* 14th Edw. III, no. 97.

[22] Book of *Aids*.

[23] Inq. P.M., 35th Edw. III, 2nd Nos., no. 35.

[24] Plac. Cor. Reg., 15th Edw. III ; Close Rolls, 28th Edwd. III.

[25] Inq. P.M.. 36th Edw. III, pt. i, no. 3 ; Somerset Fines, 42nd Edw. III, no. 30.

The remaining one-third part appears to have been still held in demesne as part of the barony in the time of William Malet, who granted it to Godfrey de St. Martin. Godfrey or Geoffry de St. Martin flourished in the reign of Richard I, and was one of the witnesses to a charter of William [Fitz Patrick], Earl of Salisbury, confirming the endowment of the Priory of Bradenstoke, Wilts, to which he himself became a subsequent benefactor ; for by charter without date, he, Geoffry de St. Martin, for the salvation of himself and Constance his wife, grants in perpetual alms to the Priory of Bradenstoke, that land of his in Limington which William Malet had granted to him for his homage, and this grant was confirmed by Jordan de St. Martin, brother of the said Geoffry, and also by Hugh de Vivonia, the successor, by the King's grant, of William Malet. Subsequently, the customary suit of Court for this land, due at the Lord's Court at Dundene (Compton Dunden, near Somerton, the seat of the Beauchamps), was released by William de Fortibus and John de Beauchamp and Cecilia, his wife.[26] 8th Edw. I, the Priory was defeated in a *quo warranto* for withdrawing the service of one-third of the tything of Limington from the Hundred of Stone,[27] and was assessed for one-third of Limington in Kirby's Quest a few years after. After the dissolution of monasteries this part was granted, 38th Henry VIII, to Richard Savage and George Strangwaies, to hold by the service of one-fortieth part of a knight's fee.

---

[26] Bradenstoke Cartulary, Cott. MS., Vitell A. xi.

[27] Ass. Rolls, Somerset, 8th Edw. I.

FINIS.

INDEX OF PLACES.

INDEX OF PERSONS.

CORRECTIONS.

p. 43, line 4, for " Odcome " read Odcombe.

p. 152, line 16, for " whimpe " read wimple.

Mandeville Pedigree, facing p. 114, last line, for " John s. and p. (ob. 5 p.) " read John s. and h. (ob. s. p.)